East London-born Jimmy Bullard joi
as a boy, West Ham, from non-Leagu
in 1999. He never played a first team game for The Hammers and moved to Peterborough United on a free transfer in 2001, where he started to make a name for himself under manager Barry Fry.

A move to Wigan Athletic followed in 2003 and Bullard played his part in securing promotion to the Premier League in 2005 and a League Cup final appearance in 2006. He left The Latics to join Fulham but his time there was blighted by injury, as was his spell at Hull City, the club he joined in 2009. Brief spells at Ipswich Town and Milton Keynes Dons ensued, but Bullard brought his career to an end by announcing his retirement in October 2012.

As far as international football was concerned, Bullard was called into the England squad in August 2008 for the World Cup qualifiers against Andorra and Croatia, but did not feature in either match.

He has appeared as a pundit for the BBC and BT Sport, and in 2014 he appeared as a contestant in I'm A Celebrity . . . Get Me Out Of Here!

[illegible] ned the club he supported
[illegible] e Gravesend & Northfleet
[illegible]

BEND IT LIKE BULLARD

MY TWELVE PILLARS OF FOOTBALL WISDOM

JIMMY BULLARD

WITH
GERSHON PORTNOI

headline

First published in Great Britain in 2014
by HEADLINE PUBLISHING GROUP

First published in paperback in 2015
by HEADLINE PUBLISHING GROUP

1

Cataloguing in Publication Data is available from the British Library

Paperback ISBN 978 0 7553 6552 4

Typeset in Cronos Pro by Palimpsest Book Production Limited,
Falkirk, Stirlingshire
Printed and bound in by
Clays Ltd, St Ives plc

Headline's policy is to use papers that are natural, renewable and recyclable products and made from wood grown in sustainable forests. The logging and manufacturing processes are expected to conform to the environmental regulations of the country of origin.

FSC www.fsc.org MIX Paper from responsible sources FSC® C104740

HEADLINE PUBLISHING GROUP
An Hachette UK Company
Carmelite House
50 Victoria Embankment
London EC4Y 0DZ

www.headline.co.uk
www.hachette.co.uk

For Diane, Archie, Beau, Mum, Dad, John, Shelley and my nans and grandads; in loving memory of my uncle Johnny Hall

Acknowledgements

The publishers told me I could thank everyone involved with the book on this page so this is a bit like my Oscars speech – or the closest I'll get anyway. Bear with me.

There are two Jonathans without whom you wouldn't be reading the book right now and they deserve a massive slap on the back (in a good way), so take a bow Jonathan Conway, my literary agent, and Jonathan Taylor, my publisher at Headline.

Staying at the publishers, my editors Justyn Barnes and Richard Roper did a great job of correcting all my terrible spelling and grammar, while Tom Noble, Beau Merchant, Ben Willis and Richard (aka Men Who Stare At Books) have all been legends for making sure you found out about the book so you could go and buy it. Also, my manager Jim Erwood deserves a nod for making sure I actually got out of bed and turned up at important meetings.

Some of my former team-mates, gaffers and friends have been legends for helping me remember stories that I didn't even realise I'd forgotten, and making sure I embarrassed myself even more. So a huge thanks to Barry Fry, Paul Jewell, Phil Brown, Mike Pollitt, Dean Hooper, Mitchell Crawley and Weirsy.

I suppose I should also thank my ghostwriter Gershon Portnoi for coming up with the book idea in the first place and helping me to write it – I was hardly going to do it all myself, was I?

But, most of all, I want to thank my amazing family, without whom my entire career wouldn't have happened – I'm getting right into the Oscars thing now, aren't I?

My mum and dad, Jim and Linda, have always given me the most incredible support and love. Where would I be without them? Well, I wouldn't have been born for starters.

My amazing missus Diane, along with my two fantastic kids, Archie and Beau, are the greatest things that ever happened to me. Diane has been there for me before, during and after the rollercoaster ride of my career; she's an absolute diamond.

Finally, I'd like to thank Fabio Capello for calling me up to the England squad, but not for giving me a cap. Because he never did. What were you thinking, Fab?

Oh yeah, one more thing. If I've forgotten to thank anyone, forgive me – you know what I'm like.

PILLAR 1

CELEBRATE EVERY GOAL AS IF IT'S YOUR LAST; DO SO BY MOCKING YOUR MANAGER AND IT PROBABLY WILL BE

'Pleasure in the job puts perfection in the work.' ***Aristotle***

Why always me? Mario Balotelli may have claimed that one for himself but I reckon I could justifiably wear that T-shirt too – as long as he washed it first.

You know your mate who you can always convince to do anything for a laugh because you haven't quite got the bottle to do it yourself? That's me. And that's why when my Hull team-mates and I hatched a plan to perform the goal celebration to end all goal celebrations, it was inevitable that I ended up being the focal point of the whole thing, despite it not even being my idea.

On the eve of our match away at Man City in 2009, we were having dinner together in the team hotel when Paul McShane came up with a plan.

'If we score tomorrow, let's rinse the gaffer by doing a celebration taking the piss out of his on-pitch team talk last season,' he said, as my team-mates and I nodded and laughed enthusiastically. 'Not if we're 3-0 down, but if it's an equalising or winning goal, whoever scores it has to do it.'

McShane was part of the Hull team who had been humiliated by our gaffer Phil Brown in the corresponding fixture the previous season. Then – playing without me obviously or it

would never have happened – Hull trailed 3-0 at the break and Brownie decided to keep the players on the pitch and delivered his half-time words of wisdom to them in front of the stunned visiting supporters.

If you ask me, that was a liberty and if I'd been a Hull player then I would have walked off the pitch and gone to the toilet. A lot of my future team-mates said he lost the dressing room at that point, and that's why they were up for a small dose of revenge. But that was Brownie – he was unpredictable and did the most ridiculous things sometimes.

For better or worse, his very public team talk became one of the most talked-about incidents of the season. What was it that Oscar Wilde said about being talked about or not being talked about? I've got no idea. Do you think I've ever read Oscar bloody Wilde?

A year later, it was me who was being talked about when, with eight minutes left and Hull trailing 1-0, we were awarded a penalty in front of thousands of our fans who had travelled to Eastlands.

Shortly before, Brownie had asked me to play further up the pitch as we tried to claw something out of the game. I'd been playing in the deepest position of our three-man midfield, but the gaffer encouraged me to get forward and try to cause a few problems for the City defence, or at least give them something else to think about.

Who knows whether it was that or just fate, but a few minutes later Kolo Touré bundled over Jan Vennegoor of Hesselink and the ref Lee Probert gave us the pen. The City boys went absolutely mental, arguing with him, but I tried to shut all that out.

I just picked up the ball with only one thing on my mind – scoring and going crazy in front of our fans. I'd completely forgotten about the 'half-time bollocking' celebration. I stepped up and smashed the ball to Shay Given's right to draw us level and reeled off yelling and screaming to the Hull fans.

I'd completely lost the plot, as I do whenever I score, until one of the boys reminded me about the special celebration. Within a couple of seconds, all my team-mates were sat around me in a circle while I stood in the middle, gesturing, pointing and finger-wagging at the lot of them. It was a pretty convincing impression of the gaffer even if I do say so myself.

To add to the authenticity of this performance, it was in exactly the same spot at the same end as Brown's barmy moment the season before – Laurence bloody Olivier couldn't have done any better.

I love scoring goals and I love celebrating them. I'd done my bit for the lads and I still wanted to do my own little piece where I run to all four corners of the ground acknowledging the crowd. Unfortunately, there wasn't much time for that – I once did pretty much that while I was at Peterborough and got booked for my trouble – as, for some weird reason, the referee who had so kindly given us the penalty was now insisting that we should carry on with the last eight minutes of the game.

As City kicked off again my only thought was 'I fucking hope this stays 1-1 after that celebration! Imagine if we lost 2-1 now . . .'

Fortunately we held on. I still had to face the gaffer back in the dressing room . . . but only after I'd milked the

celebrations with the away fans even more at the final whistle, naturally.

With Brownie there was no way of second-guessing how he'd react to something like that. He could either be absolutely fine and good-humoured or he could come down on you like a ton of bricks.

At City the dressing room is split into two, with an area for the coaches and all their technical equipment and a space for us to get changed. By the time I got back there, most of the boys were crowded round a laptop in the coaches' half watching replays of my celebration. Then the gaffer walked in.

Brownie looked into the area where all the players would normally be and seemed puzzled that nobody was there, but then he looked round and saw most of us stood by one of the computers. It wouldn't have been hard for him to spot us seeing as most of the boys were pissing themselves laughing.

'Oh shit,' I thought as he strode over to see what all the fuss was about.

A few of us shuffled back into our half of the room as the gaffer watched the incident.

Then it went silent.

'Oh shit,' I thought again.

'Oi, Bullard,' he yelled. 'What have you been doing?'

I looked up and was mightily relieved to see a broad smile across his chops. He thought it was absolutely hilarious.

(As it happens, he hadn't seen my celebration at the time. He told me later that while I was busy taking the piss out of him, he'd grabbed hold of Richard Garcia to tell him to drop deeper so we'd have a five-man midfield and keep hold of our hard-earned point.)

'That was blinding,' he said. 'But that'll be the end of that though, eh?'

Message received loud and clear.

But not before I did a post-match interview about it on *Soccer Saturday* in which I explained how it had come about and told the reporter, 'Whoever scored had to do the pointing. Trust it to be me!'

The press asked the gaffer a lot of questions about it after the game as they were hoping he'd be furious with me and the boys. They'd have been disappointed with Phil's reaction as he maintained his good-humoured way of looking at it. If anything, he felt that it exorcised the ghost of what he'd done the season before and that we could now all move on.

I wasn't that bothered about what he felt; I was just relieved that I'd gotten away with it.

And not just that, the following day I was on the back pages of pretty much every newspaper and all over the telly. Football fans could not get enough of it – I even picked up a *Nuts* magazine award for the celebration despite the fact it wasn't my idea. In reality, Paul McShane and the other lads should also have won it but I just took that one for myself, thanks very much!

Would any of the other lads have done the celebration if they'd scored? It's hard to be sure. But it was typical that I was the person in the spotlight at that precise moment.

The truth is I'm not wired right. At least, I'm wired just a little bit differently to other people and that meant I had an absolute ball as a professional footballer. I can honestly say that not a day went past where I didn't appreciate what it was that I was doing. Make no mistake, I lived a dream and I loved every second of it.

Unlike most other Premier League players, I grafted as a part-time footballer, cable TV technician, carpet fitter and painter-decorator while trying to get my big break. And that's why I was so determined to take it all in, soak it all up and, most importantly, entertain for every minute I was on the pitch.

I couldn't help but perform, whether it meant with the ball or just by acting the fool – and if that enhanced people's enjoyment of the game then so be it.

To some players football was just a job, to me it was the realisation of a boyhood dream, of hard work, tears, tantrums and plenty more besides.

That goal celebration is one of three things that football fans always ask me about. There's that, being on *Soccer AM* and my, ahem, confrontation with Duncan Ferguson.

I came. I saw. I went bonkers.

PILLAR 2

CONFUSE THE OPPOSITION BY HAVING GIRL'S HAIR; BUT NEVER MISTAKENLY ENTER A CONVENT TOPLESS

'Because one believes in oneself, one doesn't try to convince others. Because one is content with oneself, one doesn't need others' approval. Because one accepts oneself, the whole world accepts him or her.' ***Lao Tzu***

One October afternoon in 1978, my mum and dad went out to their local pub, The Brick, for a bit of Sunday lunch. My mum was heavily pregnant – I was only a week or two from making my first appearance in the world – but she struggled down there with my old man for a drink at the East End boozer which was owned by Frank Lampard Sr. My dad was meeting his cousin, former West Ham player Tommy Taylor, down there and they were all tucking into their Sunday roast, when Bobby Moore walked in.

He said hello to Tommy, his former team-mate, and then clocked my mum's bulging stomach – most probably that big because it was full of my curly hair.

'I hope you have a footballer in there,' said England's World Cup-winning captain to my parents.

A couple of weeks later, on 23 October, I made my world debut. Bobby Moore wasn't there to greet me, but my dad was on hand to inform anyone who cared that his boy had been born on the same day as his football idol, Pelé.

A blessing from Bobby Moore and a shared birthday with

Pelé – could I ever have been anything else but a footballer? (Well yes, I could very easily have been a fireman or the, er, Milkybar Kid, but those are different stories . . .)

A year later on 23 October 1979 I celebrated my first birthday. What a night that was.

Okay, I don't remember a second of it, but I'm reliably informed that it was the first time I kicked a ball.

Until that day, I'd never bothered standing up. I just couldn't see the point – my parents brought me everything I needed anyway so why move? I had a little football in my pram and one in my cot, what more did I need?

Another one, apparently – that was my dad's first birthday present to me and I was sitting there quite happily with my new ball in front of me, when another little boy walked in. That's right, he *walked* in.

He might as well have been wearing a sign saying 'Look at me'.

It was my birthday and I wasn't having it, so I chose that moment to get up on my feet for the first time and, in the process, I made my first contact with a ball as I walked straight into the new one that had been sitting in front of me.

From a sporting point of view, I never looked back. Luckily for me, sport was the only pastime that existed for my old man and he shared his love of every single one with me.

You name it, we played it together: pool, snooker, darts, fishing, golf and, of course, football.

I was a competitive little sod, too, and did not take kindly to losing. Pool cues would get hurled across a room or snapped in two; I'd often walk off a football pitch in tears, threatening to kill everyone in the opposing team if my side had lost – that was still happening when I was fifteen years old. Seriously.

On a family holiday in Greece, a Belgian kid of my age kept beating me at table tennis. My parents never saw me that holiday because I spent the entire two weeks practising until I was good enough to beat that kid – only then was he allowed to go home.

But I was fortunate enough not to be on the losing side too often in most of the sports I played because of the facilities available to me. My old man ran the bar at West Lodge, the local working men's club in Bexleyheath, where my parents had moved to when I was three, leaving behind the East End they'd known and loved their whole lives. And my old man being in charge at West Lodge meant I was allowed unlimited games of pool and darts. I wasted little time in trying to perfect both games, despite being even smaller than knee-high to a grasshopper.

My talent was not just confined to south-east London – when I was four we went to Leysdown-on-Sea on holiday and I used a beer crate to stand on so I could reach the pool table, which drew the attention of plenty of interested punters. I would say I beat allcomers, but I let one or two win as I didn't want any trouble.

My little six-by-three-feet snooker table at home was far easier to reach as that was laid on the floor. That kept me busy for hours and the practice must have paid off as I managed a century break when I was in my teens (it was 102, trivia fans).

Darts also came naturally to me. I may not have been Phil Taylor but I was good enough to rule the oche at West Lodge

every Friday night. Everyone paid a few quid to enter the weekly contest and the winner took home £40. I was fourteen and I was taking that money home with me every week. It got to the point where people would ask if I was playing before they entered the competition – and if they were told I was, they wouldn't bother.

Fishing was another passion of mine and it still is. From the age of seven or eight, I'd spend hours on the river banks watching other people fish, trying to pick up tips. I knew that I'd learn more from watching others than fishing myself at that stage.

I must've cost my old man a fortune though as not only was he paying £12 for me to attend the fishing club every week, but in my eagerness to see how other people did it, I was always tripping over their rods and breaking them because I was a clumsy sod; and my dad would always replace the gear I broke.

I didn't realise it at the time, but fishing gave me an amazing sanctuary away from all the temptations on offer to bored kids. All my mates – and most normal kids – had their dossing places where they'd just hang out and do what kids do. Some of them would be outside the chippy or McDonald's, while the bigger lads would even be in the pub trying to convince the barman they were eighteen, when some of their voices hadn't even broken.

Me? I was always down the River Cray on my own. Generally speaking, I hated being on my own and still do, but being by the water always made me feel good. Even now, whenever I see a stretch of water, I feel calmed by it and try to work out how I'd fish it.

But for everything I learned about rods, reels and bait by the river, the most important thing I picked up was confirmation that my hair looked great.

My angling idol was Jan Porter, a fishing competition champion and huge character of the sport. I didn't know Jan but I'd seen pictures of him in the fishing magazines I used to spend hours reading. He probably stood out a mile as he always wore bright red and had long, flowing blond hair crawling down his back. I too sported a wonderful white-blond mullet, although calling it a mullet probably doesn't do it justice. My hair was seriously long. So long that people had to look twice at me to work out what I was. Yes, *what* I was.

Often when I played football, I'd hear the other team making comments like 'They've got a girl on their team and she ain't half good'.

Once, my uncle and I were larking around in the grounds of the convent school that backed on to my parents' house. It was a hot day so I took my shirt off to cool down, only for one of the nuns to come over and say to my uncle, 'Would you mind telling your daughter to put her top on?'

Before my hair had taken on a life of its own, I had looked like a small boy. And at the age of seven, my mum decided that my blond hair and saintly smile would give me a good shot at landing the dream role of the Milkybar Kid. She wasn't wrong. Hundreds of kids auditioned but I made it down to the final six.

Although I loved playing to a crowd when I was older, I wasn't the most confident in those situations at that age and I was shitting myself as I waited to go on stage and do my bit in front of the Milkybar Kid selection panel. I was more or less dragged out there as one of the casting crew took my hand. Then it was time for me to deliver.

'My name's Jimmy from Bexleyheath,' I said as loudly and clearly as I could. Followed by the killer line: 'The Milkybars are on me!'

A completely different future beckoned at that moment; a future where people would shout 'The Milkybars are on me' at me in the street every day, instead of something about Duncan Ferguson or *Soccer AM*.

But it wasn't to be – the kid who went after me got the gig and I was left to pick up the shards of my shattered dreams and become a professional footballer instead. Tough break.

I cried Milkybar tears when I narrowly missed out on the role as I took any defeat personally; the only times I never cried loser's tears were on the golf course or in the boxing ring.

For three years between the ages of eight and eleven – I told you I played a lot of sport – I was schooled in the noble art of boxing; keep your guard up, wait to make your move, respect your opponent.

But when it came to my first fight I couldn't wait to get out of my corner. I practically sprinted to the boy I was up against and took the biggest swing at him possible. I wanted to knock his head off, but instead I missed, went arse over tit and knocked myself over.

It wasn't the most glorious start to my fighting career, but things improved a few years later on my street. My younger brother John and I were being hassled by a couple of older and far bigger boys who lived nearby. John was no shrinking violet and we ended up scrapping with these lads – I say we, but my brother did most of the scrapping and sorted the pair of them out. The lads' mother was far from happy with the state of her kids and called the police to complain.

John and I had run back home and told our mum breathlessly, 'Mum, the lady's going to get the police because we bashed her kids up.'

Showing all of her true Eastender spirit, she told us not to worry about it. This was her fight now so we retreated to the living room, knowing we had strength and justice on our side.

Sure enough, the Old Bill knocked on the door shortly afterwards. My mum answered and told the police she knew why they were there. She invited the coppers into the living room and they asked to speak to the lads who'd been in the fight.

'It's them!' explained my mother, causing the coppers to do a double take as they eyed us up and down properly for the first time.

'You're telling me they beat those bigger kids up?' asked one of them.

'They didn't beat them up,' my mum informed the policeman. 'They stood up for themselves.'

There was no way a couple of skinny runts like us could get in trouble for beating up two bigger kids. And luckily, that's how the police also saw it.

'I don't know what to say,' said the copper as he and his colleague began to leave the premises. Job done.

When I wasn't boxing (in or out of the club), being mistaken for a girl, playing pool, darts or fishing, I could always be found on the green in front of our house playing football.

I knew every bump of that patch of grass where I'd play with mates or on my own. It didn't bother me either way.

The only time I wouldn't be there would be when I was called in for tea by my mum through the open window that looked out on to the green so she could keep an eye on me. I would then race into the house, wolf down my supper as fast as humanly possible, then sprint back out on to the green to carry on playing. And because of that, throughout my career I was always happier playing on a full stomach. It just felt right to me and I'd always make sure I ate something substantial quite close to a game.

Luckily, although my parents were strict with me, I was always allowed to have something to eat if I was hungry. Not that you'd have known it by my size – I was a skinny little thing who was always about three years behind other players my age in terms of physical development. Which meant I was always trying to prove myself right up until I made it into the Premier League.

⚽

It all started when I was six and my dad took over as coach of the local YMCA team. My old man was a football man through and through, although he'd never played professionally. He'd played for district and county teams as a right winger, he'd gone to school with Frank Lampard Sr and was coached by Harry Redknapp and John Bond.

He was old school in his approach and as we got older he'd employ some questionable coaching methods. We trained on Thursdays and, because we were kids, we just wanted to play. But he had other ideas, most of them starting and finishing with running. He would even make us run through stinging nettles. As we all pissed and moaned, he yelled, 'Run through 'em!'

If he coached kids like that today, he'd end up in prison.

But for all that, he drove me and inspired me to become a footballer. He was always convinced I was going to make it as a pro and his confidence in me gave me huge amounts of self-belief on the pitch. In one game against Crayford Arrows, I gave away a penalty. I was absolutely livid and my eyes filled with tears.

Through a mixture of aggravation, determination and belief, I soon made up for my mistake.

The ball was rolled back to me from the resulting kick-off and, with tears still in my eyes, I struck it as hard as I could from inside my own half. Suddenly the other team were screaming at their goalkeeper to get back on his line but he would have been wasting his time as the ball sailed straight over his head and into the net. Apparently, David Beckham tried the same thing a few years later down the road at Selhurst Park but that's probably just one of those urban myths you hear about.

Despite my skinny legs, I had a hell of a kick on me, the hardest in my team apart from my mate Richard Dimmock. But then he was one of those kids who had a beard when he was ten so that was hardly a fair comparison.

I also played centre-back even though I was smaller than most of the other kids. I loved mixing it with bigger lads although it soon became a boring job as our team was thrashing everyone else and I barely got a kick all game.

I nagged my dad for ages to move me into midfield and he finally agreed – it was the best decision he or I ever made.

Playing in the middle of the park was also much more in keeping with my footballing idols. As a kid, Paul Gascoigne was the English player I looked up to the most and styled my game on. The 1990 World Cup made a big impression on me and Gazza was the star of that show. That was the point where I started to understand football far better and he remained England's best player for a few years after that, so was always someone I'd try to learn from – on the pitch.

I also loved George Best as a kid even though his playing days had long since finished by the time I was growing up. My old man always told me what a fantastic player he was – Bestie, not my dad – and whenever old footage of him was shown on the telly, I always used to watch him and marvel at his ridiculous skill.

One Saturday morning when I was a little bit older, my old man was watching the telly when he called out to me: 'Jim, you've got to see this player.'

I looked up from whatever I was doing – most probably reading a fishing magazine – and he said again: 'Come and watch this boy play. His name's Zeezee Zouzou, or something like that.'

I sat down next to him and watched this extraordinary player with a hell of an engine and the most amazing balance on the ball (as pointed out by my dad).

Zinedine Zidane became a big idol of mine as I got older. I tried to copy him on the pitch – although thankfully I never nutted anyone – by controlling the ball in exactly the same way as he did. I even got a pair of his boots to be like him even though we were completely different physiques and I never stood a chance of being anything like him. I believed I was like him and that was enough to help me progress.

The other player I tried to copy was Juan Román Riquelme, also one of the major foreign stars of the time. We were a similar age, but he'd been playing for Boca Juniors since he was eighteen, eventually moving to Barcelona, then playing for Villarreal.

Riquelme is one of those players who just has pure talent. A naturally gifted bloke who scores some outrageous goals thanks to his pure football ability. I always remember one game where he ran the show for Boca against Real Madrid in the 2000 Intercontinental Cup. He was only twenty-two and his skill was frightening.

My progress was slightly slower although by the time I was ten, despite all the other sporting distractions, football had become the most important thing in my life, even overtaking fishing – but I kept the Jan Porter haircut.

I played for Millwall boys between the ages of ten and thirteen and I also represented Kent schools, district and county teams. My size and shape meant I was never actually on the books of a professional club when I was in my teens. But I was still playing against some of the best young players in the district – I once came up against Bobby Zamora, who played against my YMCA team for Senrab, where many future stars started out.

I took a step up when I started playing youth football for Corinthian FC in a Kent youth league, who were coached by former Charlton goalkeeper Nicky Johns. By the time I was sixteen, I'd managed to break through into the club's first team, which meant playing on Saturday afternoons. When I finished playing, I used to work at Tony's Fish and Chips in Crayford High Street.

I'd peel potatoes for five hours every Saturday evening, while my mates were on the streets doing goodness knows what. I was at the age when blokes start getting into stuff that perhaps they shouldn't. All I was into was chips – but they were unbelievable chips.

Take away the cab fare to and from the chippy from the £15 I was earning and it almost cost my parents money for me to work there. But they wanted me to understand the importance of working so I would always appreciate becoming a footballer if and when that might happen.

After my football and fish 'n' chip shift on a Saturday, I'd be up early on a Sunday morning to play again for the Corinthian youth team – you can get away with that in your teens, especially when you're chasing a dream.

My dad was doing everything he could to make that dream a reality and a phone call to his cousin Tommy Taylor, who by then was the Leyton Orient manager, set up a two-week trial which would be my first taste of the professional game.

I was sixteen years old when I turned up at Orient's training ground. My football ability was sound but physically I was no more developed than a thirteen-year-old. And you don't tend to get many thirteen-year-olds playing professional football.

A game was quickly set up and I lined up alongside other youth and reserve players against the first team. I went in for a challenge with one of the Orient regulars who went straight through me and left his boot in as I lay in a heap on the ground.

'Welcome to the professional game,' I thought.

There was no need for him to have gone in on me like that. It was a one hundred per cent liberty challenge that could have caused me damage, but it really opened my eyes and was a moment I'd never forget. What that pro was saying to me with that nasty tackle was that it doesn't matter if you're a trialist, a youth teamer or the manager's cousin's son – this is football and nobody's going to give you anything; it's dog eat dog. That's the game and that's what some players are like.

The two weeks came and went and there was no deal for me. It was more a case of Tommy doing my dad a favour – but I'd also been done a favour as the experience toughened me up mentally and I was never as scared going into a tackle after that.

By the time I was seventeen, I'd left school and had started working. Unsurprisingly, I wasn't the most academic kid, but I certainly wasn't thick either, which couldn't be said about a fair few footballers I played with. At school, most teachers paid no attention to me when I told them that my future lay in football, rather than chemistry or geography.

'Jim, do you know how many kids want to be a professional football player?' they would say.

'Yeah, I know but I really think I can do it,' I'd reply.

'Jim, give it a rest.'

There was only one teacher who believed in me and I still have a card from Mr Marquois which says: 'Jim, one day I know you're going to be a professional footballer.'

Part of me thought that most of my teachers were right, though. And when I got my first job laying TV cables, complete with my own van, I remember thinking I'd really cracked it in life anyway as me and my mate zipped about town.

At that point, I signed for Dartford, a decent non-league team who offered me £30 per game. I was getting paid to play football. Well, I would've done if my manager Gary Julians had ever picked me to play in my favourite position.

Gary could be a right old grumpy bastard at times but that didn't stop one of my team-mates, Mitchell Crawley, and myself larking around whenever we could. One evening after training we were chucking things at each other in the empty car park outside the club – as you do. I lobbed something at Mitchell and then jumped straight into my motor, a huge Sierra Ghia estate car complete with towbar at the back, to escape. I switched on the engine, stuck it in reverse and slammed on the gas. As I sped round the corner, I could suddenly see the gaffer's car behind me but it was too late and I smacked straight into his motor.

If that wasn't bad enough, I then tried to drive forwards but the towbar had gone straight through Gary's passenger door and I started dragging his car along with mine!

'What are you doing, you soppy git?!' he yelled.

We both got out of our cars and as soon as he saw Mitchell, he started blaming him, saying he might have known he'd be involved in this. Result.

That little incident wasn't why Julians didn't pick me. It was the old size and shape problem rearing its head again as he felt I was getting pushed off the ball too easily in central midfield so, when I did get a game, he stuck me out on the wing.

My dad tried to compensate for my size by making sure I was the fittest player in the team. He pushed me hard and I hated it at the time but I soon came to appreciate it as I was always the fittest player in every squad I was a part of. I used to take it for granted, but it didn't happen by accident. It was down to bloody hard work.

One of my old man's favourite training drills – when he couldn't find stinging nettles – was interval training. His brutal version of it, that is. He'd drive down Bourne Road and I'd be jogging along next to the car. Then, he'd hoot and accelerate and I'd have to sprint hard to catch up. Only then would he slow down. This would be repeated until I couldn't take it anymore.

Sometimes, he'd make me run in ankle weights to really make me suffer. But the more I suffered the fitter I became.

Working long days laying all that cable, training twice a week with Dartford and then playing at the weekend was taking its toll so I started working with my dad, mainly in the City doing painting and decorating. I used to help rub down skirting boards, prepare walls for painting and I progressed from there, although I never hung any wallpaper – even off the pitch, I played to my strengths.

I was earning £30 a day but I was working very hard and grafting away. I didn't enjoy it at all, but I knew I had no choice.

Fortunately, my old man made things easier for me on the football front. His attitude had always been fantastic. Since I was a young kid, I don't think I can ever remember him being grumpy or in a bad mood.

'Dad, surely you can't be in a good mood every day?' I used to ask him.

'Yeaaaaah, why not?' he'd reply.

He just loves life and was always happy with his lot – he might work from 6am to 6pm but he would still come home happy. And I was just as delighted with his idea to give me days off whenever I had games for Dartford.

He thought that by keeping me fresh, my performances would improve and therefore any watching scouts would see me at my best. As long as I trained in my spare time, he was happy to let me work less. Those extra hours gave me an advantage over the other semi-pro players and it is little things like that which can make a difference between those who advance to the pro game and those who don't.

It wasn't just the physical side of my game that my dad was taking care of. Psychologically, he knew exactly how to handle me. Even if I'd had a poor game, he'd tell me I'd played okay. And if I was bang average, he'd say I'd played a blinder because he knew what I needed to hear.

The fact is, as he has always told me, whenever I came off a pitch in the early days, I never really knew if I'd played well or not. Sometimes I'd come off the pitch after a big game and be awarded the man of the match and I had no idea why. Honestly, I could barely remember the game.

I played minute to minute only focusing on what was happening at that very moment. If there was a ball to be won, I'd win it. Likewise, a corner or free kick to be taken, or a run into space to be made. My focus was intense partly because I was never the quickest player so I made up for that by trying to be the sharpest mentally and anticipating things before others. I saw the game as individual incidents of action rather than as a whole and somehow that worked for me.

While I was playing for Dartford, there were plenty of people doubting me, not that I knew it because my dad always protected me. But he had to deal with plenty of friends and football acquaintances telling him that I wasn't going to make it, that we'd left it too late. His standard reaction was to tell them they didn't know what they were talking about. Of course I was going to make it. His confidence was my confidence.

But I had doubts myself. So much so that I decided to become a fireman.

My dad backed the plan as he thought I'd still be able to develop my football as the fire brigade had a good, amateur set-up. But I was getting fed up with not playing enough for Dartford and saw the fire brigade as a career in which I could really progress.

I passed the fitness test with ease – it involved plenty of running which suited me fine. I even did the rat run which was probably the most terrifying experience of my life to that point. I wasn't that strong and I was weighed down by all the fireman's gear I was wearing and carrying while I had to scurry around a steel structure with a smokescreen glass mask on my face. The mask meant I could hardly see a thing as I looked for a dummy which I had to pull out of this maze-like structure.

There was also a lot of noise with the firemen yelling at you to do this or that, and I couldn't help panicking. I did it, though, which was a great feeling. The trouble was I also had to do a sit-down written test which was where I came unstuck.

It's hard to know what might have been had I passed that exam. It's possible that the Premier League and all that might have never happened. Thankfully, my academic shortcomings stood me in good stead. The head of Bexley Fire Brigade invited me to try again the following year but I wasn't able to take him up on his offer as, by then, my football career had gone mental.

After one of my better games for Dartford in which I'd also scored, Gravesend & Northfleet manager, Andy Ford, the opposition gaffer that day, approached me straight after the game.

He asked me if I fancied playing for his team and offered to double my wages – £60 per game seemed like a lot of money.

And that all led to the showdown in my parents' front room where I had to pluck up the courage to call Gary Julians and let him know I wanted to leave.

Back then, making any phone call was a hard thing for me to do. You can't get me off the bloody thing nowadays, but I was still young and slightly retiring then. Calling my manager to say I wanted out filled me with fear. I had to do it, though. Gravesend were playing a higher level of non-league football than Dartford, where I wasn't playing enough in any case.

Shaking and sweating, with my parents stood right next to me, I dialled Gary's number.

'Gary, I hope you don't mind but I feel like I want to move on with my football and Gravesend have approached me . . .' I said.

But he did mind.

'I don't agree with that Jimmy,' he said, sounding like he had the right hump.

'Hang on a minute, Gal, you don't even play me!' I said.

When my dad heard me say that, he took a step towards me, chomping at the bit, saying 'Give me the phone, I'll tell him!'

'No,' I said. I had to do this one myself.

I continued to explain my position and Gary got the message. I was going to Gravesend.

There I was reunited with my old schoolboy football pal Richard Dimmock. He was still ridiculously overdeveloped for his age while at nineteen going on twenty I was struggling to do a passing impression of an adult. Together we ran riot at that club. We were a good combination off the pitch and the manager loved the havoc – all good-natured, of course – we used to cause.

On the pitch, my performances were good, so I was told. I was scoring goals regularly and it was that form which saved me from getting the sack.

Richard and I had been playing for my dad's West Lodge pub team on a Sunday, which we weren't supposed to do now that we were being paid to play by Gravesend. We got rumbled and the club were not happy. Richard got sacked, but because I'd been playing well, they gave me a bollocking and that was the end of it.

But I was soon bidding farewell to the club anyway.

I'd heard that lots of scouts had been watching me but I didn't really believe it. I just presumed that they were watching someone else as there were twenty-one other players out there. Then, one afternoon, we played Purfleet and I had an absolute blinder. I scored a free kick which went in off the post after a team-mate had told me not to take it and then made another goal.

After that game, Andy Ford had a chat with my old man. It turns out that I was being watched – in a good way. Both QPR and West Ham had scouts there and were both interested in offering me a trial with a view to a permanent move.

Run that by me again?

A permanent move.

A professional contract.

No more painting and decorating.

No more stinging nettles.

No more chasing after a honking car.

And definitely no more playing football on the green in front of my parents' house. Because at the age of twenty, I was still doing that. I shit you not.

It was an incredible feeling to be within touching distance of that thing I'd craved and worked towards my whole life. For my dad, it meant as much as he had kept faith and never stopped believing in me.

And to top it all off, the club my dad and I had grown up supporting, West Ham, wanted to sign me. The only problem was that Andy Ford wanted me to go to QPR as he knew the scout, Roger Cross, a former Hammer too. There was no way my old man was going to allow that. He wanted me to go to West Ham so I could learn my trade at a much bigger club with a good footballing tradition. Andy warned him that I wouldn't get a game there but my dad wasn't fussed about that due to the experience I would have.

There was a bit of a stalemate as Gravesend still had a year pending on my contract so my dad called Hammers' boss Harry Redknapp, who was very encouraging and told him not to worry, they would wait a year to sign me.

It was a shrewd move because that meant Gravesend wouldn't get any money for me if my contract was up so Andy Ford gave me permission to leave then in return for a £35,000 transfer fee from West Ham – subject to my two-week trial going well, of course.

Remember Bobby Moore's blessing? Remember sharing Pelé's birthday? Remember my dad's cast-iron will for me to succeed?

Of course that trial would go well.

PILLAR 3

NEVER PANIC WHEN YOU'RE NOT SELECTED; ALTHOUGH MAYBE DO SOMETHING ABOUT IT AFTER TWO YEARS

'All things appear and disappear because of the concurrence of causes and conditions. Nothing ever exists entirely alone; everything is in relation to everything else.' ***Buddha***

So there I was sitting on the bench at Anfield. Yeah, Anfield – home of the five-time European and eighteen-time English champions. I wasn't part of an official club tour nor had I managed to hoax my way in – I was there on merit as a West Ham United substitute, having been selected by the club's manager Harry Redknapp. The team that I supported as a boy – in fact, at twenty years old I was pretty much still a boy – had signed me on a three-year contract and all I could think was 'How the hell has this all happened?'

Two weeks earlier, I was still a painter and decorator.

As I sat there in my comfy West Ham tracksuit and the Liverpool crowd finished singing 'You'll Never Walk Alone', there were probably still paint stains on my hands and, if you got really close, I may have even still smelled of turps, yet there I was, a Redknapp decision away from playing in the Premier League.

I'd been in a daze ever since I'd arrived at Chadwell Heath, West Ham's training ground, one Monday morning in February 1999. Part of me was still expecting the whole thing to be a ridiculous wind-up and that I'd be laughed out of there, but within fifteen minutes I was going one-on-one with Frank Lampard and there was nothing funny about that – unless your idea of fun is potential humiliation. In which case it was bloody hilarious.

I walked into the dressing room and I seemed to recognise everyone – Michael Carrick, Joe Cole, Rio Ferdinand, Trevor Sinclair, Neil Ruddock, Ian Wright, Paul Kitson, John Moncur and Lampard – except not one bloody sod recognised me. And why should they?

I was an unknown kid going into a Premier League club for the first time and I was petrified. Imagine your first day at a new job, going into a new office, full of people who already know each other and you're the stranger. It can be a horrible feeling. Now multiply that by a hundred and you're not even close to what it's like stepping into a professional football dressing room for the first time.

All I could think that morning was 'Wow!' and 'Shit!', the two words echoing around my head like a broken record. That 'new club' feeling never got any easier throughout my career. Even when I joined MK Dons at the age of thirty-three, I still hated that first day.

What made matters worse was that I'd turned up in my own knackered Umbro training gear and didn't have the balls to ask the kit man for some official club clobber. So as we all strolled out on to the training ground, I looked and felt right out of place.

'Wow! Shit!'

Mind you, I'd already felt like a fish out of water earlier that morning when I'd chugged into the players' car park in my dad's gold Granada Ghia, grinding to a halt alongside Rio Ferdinand's Aston Martin. That was a hell of a way to announce myself. The Granada Ghia was probably the longest car ever built that wasn't actually a limo and there it was, getting up close and personal with Rio's Aston.

Over time, that glorious Granada became a regular sight in the West Ham car park. The boys would look at me and say, 'How do you get away with that?' and I'd just laugh it off and reply, 'Don't worry, it's quality'.

When I joined Peterborough, I replaced Dad's Granada with my very own brand-new Ford Fiesta. I was never one for flash cars. Where I might go and spend £3,000 on a fishing pole, other players would spend £4,000 on new wheels for their supercar. For years, team-mates would say to me, 'Er, your motor, Jim?' and I'd say, 'Don't worry about it, I've got to drive it, you ain't.' But I wasn't that confident on my first day at West Ham.

We were out on the training ground. Everyone looked the part except me in my battered old gear. I couldn't stop looking at all those players and trying to pretend I was taking it all in my stride when, in fact, my heart was pumping so fast I was pretty sure Harry Redknapp could hear it – and he was still in his office.

'Wow! Shit!'

Eventually, the gaffer joined us. The first team had lost on Saturday and, despite what you might see on the telly and read in the papers, Harry is a hard man and his reaction to that defeat was to set up one-on-ones for all of us. It's a gruelling exercise where two players, each with a goalkeeper in nets behind them, go head-to-head on a small pitch. There's

a lot of running, a lot of huffing and puffing, and a lot of sweating.

Before I knew it, Harry had put me up against Lampard. How's your luck? It's just me and him in front of everyone.

'Wow! Shit!'

I could feel the tension but my racing heart meant the adrenaline was pumping at the same time. This was what I'd always dreamed about.

Fortunately, I managed to hold my own and, despite my awful kit, not embarrass myself at all. After that, the training session raced by and, before I knew it, I was back in the Granada Ghia heading home to my mum and dad's place in Bexleyheath, where I still lived. In the weeks and months that followed I'd make life a lot easier for myself by staying at my nan and grandad's in Canning Town after training, with the added bonus that the place was like the story of my football career as my nan kept every medal and trophy I'd ever won.

But that first day I collapsed into my own bed at about 4pm and slept right through until the following morning when it was time to go through the whole process again.

'Wow! Shit!'

It was only at that point that I realised just how fit footballers are – I thought the graft of painting and decorating was tough, but I remember thinking that first training session was physically ten times harder. It made me even more determined to improve my fitness.

The two-week trial period rocketed by in a flash and I must've done something right because suddenly I was sitting at a packed press conference alongside fellow new signings Paolo Di Canio (fresh from his eleven-game ban for shoving over referee Paul Alcock), Marc-Vivien Foé, Gavin Holligan (a non-league player from Kingstonian) and Harry.

'Wow! Shit!'

There must've been at least a dozen cameras flashing and clicking away as I sat there like a rabbit in the headlights, a little kid in front of all the grown-ups.

After what felt like forever, Harry introduced us to the press. 'Afternoon everyone, thanks for coming. I'm pleased to be able to present our new signings. We have Paolo Di Canio, Marc-Vivien Foé, Gavin Holligan and er . . . what's your name?'

Silence. You could have heard a pin drop.

He'd forgotten my name. I was utterly devastated. But, before I could announce myself to the world, Harry's brain clicked into gear and it came to him.

'Er, Jim. Jimmy Bullard.'

The world now knew my name. There was no turning back from this point. Fame and glory awaited – all I had to do was get on the pitch. Unfortunately, that proved to be a lot harder than I thought.

As it turned out, Anfield was the highlight of my two years at West Ham, although on that February afternoon on Merseyside I had no idea that would be the case. The thrill and buzz of that day was extraordinary. I can still remember pulling up outside the ground, seeing all the fans milling around, touching the 'This is Anfield' sign as I walked out of the tunnel and feeling the hairs on the back of my neck stand up and do a little dance as the supporters sang. I even got goosebumps in the dressing room as Anfield is one of those old grounds where you can hear the crowd singing while you're getting changed. Fortunately, that was all quite similar to most Gravesend & Northfleet home games so I took it all in my stride. Yeah, right.

Seeing my name on the squad sheet had given me my first huge buzz. My dad had been watching us train that morning and I sprinted across the pitch to tell him the news: 'Dad! Dad! I'm squadding tomorrow!'

He beamed from ear to ear. What a moment for my old man and my mum, after everything they'd done for me. But there was no time to get all soppy as I had to peg it back to Bexleyheath to pick up the gear I needed for the overnight trip, then bomb it back to the training ground to join the team on the bus to the North West.

Here's what all the fuss was about. That Saturday at Anfield, West Ham lined up as follows: Hislop, Sinclair, Potts, Ferdinand, Pearce, Minto, Lampard, Foé, Lomas, Berkovic, Cole; Subs: Lazaridis, Keller, Holligan, BULLARD, Forrest.

'Wow! Shit!'

I stared at that team sheet for far too long, then glanced at the Liverpool line-up: James, Heggem, Song, Staunton, Babb, Bjørnebye, Carragher, Redknapp, McManaman, Fowler, Owen; Subs: Riedle, Berger, Friedel, Harkness, Ferri.

'Wow! Shit!'

Probably the most exciting thing about that day was that I would finally get to find out what went on inside a Premier League dressing room and how different it was to non-league.

But I was probably a bit naive because it wasn't particularly different at all. A football dressing room is similar whether you're playing Sunday League or Premier League – other than an extra lick of paint and a bit more space of course.

The familiar football smell of Ralgex was the same.

There were men's cocks out everywhere, which was the same too.

And the actual talking from the manager was fairly similar with Harry saying things like 'We need to get it into Paolo more' or 'Rio, bob Eyal [Berkovic] the ball a bit quicker'. Change Paolo to Paul, Rio to Rob and Eyal to Ian, and it could've been any non-league dressing room.

The main difference, however, was everything that was laid on for you in there. All the energy drinks and food you could ever need were ready and waiting when you got into the changing room, as were the neatly laid-out shirts. Seeing mine with my name on was a massive buzz. The tie-ups for the socks were all cut up and ready as were any bits of tape you might need. From that point of view, it was like moving into the Dorchester from a youth hostel.

Once I'd got over the fact I was a professional footballer at Anfield – the memory of which is something I'm probably still coming to terms with to this very day – I was off to the bench to watch the game.

It was an exciting match, not that I'd have known that much about it. I'm far more of a football player than a watcher and I was just itching to get on – all footballers will tell you that, but whenever I was on the bench, I would do absolutely anything I could to get on. Short of asking the manager directly (which I did, sometimes), whenever I was within sight of the gaffer, I'd fiddle with my shinpads as if to say, 'Yes boss, I have the correct attire to play association football so you just throw me in at the first available opportunity.'

My stretching would also be as deliberately over the top

as possible in order to catch the manager's eye, whether it was Harry Redknapp or Fabio Capello.

At Anfield, I was sitting next to Holligan, a promising striker, and with the match finely poised at 2-2 with ten minutes left, Harry turned to the bench to look at his options: promising striker plucked out of non-league (Holligan) or promising winger plucked out of non-league (Bullard)? Or as Harry might have thought, 'Gavin Holligan or, er, whassisname?'

'Please choose me, please choose me' I thought as I was temporarily transported back to my regular lunchtime games at the school playground. Except in those days, I was always picked early doors. Unlike this time when Harry opted to replace Joe Cole with Holligan.

'Wow! Shit!'

In fairness, I could see why Harry wanted to go with a striker and try to win the game. And Gavin made an instant impact, almost scoring. I was gutted but, being naive, I assumed my chance would come sooner rather than later – after all, he could so easily have chosen me that day.

I had to wait a couple of months for my next opportunity but the adrenaline started pumping again when I saw my name at the bottom of the squad list for our away match at Tottenham. Like the Liverpool game, Harry was short of options because of injuries and suspensions but I still saw it as another massive opportunity for me to grab.

In the dressing room before the game, Harry was talking about the Spurs star David Ginola and how crucial it was to try to keep him quiet.

'He's a superstar,' he told us. 'He looks like a model, you won't miss him. He'll be on the left so Steve Lomas, you need to get as close to him as possible from right-back. If he takes you on, I want the centre-back on him, then the other centre-back on him. You've got to be on this man.'

Shortly after, we were in the tunnel waiting to walk on to the White Hart Lane pitch – another wonderful and surreal moment for me. The Spurs boys were stood alongside us and there was the Frenchman Ginola, six feet tall with his long, L'Oréal-coiffured hair resting on broad, muscular shoulders, his manicured hands on his hips, looking worth it in every way. He smelled incredible, as if he'd just been bathing in Jean Paul Gaultier's new scent – even I couldn't help thinking what an absolute knockout he was.

Ian Wright didn't just think it though, he told Ginola.

'You smell like a million dollars, son.'

'Sank you,' replied Ginola in his thick French accent.

Watching from the bench, I had a bird's-eye view of the man's football skills too when Tottenham's right-back Stephen Carr launched a long ball from the right towards Ginola. It looked like it was going out of play and Harry even got up to catch it, but the Frenchman launched himself in the air and controlled it with his chest. In a couple of seconds, he'd gone inside two players and bent an incredible shot right into the stanchion.

Even Harry couldn't help but applaud that skill. We all did as it was a ridiculous goal, scored by a marvellous player. 'Fuck me,' I thought as I stood there clapping, a bit stunned. 'I've got a hell of a lot of improving to do to reach anywhere near that kind of level.'

Putting me into that situation was very much like putting a fan in there. I'm not ashamed to admit I was completely awestruck and with good reason too. I'd come from the reality of being a semi-pro to the fringes of the fantasy, the Premier League, in such a short space of time that I had to stop and pinch myself if I was at White Hart Lane or Anfield. And that was the attitude I took with me throughout my career. I would never take anything for granted and was always determined to take in every moment, whether it was pulling up in the team bus outside every ground, seeing and hearing the fans, or just the feeling of being in the dressing room before a match when three points were at stake.

I would never be one of those players who puts the oversized headphones on and zones out. I wanted to hear, see and smell everything – even if that meant breathing in the burgers, getting the middle finger from rival fans or listening to them telling me to fuck off. It's what I'd craved from a very young age and I was determined not to let any of it slip through my fingers – although I wasn't that keen on all the insults; my hair's lovely, just ask the good people at Wash & Go.

I never got on the pitch at Spurs and that was it for me in terms of my West Ham career highlights – two games on the bench.

Looking back, we had such a strong team at that time that it was little surprise I hardly got a sniff. In the early stages, I was still living the dream, feeling like my chance would come. But realistically, I was trying to compete for a first-team place with players like Joe Cole, Michael Carrick and Trevor Sinclair. Even youth players like Adam Newton and Richard Garcia were really promising prospects so I had my work cut out just to get a reserve-team game. Lionel Messi would have had a tough time getting a start there – mind you, he would have been aged twelve at the time.

To me as a young pro, Harry came across as very strict and I found it hard to play under him. I know that might be at odds with the public perception of him, but he was never going to treat a rookie like me in the same way he would senior pros like Wright or Di Canio.

In fact, Di Canio was almost part of the management team there; he changed everything when he arrived at Upton Park. He came with a bad reputation – pushing over a referee in the middle of the park was never going to go down well, even if the ref did tumble like Charlie Chaplin – but it couldn't have been further from the real Paolo. The bloke was immaculate. His kit was tight and fitted him perfectly. He became club captain and his skipper's armband had claret and blue tassles hanging off it, making him look like a warrior. His socks were rolled up perfectly over his permanently shaved, well-oiled legs. He oozed Italian class and style. He was a real man. And he was also an utterly terrifying nutcase.

When he first joined the club he was far from impressed with how we warmed up before training and matches, especially if one of the other lads started taking the piss. He took Harry to one side and said, 'This warm-up is shit! We are supposed to be stretching and Razor Ruddock is talking about drinking last night. He's talking about shitting! This is not right!'

Before long, Paolo had brought over his own fitness coach from Italy to put us through our paces. The guy ended up staying at West Ham for a few years.

Perhaps I should have taken the bull by the horns like Paolo and insisted that one of my mates looked after training. I'm not sure we would have got much further than the pub, which probably would have suited Razor Ruddock down to the ground.

He was another senior pro whom Harry treated very differently to the younger players. When we returned for pre-season, Harry had us running circuits of the training ground pitches. Big Razor did one circuit, ran straight back to the dressing room without breaking his stride and yelled to Harry 'That'll do for me boss'.

Razor struggled with his weight throughout his career. I heard one story about how he'd kept a food diary while he was at Liverpool and they worked out that he ate 212 steak and kidney pies per year. He was a law unto himself and, alongside the likes of Wright, Moncur and Kitson, ruled the roost. One of his trademark acts was marking his territory in the dressing room after training.

He'd walk straight up to one of the enormous team baths, piss straight into it and say: 'That's Razor's bath, no-one's getting in it.' Ridiculous behaviour, but it used to make me laugh.

As did the time he nicked our goalkeeper Shaka Hislop's motor. Razor was injured that day – I think he'd probably had one too many the night before, a common 'injury' in that era – so he was roaming around the dressing room while everyone else was out on the pitch and decided to help himself to the keys to Shaka's Maserati. The car was his pride and joy and even had 'Shak' on the number plate, but Razor wasn't bothered about any of that and drove the car up the road, walked back to the training ground and put the keys back in Shaka's pocket.

Ruddock would have made a great criminal because he looked as cool as a cucumber a couple of hours later when Shaka was desperately asking everyone to help search for his motor. The keeper even called the police to tell them it had gone missing until Razor put him out of his misery and told him what he'd done. Hilarious.

But I wasn't laughing that much before my first pre-season, when Harry asked me to do some work on building my physique. 'You have to come back bigger' he told me as he wasn't a fan of my slight build. My body was closer to a sixteen-year-old's than a twenty-year-old's and Harry was convinced that the Premier League required players to have a physical presence as well as ability.

I wasn't so sure and I felt that he lacked belief in me. He was always after perfection, which I just didn't have. Whenever I put in a bad cross in training he would be right on my case. With hindsight I can understand that he wanted me to learn so he could get the best out of me, but the longer I stayed at West Ham, the more of an outcast and reject I felt.

The fact is that most of the younger players and me found Harry to be a very harsh bloke. He was more like a headmaster than a manager to us. We were scared shitless of him and we saw less of him when Glenn Roeder came into coach us because with about forty pros on the books, it was impossible for Harry to take a session with all of us.

Harry demanded that all the reserve players turn up at the weekend to watch the first team so we could learn from them and improve our games. But, rightly or wrongly, that didn't interest me in the slightest.

I've never been a great watcher of football. I loved the

game and understood it inside out, but I always wanted to play. That's why when training was over on a Friday, unless some of my mates were involved in the first team, that was it until after the weekend for me.

One Monday morning, Harry confronted me. He had the right hump because we'd been stuffed 4-0 at the weekend. It was best to stay out of his way after a defeat for at least a couple of days, but he had me cornered so I had to engage.

'Where was you at the weekend? At the game?' he asked me.

'No,' I replied. Honesty was always my policy.

'Where was ya then?'

'Fishing!'

His face turned to thunder, whatever that actually looks like.

He marched over to Roeder and said, 'Him! Fucking fishing. Not even watching the game. Fucking fishing!'

Then he turned round to me and added: 'And get your fucking hair cut as well, you can't even see!'

Harry must've seen me constantly flicking my gorgeous, flowing locks away from my face during training. The Alice band hadn't yet made it into my on-pitch wardrobe as I didn't have the confidence to wear one. It was only when I started thinking I was a bit of a player while at Wigan that I started to wear it regularly.

I was tempted to tell Harry that I didn't like watching football, just playing it, but I thought I'd better bite my lip. It would be one thing if Di Canio had said something like that to him, but not a twenty-one-year-old without a first-team appearance to his name.

So I swallowed that and made sure I turned up to matches for a few weeks. But I wasn't getting my hair cut. No bloody chance. I actually grew it longer. My hair was personal, none of his business. I can't imagine he would ever have said something like that to David Ginola, if he was on our books.

I was desperate to show Harry that I could play, but my situation wasn't helped by the fact I didn't have an agent, which hindered my chances of getting out on loan.

After six months I started to wonder if it was ever going to happen for me at West Ham.

After a year, I was certain it never would. But I remained determined to prove myself every time I stepped on to the training pitch or crossed the white line for a reserve game.

Despite the issues I faced, I remained grateful for my privileged position. There were some extraordinary times in that Hammers changing room, and enjoying the antics of the lunatic senior pros helped my non-playing time pass by far quicker.

There were two cliques at West Ham. The first was made up of the younger players like Rio, Lampard, Cole and Carrick, who were all quite serious about their football. Rio was only twenty-one but he was already one of the club's best players so he could afford to muck about a bit. But none of them dared to overstep the mark with the other clique, the senior pros.

Except Jermain Defoe that is, who took no shit from anyone.

Jermain was signed from Charlton as a sixteen-year-old and although he was the same age as the youth players, he was on a professional contract. So when Razor asked Jermain to clean his boots, the teenager was having none of it. 'You come and clean my boots!' he said. 'I signed here as a pro, not to clean anyone's boots.'

But that kind of thing was very much the exception as those older players were the governors and watching them larking about on a daily basis shaped my career and reputation more than I ever realised at the time.

Those lads were mad. There were at least half a dozen big characters and to this day, I have no idea how Harry kept them together. They were a dying breed, the last of the old school and I learned so much by watching them from the outside because I was only on the fringes of the first team.

In a weird way, I probably carried a little bit of their old-school attitude with me throughout my career although I could never have got away with some of their behaviour.

One cold January morning there was a press call at the training ground and John Moncur asked Eddie the kit man for his gear. Moncs looked through the clothing he was given and noticed he hadn't been given a hat.

'If you don't give me a hat, I'm going out there naked,' he told Eddie.

It only took a little thing like that to set Moncur off. Once he was riled, he'd go off on one and do anything. I was always very wary of him as he was completely unpredictable.

'You ain't gonna do that,' said Eddie, knowing how many journos and cameramen were waiting outside.

That was a challenge that Moncur couldn't resist, especially with Razor egging him on. He blew up a surgical glove, wrapped it around his head so he looked like a chicken, then sprinted on to the training pitches wearing just his jock strap.

The gaffer was already out there chatting to the press when he was interrupted by Moncur yelling, 'Harry, sort your fucking kit man out, he won't even give me a hat!'

A shocked Redknapp spluttered, 'Moncy, get back in son. What's the matter with you? You're showing me up!'

If I'd done something like that at Fulham under Roy Hodgson it would have gone down like a shit sandwich – and that's not something that tends to go down that well.

Once Di Canio joined there was always tension between him and Moncur which took up a lot of Harry's time. I remember soon after Paolo signed, he walked into the dressing room and Moncur was holding court.

'Paolo might be here,' he told everyone, 'but it don't matter how many wands they bring to this football club, I'm still the magician.' The lads loved it and fell about laughing, but Di Canio wasn't that impressed and the pair clashed regularly.

Paolo was big on respect and he would lose the plot if he felt he wasn't being shown any. We had two masseurs at the training ground, Rupert and Russ, and we'd often go for a rubdown after training. But if it was the day after a game and Paolo came in for a massage to find both tables with reserve players on them, he would do his absolute bollocks, ranting and raving until one of the beds was vacated. Which never took long because if he came in wanting a massage and you were on one of the beds, you moved off it pretty sharpish.

He was always blowing a gasket about something. After one training session he came into the changing room to find his slightly loud, yellow paisley shirt hanging from one of the aircon ducts on the ceiling.

Di Canio took his clothes very seriously. He would usually be dressed in tight jeans or trousers, pointed shoes and a funky shirt. I often sat next to him and I would never dream of touching any of his gear. So when he saw his shirt had been moved he went apeshit.

'Who put my shirt up there?' he roared as we pissed ourselves laughing.

'You fucking bastards! Don't show me disrespect like that!'

He marched off upstairs to Harry's office and made the gaffer come down to the changing room to resolve the matter. He didn't calm down until the culprit was found, an apology was made and he had made sure no-one ever touched his clothes again.

'If anyone ever does that to me again,' he seethed, 'I'm not playing.'

A minute later, the nutcase was in the shower, dancing and singing away.

It was the same during training as Paolo hated to lose and would often just walk off the pitch if things weren't going his way, especially if he was on the opposite side to Moncur.

It got to the point where Harry always had to put them on the same team whenever he set up a game during training or World War Three would have kicked off.

If they were on opposing teams, any free kick given for a foul on Di Canio would be met by Moncur screaming, 'You're a fucking cheat!'

To avoid a situation he could not possibly manage, Harry always put them together. Even then, there would be murders as whichever team lost would go off their heads. It was an absolute nightmare for Harry, but it was extremely funny for me to watch.

When people talk about man-management these days, I always think back to that dressing room and I still have no idea how Harry kept everyone happy – that's why I think Roberto Mancini did such a good job at Man City; that must have been an impossible changing room to control.

Paolo was sometimes just as hard to control on the pitch – there was one game I turned up to watch, after Harry had given me a bollocking, which was crazy. We were losing at home to Bradford, when Paolo went down in the box. It looked like a penalty but the ref waved away our protests for the third time that afternoon. Di Canio felt like the world was against him and he walked over to the bench and started making the substitution sign to the gaffer.

'What the fuck is he doing?' I thought, and so did Harry, who tells the story brilliantly.

'I don't play,' said Paolo, as he sat himself down in front of the dug-out, folded his arms and put his head in his hands.

'Come on, Paolo!' said Harry.

'I don't play no more!'

'Paolo, get up quick, we're losing 4-2!' urged Harry.

While they were debating the issue, the Bradford players were dribbling the ball around him and Dean Saunders missed a glorious chance to add to the visitors' lead.

The fans started chanting Di Canio's name and he suddenly ended his on-pitch sit-in and got on with the game, which meant having a huge row with Frank Lampard when we were awarded a penalty soon after. The pair of them both had their hands on the ball and Paolo wouldn't let go of it until he was the man placing it on the spot. He ran up and smashed it confidently past the keeper. The comeback was on and two further goals meant we won, but it was all about Paolo.

It was more of the same later that year when we played Everton away and Paolo gave up the chance to score a last-minute winner because the home keeper Paul Gerrard was down injured. It was an extraordinary moment as the perfect cross came in and all Di Canio had to do was put the ball in the empty goal – but he caught it instead and signalled that Gerrard should get some treatment to the astonishment of pretty much everyone.

Apparently, Stuart Pearce was absolutely livid after the match and was prowling around the dressing room urging Harry not to let him near Paolo when he came back in, in case he killed him. To make matters worse, the gaffer then had to do all the post-match interviews praising Paolo when he was just as pissed off that we'd missed out on the chance of three points – Di Canio even won a special Fifa Fair Play award for it, but then that's Fifa.

I can't imagine they would have lauded his actions during half time of a League Cup tie at Birmingham. All the boys were full of it at training the next morning, as Paolo had supposedly not lined up correctly in the wall for a Birmingham free kick from which they scored to lead at the break. When Shaka came into the changing room he asked Paolo what he'd been doing – and the Italian lost it.

'Oh, you blame me?' he said, as he got up, picked up one of those huge Gatorade buckets and started swinging it around the dressing room, angrily muttering to himself. Everyone ducked for cover trying to get out of the way of the bucket – and its contents – before Paolo eventually chucked it all over the place, making sure Shaka's gear got a good soaking.

'I don't play no more,' he sulked, not for the last time in his career, and pulled off his boots. But, funnily enough, he was back out on the pitch for the second half and we turned it around to win the game.

Paolo wasn't the only great character during my time at

Upton Park. Harry was never shy when it came to signing players, which meant I was lucky enough to experience training with a colourful cast of footballers.

Davor Šuker was a European football legend and he turned up towards the end of his brilliant career. I can't think of a more skilful player I've ever shared a pitch with – he was unbelievable. He brought another Croatian star with him in Igor Štimac, the hardest defender I'd ever seen, a total animal on the pitch.

But for all his ability, Šuker had this crazy habit of insisting on chipping the goalkeeper from wherever he was on the pitch. He could be seventy yards away from goal during training and he'd have a go at catching the keeper off his line.

It would wind the boys up something rotten and Harry would do his pieces on the sidelines, saying 'Stop fucking doing that!' but Šuker couldn't help himself.

I think it stemmed back to that amazing Euro 96 goal he scored when he chipped Peter Schmeichel from the edge of the box. He'd obviously been ripping the arse out of it ever since and it must've become his trademark. It was almost as if his attitude was 'Nobody can tell me not to do that now – did you not see that goal I scored against Schmeichel?'

But he was a top lad as he proved when I went to Croatia with England in 2008. I wouldn't have even been certain that he would've remembered me – I'm sure I wouldn't have remembered him if the roles had been reversed – but he went out of his way to come over and shake my hand. 'Jimmy!' he said with a smile on his face when we arrived at the stadium that night. Fortunately, we were in the stands watching so he didn't have an opportunity to try a chip on that occasion.

Samassi Abou also turned up at a similar time and he was an out-and-out lunatic, who nobody dared to cross. He was another absurdly talented player, who spoke with a broad African accent as he was from Ivory Coast. In training, you never knew what he was going to do. His feet were so quick, they were an absolute joke, and I don't think even he knew what he was going to do either. And if he didn't know there was no way a defender was going to have a clue how to handle him so he proved to be a very tricky customer on the pitch.

And then there was Manny Omoyinmi, one of my reserve team-mates, who got us thrown out of the League Cup – although it was hardly his fault. Most West Ham fans would remember him for playing seven minutes as a substitute in the League Cup quarter-final which West Ham won on penalties against Aston Villa. But we were then forced to replay the game because Manny had played earlier in the competition while on loan at Gillingham. He was cup-tied and shouldn't have played, but he was made the scapegoat for that shambles as he was sent out on loan after that and never played for the club again. The club secretary also had to resign. Manny was just trying to break into the first team like me and he told us afterwards, 'I didn't know the rules. If I'm lucky enough to get a chance for the first team, I'm just going to play'.

Being perfectly honest, if that had happened to me I wouldn't have known the rules either – when did we go to football school and get taught all that stuff? I must have missed that one.

It wasn't just the West Ham players who were quirky,

there was also Stan, the hilarious reserve team kit man and minibus driver. The poor bloke was so old he probably should have retired but he loved it too much. He was at the ground at six or seven every morning, washing kit and clearing up. Later in the day, he'd drive us to somewhere like Norwich for a game and by 11pm he'd be driving us back to London.

But he could never stay awake, which is not ideal if you're a passenger on his bus. He fell asleep at the wheel so often it was frightening and there was always the same tell-tale sign. We'd be cruising along then suddenly we'd all hear the noise of the minibus wheels bumping over the cat's eyes on the road – de-de-de-de-de-de-de-de-de-de-de-de.

'Stanley!' we'd all yell. 'Wake up, for fuck's sake!'

It's hard to believe these things went on, but we just accepted it. It was my first experience of professional football and I suppose I didn't know any better.

But what I did know was those reserve games were not helping my career and not just because of Stanley's driving. I felt like I was going nowhere. After two years at West Ham, it was fight or flight time, but the decision was out of my hands as Harry had already decided I had no future at the club – which was about as surprising as a Paul Scholes yellow card.

I was convinced I hadn't ever been given a proper chance at West Ham so there was no way Harry could have known what I was capable of. The confirmation of what I'd known all along simply made me extra hungry to make it as a pro footballer. I just needed to find a club that believed in me.

I think the first and only time I'd ever been in Harry's office was when he told me I wouldn't be getting a new deal at Upton Park.

I was in there with my dad and there were no hard feelings although I was determined to prove him wrong – and I told him that one day I'd line up for an opposing side against one of his.

Years later, I was proved right when I played against Portsmouth and Spurs. On both occasions, Harry came over to shake my hand. There was never any bitterness there and, if anything, I owe a hell of a lot to the Redknapp family. Harry made my career, and about five years later Jamie saved it. But that's a different story.

PILLAR 4

REFUEL WISELY WITH YOUR HALF-TIME CUPPA; UNLESS BARRY FRY HAS KICKED IT ALL OVER THE FLOOR

'Remember, no human condition is ever permanent; then you will not be overjoyed in good fortune, not too sorrowful in misfortune.'
Socrates (The philosopher, not the Brazilian footballer)

The Peterborough team bus on the way to play Wigan at the JJB Stadium was running late.

Usually, we'd arrive at an away ground about ninety minutes before kick-off so there was enough time to get changed and warm up properly before the game. But, that Saturday afternoon we were behind schedule and we finally pulled into the ground at about 1.45pm.

On the way there, a few of us had been playing three-card brag, including myself, Neale Fenn, Jon Cullen, Gareth Jelleyman and the physio Paul Showler. Never one to be far away from the action, our larger-than-life manager Barry Fry also joined us for a few hands. Imagine Arsène Wenger joining the Arsenal boys for cards – it's never going to happen. But this was Peterborough and this was Barry Fry, so we all went along with it.

The bus stopped outside the stadium while we were in the middle of a hand and I was thinking we needed to pack this game up and get into the ground. But Barry didn't move. He was looking at his cards closely and thinking.

We gave each other a few puzzled looks and someone piped up and said: 'Gaffer, are we getting off the bus or what?'

'Hang on!' yelled Barry. 'No! Nobody's getting off while I've got money in the middle! We'll finish playing this hand first.'

I looked round at the boys. I mouthed the words 'This geezer's mad!' to one of the lads, but we had no choice but to finish the hand we were playing. And only then, twenty-five minutes later than planned, did we actually make it into the stadium. Madness. As Barry said to me later, 'You've got to get your priorities right.'

Looking back on it now, it's funny how we all just went along with it. We're professional footballers and he didn't let us off the coach because he was playing cards with us.

Bazza was clearly an unusual manager, but he was part and parcel of the Peterborough experience. Without a doubt, Bazza was one of the biggest influences on my career – there's no way I would have gone on to enjoy the success I had without him.

Bazza was a unique character, unlike anyone else I've ever met in football. But forget about all the stories you've ever heard about him being a bit of a nutter, it's all bollocks. In real life, Bazza is the maddest bastard of them all. He's a little powerhouse of a bloke, who probably only stands about five feet off the ground, but he's all energy, emotion and passion. Reminds me a lot of myself actually, although I'm not short and fat.

I love hearing about the meticulous preparation and strict rules of today's modern managers – and I even experienced England under Fabio Capello for a bit too which was no picnic – and then comparing them to Bazza and some of his antics.

You never really knew what was coming next with him. Apart from the fact that if we were losing at half time, the tray of tea on the dressing room table would not stay there for long – and not because anyone was drinking it.

Baz would lose it with us big time if he had the hump with our performance. He was very old school like that. If he was waiting for us when we got to the dressing room, it wasn't because he wanted to give us all a pat on the back to say well done, it was because he wanted to knock our blocks off.

Every home game, a lovely old dear would come into the changing room and put the tea on a rickety old table near where we were all sitting. And without fail, if Baz had the hump, that table would be the first to feel his anger as he'd give it a kicking and the tea would fly everywhere. It got to the point where I wondered why the old girl even bothered bringing it in.

Barry's view was that if we'd been useless we didn't deserve the tea, so we weren't having it. End of discussion. Given his size and stature, it was a miracle that he managed to raise his leg high enough to kick that tray over at all and I can't imagine he'd be able to do it today – not without a crane to help him.

We often had sandwiches straight after a game and on one occasion when the gaffer exploded after we'd lost, he booted the table, sending the sarnies spiralling through the air and a couple of them actually landed on our captain Andy Edwards's head. The place erupted, we were all on the floor laughing; I was actually crying. Never mind Fergie kicking a football boot at Becks, this was the real deal – the gaffer landing a prawn sandwich on the skipper's head; deal with that!

Luckily, Andy was a mild-mannered enough guy to take it on the chin – literally – and he didn't make too much of a fuss. He was without doubt the softest captain I've ever played alongside, completely unlike our right-back Dean Hooper, who took no shit from anyone. Even Baz.

The pair of them used to squabble all the time as Dean was a bit of a nutter. In fact, he was the biggest lunatic I've ever met in football. And I've met Duncan Ferguson.

He was a bricklayer with his own building firm as well as a footballer, a proper hard bastard who you were always glad was on your side. He didn't know the meaning of 'riding a tackle' – if an opposition player was anywhere near the ball he was going for he'd go straight through them. Once, we'd come in at half time to find Barry waiting for us and we all waited for the inevitable – as did the old dear and her tea. The gaffer upped the tea, pointed at Dean and said: 'You've got to pull your fucking finger out today!'

Immediately I thought 'This is going to go off' and I tried to look anywhere but at the pair of them. Dean jumped straight up and him and Baz were nose to nose with Dean yelling: 'Don't you fucking talk to me like that, I'm trying my best.'

Baz had him by the scruff of the neck and it looked for all the world like he was going to give him a right-hander. I looked on at this incredible match-up. In the blue corner, our psycho bricklaying, brick-shithouse right-back; in the red corner, our fifty-eight-year-old, short, fat, ferocious manager.

Barry still had Dean by the scruff of the neck and, using his head, managed to push my team-mate back towards his seat.

'You fucking sit down,' growled the gaffer and that was the end of it.

It was the first time I'd ever seen a player get up and confront the manager like that and it was frightening and exhilarating at the same time.

It's hard to explain what it's like in the dressing room, especially at half time. Passions can run high. The adrenaline is still flowing from the first forty-five minutes and there are a load of testosterone-fuelled blokes all sitting very close together.

Barry and Dean both hated losing so that confrontation was a recipe for disaster. It just boiled down to who was madder and Baz was mad enough not to be afraid of Dean. I would have been and so would most people, but that's Barry.

He'd do anything to win. He once told me a great story about when he was manager of Birmingham and results weren't going his way. He discovered there was a curse on the St Andrews pitch as the stadium had been built on Romany land, so Bazza decided to lift the spell by pissing on all four corners of the pitch. As you do.

I could just picture him waddling around the pitch, doing a bit of wee then holding it and waddling some more. Amazingly, it almost worked as a three-month winless streak was broken soon after. Bazza's luck didn't last, though, and it wasn't long before he was sacked.

We all suffered whenever we lost and not just because we were down about it, but because Barry made sure post-defeat training was never a pleasant experience. He had a special running session which he'd treat us to on a Monday after a defeat. He'd mark out a huge circle on the training pitches, probably about 500 metres all the way round. He'd then send us running around it and we'd have to change direction when he blew his whistle. And that was it. He'd have us running for an hour as a form of punishment but it didn't bother me particularly as I was always fit enough to cope with anything like that.

For all his wacky ways, Barry was someone you could always turn to. He had your back. If you were in trouble, he'd stand by you and help you out. He was a very loyal man – you couldn't wish for better qualities in a manager. Okay, it might have been nice if he'd let us off the coach to play the odd game instead of playing cards, but I suppose I'm just being picky.

And now that I was in the team every week, I couldn't have cared less if he'd made us run a marathon every day in between games. This was what I'd always wanted and Barry had saved me from that bleak period when West Ham had shown me the door.

When people talk about the glamour of being a professional footballer, I don't think they quite understand that it isn't all setting £50 notes alight while cruising around in a sports car. I only ever did that on Thursdays.

On other days life could be tough, as I found out when my missus Diane and I went over to Norwich where I hoped to impress their manager Nigel Worthington into offering me a deal. After Frank Lampard Sr had confirmed to me and my old man that the Hammers were letting me go, I had three months to find a new club and the pressure was on. I remained convinced that I was a far better footballer than I was a painter-decorator. And hundreds of customers with paint peeling off their walls would have agreed with me.

Diane had been my childhood sweetheart and I could never imagine life without her. She's always been there for me through thick and thin – fortunately mostly thick – and there's no way I could have coped with all the ups and downs of my career without her love and encouragement.

In the early part of my career, Diane was by my side when I needed her most – none more so than when I had to go over to Norwich for a trial and she almost froze solid watching me in the stands.

When we arrived in Norwich we didn't check straight in to the local Hilton and order room service. We didn't even get an Alan Partridge-style Travel Tavern. Instead, we made our way to a lovely old lady's house on the outskirts of town where we would lodge for the next two weeks – it was the best that the club could do for us.

I worked my nuts off in training with Norwich for the next fortnight, determined to prove I was good enough to play for the club. Carrow Road was a lovely ground and when I watched a game with my old man while I was there, the atmosphere was superb. I really started to think that this could be for me. As usual, I was a terrible watcher, though, and I just got restless so began to whack my dad on the head for a laugh. 'Behave,' he said. 'There might be cameras on us, you never know.'

I was just full of nervous energy ahead of my trial game.

By then, the weather had turned ridiculously cold and the pitch was covered in snow. It was absolutely freezing but the club managed to get the game on so I couldn't use the temperature as an excuse – I knew I had to produce as this was the crunch for me.

Fortunately, I played really well in front of Nigel Worthington and Steve Foley – and also in front of poor Diane, who was sitting in the stands with about ten others, going numb with the cold. And did she complain? Of course she did, but that's not the point.

I was convinced it would all be worth it – although Diane, whose feet took about a day to thaw out, probably disagreed – after I'd performed so well, but Norwich were not quite in agreement and they informed me they couldn't offer me a deal.

BANG! OOF!

That was an absolute killer. A real kick in the balls. I could not believe that they didn't want me after all that time I'd spent with them and playing so well in the trial.

Later on, I heard that Norwich had been interested in signing me but that West Ham had asked for £68,000, which they didn't want to pay. I wasn't sure who to believe and it didn't really matter because either way I didn't have a club.

There was a glimmer of hope when Frank Lampard Sr told my dad that Harry was going to be leaving the Hammers, meaning I might be able to go on a free transfer, but when we got back in touch with Nigel Worthington, he'd already signed a midfielder so no longer needed me.

My dad tried to keep me positive and we set up a trial at Gillingham. It was just the one match, I didn't know any of the players' names and couldn't get on the ball so just ran around a lot. Apart from that, it went really well. The message back from them was that they didn't think I was better than what they already had.

But my luck was about to change.

When I returned to West Ham I played up front in a reserve team game and did quite well. My phone rang later that night and it was someone from West Ham saying that a scout from Peterborough had asked if I could play in a second-string game for them the next day. 'I've just played!' were my first words, but within seconds I'd agreed to play again the following day as I couldn't afford to miss the opportunity.

This time, there was no old lady's house, just a short trip up to London Road to play my second game inside twenty-four hours. Although I was feeling a bit leggy, back then I still had the energy levels of a kid in a school playground. I could have played four games a day and still never have been outrun by anybody on the pitch.

'Posh' reserves were playing Bournemouth that day and the weirdest thing about it was that I was lining up in central midfield against my best mate Sam Keevill. I'd asked Barry Fry if I could play in central midfield, even though, in theory, I played on the right for West Ham.

I never got on the ball enough with the Hammers so I thought it would be a good idea to show Barry what I could do – after the Norwich fiasco, I felt that it was now or never for me. If I didn't perform I could have been out of football and there would be no money-burning Thursdays for me.

If I'd played well in the Norwich trial game, I absolutely bossed the Peterborough one from start to finish. I honestly

think it's the best I've ever played at any level. At one point my mate Sam said to me 'You're on fire!' and when he came off the pitch later, he told me he'd never played against anyone who'd performed like I just had.

After the game, Barry Fry called my dad and I into his office. He sat in his chair with an oversized, steaming cup of tea and asked my dad if he wanted a coffee. Wayne Turner, the Posh assistant coach, brought my dad over a coffee in a plastic cup and Baz didn't look happy.

'Put it in a china cup, he ain't signed yet, dopey!' joked Barry as he offered me a contract then and there. I didn't even bother to consult my old man. It was time to start playing for three points every week and if that meant dropping down two divisions then so be it.

Peterborough might have lacked the glamour of West Ham, with away trips to Liverpool and Tottenham replaced by Stockport and Bournemouth, but I was also swapping poncing about in the reserves with proper first-team professional league football.

I might miss Johnny Moncur strutting about naked, Paolo Di Canio's shaved legs, and Neil Ruddock's special baths, but I would now be treated to large helpings of Barry Fry on a daily basis.

Later on I found out that Barry had watched me a few times – he'd turn up to West Ham reserves to see me play and was always surprised to find that I wasn't in the team the next time he came. Tell me about it, Baz!

He also told me he couldn't believe he'd got me on a free transfer; for a wheeler-dealer like him, that was great business. Especially as the club would end up selling me for £275,000.

As Barry always told me, he saw Peterborough as a stepping stone for me; he knew I wouldn't be there for long – I listened when he said that, but it never went to my head. I knew I had a lot of hard work to do there before I could think about moving on.

First and foremost, Diane and I had to up sticks and move to Peterborough. For a boy whose parents wouldn't allow him to go to McDonald's on his own at the age of sixteen, moving to Peterborough was like emigrating to Australia. I had to go over to my granddad's and borrow £1,000 from under his mattress so I could pay my rent and deposit up front and then I had to deal with things like gas, electricity and water bills for the first time in my life.

But these were great problems to have and showed me that my career had finally started . . . except a week into the new season I was sitting on the sodding bench again.

I'm not sure whether you're familiar with the County Ground, home of Swindon Town. It's a small stadium in the centre of town, full of character although some of the wooden stands are ageing a bit and it can probably only hold about 15,000. But to me, on Saturday 11 August 2001, it might as well have been the Maracanã, such was the buzz I got from arriving there for my first professional league start. The records may show that 7,934 were in the ground that afternoon but I swear on my life it seemed like there were about 60,000.

When we went into the changing rooms before the warm-up, I could hear the crowd above us and I came out in goosebumps. That's how much it meant to me. This wasn't like Anfield where I could hear the crowd but knew I was on the bench with the slimmest chance of playing.

This was my chance.

I didn't want to go back to sanding down skirting boards; I was completely focused on making it as a footballer and this was my big opportunity. If I didn't make it at Peterborough, that would be curtains for me and I could dig out my old overalls again.

Sat in that dressing room, straight away I noticed that the biggest difference about starting a first-team match was playing for three points. Now, I was in a team where careers, livelihoods and contracts were at stake. It was a totally different environment. Everything was about winning, about the team. Every one of your team-mates was going to support you. You all had each other's backs. In reserve-team football, half of the players just want to get out and do it for themselves.

Even as we approached the County Ground on the team bus that afternoon, I was soaking it all up and breathing it all in as I always treated every game as if it could be my last. I know that philosophy sounds a bit sad, but appreciating my good fortune was just part of my pre-match ritual. It all came from my parents, and another thing I always did on the way to a game was speak to them. That wasn't always so easy as some managers were quite funny about players using phones once we'd left the team hotel, but I'd usually hide behind the seats towards the back of the bus and give my folks a ring.

The conversations would always be the same. My mum

would answer the phone and say: 'Jim, this won't last forever so you make sure that you enjoy it; win, lose or draw. Have your eyes and ears open and enjoy it.'

That's exactly what she said before every game whether it was Swindon v Peterborough or England v Germany – it didn't matter to her, the outlook was exactly the same. She'd say nothing about the football, but she was strong, which gave me strength and made me feel confident.

Then my old man would get on the phone. He was to the point: 'Behave yourself, no arguing with the referee and play well.'

Having done all that pre-match prep, I trotted out on to the pitch in front of – what was to me – a packed house in Rio. And my first game flew by. Well it certainly passed me by at any rate.

It's fair to say I didn't have a very good match at all. I was playing in central midfield and I did manage to hit a couple of good passes but that was about it. At the end of the game, a goalless draw, I just thought, 'Shit'. This was exactly what I didn't want. Having just come from West Ham where I felt the manager had no confidence in me, the last thing I wanted was for Barry Fry to also lose belief in me.

And my worst fears were realised when I found myself named as a substitute for the next game against Cardiff. I couldn't kick up a fuss as I'd not played well against Swindon, but to be dropped after only one game hurt. Then again, Barry knew that I'd not been playing regularly enough at West Ham so it was always going to take a bit of time for me to adjust to proper professional league football every week.

I was determined to prove myself so I sat tight as I remained on the bench for the next few games and didn't say a word – apart from on the way back from a narrow win at Chesterfield where I couldn't resist speaking to Baz's assistant Wayne.

I asked him for a chance to play in central midfield again and promised I'd show him what I had. I worked the old Bullard charm on him, leaving him with no option but to press for my inclusion in the next game. It was obvious I was exactly what Posh needed as, by and large, results had not been going our way.

But I was on the bench again for our next game, a victory against Cambridge – so much for the old Bullard charm.

The following Tuesday we were at home to Premier League Coventry in the League Cup and I was handed the start I'd been craving since the opening day. Except I was playing on the right of midfield, but beggars can't be choosers.

I was so pumped up for the game; they did everything bar put a muzzle on my face and stick me into a greyhound trap to calm me down. My parents had travelled up to watch me play, which only added to my frenzied bundle of adrenaline, nerves and excitement.

Yet the first half didn't really go according to plan. I didn't see much of the ball and just couldn't get myself involved in the game.

I returned to the dressing room at half time and went all Robert De Niro in *Taxi Driver* as I stood in the loo in front of a mirror, psyching myself up while splashing water on my face. 'You talkin' to me? You talkin' to me? Well, I'm the only one here.'

Barry Fry interrupted my Hollywood audition by informing me I was moving to centre-midfield for the second half – that charm offensive on the way back from Chesterfield had worked after all.

I went back out for the second half and played brilliantly. I was full of confidence, the adrenaline was pumping and I felt like I could take on the world. Instead, I just took on Coventry. And we nearly beat them as well, but for a late goal which took the game to extra time and eventually penalties.

I took the first spot-kick and smashed it in – I would've taken all five and scored the lot, but unfortunately the rules say that's not allowed – but we ended up losing on pens.

From a team perspective we were gutted, but on a personal level, I wasn't too down because I knew I'd arrived. Like the Gravesend game against Purfleet, that Coventry match changed my career. I never looked back from that moment.

Everything clicked for us a week later when we thrashed Bournemouth 6-0, a game in which I scored my first pro goal – an absolute scorcher it was too, although not a patch on the one I scored a few days later against Bristol City, which still ranks as the best I've ever scored.

We were 3-1 up with about fifteen minutes to go against the pre-season promotion favourites, on our way up to fourth in the league, when the ball broke to me near the halfway line. I cut inside, beat a player and the ball kept running across the middle. I was about thirty-five yards out and for some reason I decided to hit the thing. I slapped it with my laces and it flew into the top corner. Unreal. I remember watching it on a DVD and you can see the Posh fans behind the goal celebrating with the ball still about eighteen yards from the goal as they knew it was in from the moment I'd hit it. Shame I got that one out of the way so early in my career.

The City goalkeeper Mike Stowell had no chance; in fact, their manager Danny Wilson said after the game, 'If there were three keepers, none of them would have stopped that!' That was the quote of the century for me.

I think nine times out of ten, I'd have hit that shot and it would have gone miles over the bar. My team-mates would have called me a wanker and all sorts. Barry Fry might even have subbed me, but luckily for me it was that one time in ten. Unfortunately, it only encouraged me to try plenty more daft things like that in the future. I took that as a sign of my confidence; my team-mates took it as a sign of me being a greedy git.

One thing I learned very quickly was to make sure I made the most of celebrating my goals. That wasn't something I had to think about too hard. When that first one against Bournemouth nestled in the net, I went mental. Going mad came naturally.

Scoring is such a high. A completely unreal moment when you just forget yourself for a second or two. Except me, who loses it for a full minute or two.

When I score, I go properly apeshit. Barry Fry once had to tell me to curb the celebrations because I was going too insane. He said, 'Jimmy, you can't celebrate that long.'

'What?' I replied. 'Course I can!'

And I did.

I once celebrated a goal for Peterborough for fully two minutes!

It all started when Barry Fry had a go at me at half time

during a game against QPR. I'd hit the post from about forty yards in the first half and he piped up with: 'Jim, you haven't hit a good shot since the old king died!'

'How can you say that?' I shot back. 'Next time I score, you're going to know about it.'

Sure enough, three or four games later, I was on target and went so mad for so long that the referee booked me. He approached me with a puzzled look on his face, showed me a yellow card and said, 'What are you doing?'

And so did my team-mates – they had no idea what I was up to as I continued to milk the goal by going to all parts of the ground and celebrating. You'd have thought I'd just scored the winner in the World Cup final.

The buzz I got from scoring continued for hours and days afterwards, especially when I saw it replayed on the box. When I scored that corker against Bristol City I saw it on telly the next day and I remember thinking, 'Fucking hell, here we go! I'll have a slice of this.'

It was so weird to see myself playing football on TV for the first time. It was also the first time I realised how big this whole thing was for me as everyone could see my goal – and my phone soon confirmed that feeling as the text messages from my mates started flying in.

It gave me huge confidence and increased desire to go and do it all over again. I watched it again and again. 'Bloody hell,' I thought. 'I've hit that like Stevie G!' To me, the only difference was that the stage was slightly smaller, but it still counted. I'd still done it on the pitch.

And once I'd grasped on to a little bit of belief like that, there was no stopping me.

That was the time that I established myself as the Posh penalty-taker. I was bursting with belief and there was no way anyone else was going to take a spot-kick instead of me and deny me the chance of scoring a goal. I scored my first penalty in a win against Northampton a couple of weeks later and you'd have had to kill me to get the ball off me when we were awarded a penalty anytime after that.

Some players are a bit reluctant to deal with the pressure of taking a penalty and being in the spotlight for a few seconds. I looked at it differently.

For me, a penalty kick was the most fantastic opportunity to score a goal and I could never understand why anyone *wouldn't* want to take one.

In fact, I would go as far as to ask what the hell you're doing on the pitch if you don't want to take a penalty? (In normal play, not a shoot-out as I can understand that pressure isn't for everyone; even David Beckham, a slightly better midfielder than me, managed to miss one in the Euro 2004 quarter-final.)

It's one v one from twelve yards out and, as the penalty-taker, you have as much time as you like to choose when you're ready to strike the ball. Just look at the stats – far more penalties are scored than missed. I say that without having actually looked at the facts myself; I'm not Rafa Benítez. But it's obvious way more pens result in goals than saves.

Having said that, it didn't always go according to plan for me from the spot.

In one game for Peterborough against Port Vale, we were awarded a spot-kick and I confidently strolled up and struck it to the bottom right of the goal and watched as the keeper saved it – shit!

Like a gift from the gods, the referee had spotted something or other that he wasn't too keen on and ordered a retake. Get in there!

Before I'd even had a chance to put the ball back on the spot, loads of my team-mates were swarming around me like flies round shit, trying to grab the ball to take the kick.

'Not a bloody chance,' I said and I clung on to that ball like it was my newborn baby.

Once the melee had calmed, I stepped up and, this time, I smacked it bottom left. The sodding keeper has only gone and bloody saved it again. Fuck.

I looked up at the ref hopefully. 'Go on son,' I thought. 'Give us another go.' But he looked the other way and so did I as I kept my head down after that little disaster. Despite that, I remained supremely confident that I'd score the next one.

As luck would have it, we got one in our next game. None of the boys were keen on me taking it and God only knows what Barry Fry was thinking as I grabbed the ball, but I stepped up again, feeling certain I was going to score and I did just that.

I always did my homework with penalties and made sure I kept the keepers guessing. Football got all fancy thanks to technology towards the end of my career, so coaches would study all the penalty-takers, meaning goalkeepers would always have a good idea of where you were going to hit the ball.

Not with me. I switched from bottom left to bottom right, then I'd vary the speed of my run-up to the ball as well. Sometimes, I'd try to spot the keeper making a move as I ran up, just to get that little advantage.

I worked hard on things like that after training. I was really compulsive, always making one of the keepers stay out so I could smash penalties past them and try different options. I'd also practise free kicks for ages until Bazza or the groundsman would threaten to kill me if I didn't stop ruining the pitch.

And they had every right to be concerned because that London Road surface was an absolute disgrace – there was more grass in the Sahara than on our pitch. We drew Newcastle at home in the FA Cup and the match was almost called off because the pitch was so bad.

It was lucky it went ahead as it was a belting game and, without doubt, the biggest match of my life at the time. There was a ridiculous amount of talent on the pitch as Sir Bobby Robson played a strong side against us with Alan Shearer, Craig Bellamy, Sylvain Distin and Nobby Solano all in the team. We went two goals down but then stormed back in the second half with a couple of our own, including Dave Farrell's equaliser, after which Bazza raced down the touch-line to high five him. I'd never seen him move so fast. When José Mourinho did his touchline celebration with Porto at Man United a couple of years later, it was clear he'd been watching Barry.

Neale Fenn then had a great chance to win it, but Shay Given made a blinding save and, just when it looked like we'd earned a replay, they were given a soft pen and added another soon after so we went down fighting.

As good an experience as it was, it was also a very tough game to play in because the pitch was a total mudbath. Every time I tried to run with the ball, it would just stick – there's no way that game would be played in today's football. But it did mean that I came face to face with Shearer for the first time and it didn't go well for me. There was a fifty-fifty ball to be won in the middle of the pitch and we both went for it, except I ended up flat on my arse, as running into him was like sprinting straight into a hotel. He was a big man whereas I was a twenty-three-year-old in a seventeen-year-old's body. I also tried to run with Bellamy but he was an absolute rocket.

Two lessons I learned from that game: get stronger and get quicker.

The high-profile nature of the game meant that the next day was the first time I'd made the national papers, with the *Guardian* writing, 'Prompted by the quick-quick passes of the local hero Jimmy Bullard, the home side overcame the early setback . . .'

I'll have some of that thank you very much, but I think the reporter must've been drinking because I could hardly stand up on that muddy pitch, never mind pass the ball.

Our pitch was typical of some of the problems you have playing lower-league football every week where the facilities weren't a million miles away from non-league, or worse. I once played at Rotherham's Millmoor ground for Wigan. We filed off the coach and into the changing room and almost collapsed in a pile of footballers, because the room was so small. It was a box at best and I'd never seen anything like it at any level I'd played.

That was just the beginning, as Rotherham boss Ronnie Moore had made sure the heating was turned up to oven settings. The dressing room was hotter than a sauna, the showers were freezing cold and there wasn't even room for a medical bed. Our manager Paul Jewell went potty and insisted we all changed in the corridor, which we did, before going out and playing on a pitch with a slope. At least it had grass on it, unlike Peterborough's mud and sandpit.

Despite our dodgy pitch, Peterborough was a glorious yet simple time in my career. Money wasn't a big deal to me as long as I had enough for the basics like food, clothes and petrol for the Fiesta. Football was giving me such a buzz that I didn't need anything else, although sometimes that buzz could be too much.

It's hard to explain just how high I was after matches, especially if I'd played well or scored a goal. The adrenaline would pump through me for hours afterwards and there was no chance of sleeping. Sometimes, I could be awake all night and would then be in a foul mood the following day – it was like a comedown, where I didn't want anyone near me. As much as I loved playing under the lights at night because the atmosphere was so good, evening matches were a nightmare for that never-ending buzz. You could forget sleeping on a Tuesday or Wednesday night, but if we'd won it didn't really matter.

Unfortunately, winning wasn't something we did that often during my two years at Posh. The team's struggles didn't affect my performances though, and during my second season with the club, Barry told me that other teams were interested in me.

However loyal Bazza was and however much he preached about team unity, if there was a sniff of a chance of another club paying money to sign one of us, he'd drop you faster than a virgin would drop his trousers in the red-light district.

That was understandable as Barry was also the chairman of Peterborough and had put loads of his own money – and his mother-in-law's – into the club. I heard that not only did Barry remortgage his own home to help Posh, but also his wife's mum's gaff. And I'm not even sure he told her either, as he once said, 'She's got the deeds back now, she didn't even know I'd given them to the bank!'

One morning I was in bed at home when the phone rang. When I say bed, I was actually lying on a mattress on my living room floor because we were doing the place up.

I answered the phone. Immediately I heard the familiar 'Barry Fry'. He would always announce himself when he called – it didn't matter that we'd been living in a world with caller ID for five years.

'What's happening, Baz?' I said.

'Birmingham.'

'What do you mean Birmingham? The place, the football club, what?' I replied.

'Birmingham City Football Club,' he announced as if he was doing the FA Cup draw. 'They want you, do you want to go?'

Fuck me. I sank into the mattress and thought about it for a second – but Barry doesn't have a second to wait. This is business.

'Yeah, if it's going to improve my football and you're okay with it, I'll go,' I said.

'Right Jim, get your gear ready, I'll call you back in an hour,' said Baz and hung up.

I was buzzing. Birmingham played in the Championship, it would definitely be a step up and a fantastic opportunity.

That's the weirdness of football. One minute you're surrounded by a close bunch of team-mates who you could never imagine being apart from. The next you might be upping sticks and unlikely to speak to any of them for years.

It was a hard thing for me to get my head round, but I didn't have much time. I told Diane straight away. That's another hard thing. When you're married to a footballer you just have to go along with all the moving, whether you like it or not. One minute you're living in the Midlands, the next you're up north. She seemed up for the move though and I waited to hear from Barry.

And waited.

And waited.

Nothing.

The next day I went into training as usual and Baz didn't say a word to me about Birmingham. Eventually, I asked him what was going on and he said that Steve Bruce, the Birmingham manager, was interested in me and Tommy Williams, our centre-back. Tom had also come to Peterborough from West Ham so we were good mates but it sounded like only one of us was going to be leaving.

After another day of limbo, Tommy rang me and told me he was in the car on the way to Birmingham. 'You fucker!' I said. And that was the end of that. I told Diane we weren't going anywhere. Stand down. Carry on with your life as if nothing has happened.

To this day, whenever I see Steve Bruce he always tells me he signed the wrong one and should've chosen me. And I always tell him he's right. (With all due respect to Tommy, of course.)

Apparently, Bruce had called Barry about five or six times to talk about me, Tommy's name had only come up late on. And when he offered £550,000 for my mate, that was it.

I was probably quite naive at that stage of my career because that whole experience made me realise how much of a business football is – nothing new there, I know, but it was the moment the penny dropped for me.

For everything we'd been told about loyalty and the importance of the team, I saw how quickly the club were ready to let me go the minute anyone with a big pile of cash came sniffing. Sod team spirit – if the price is right, the team can fuck right off. Because flogging players is much better for business and that's what this game is.

I'm not saying I didn't enjoy my football career as much after that because anyone who saw me play would know I loved every second of it. But from then on, a tiny part of the fantasy image of being a footballer was taken away from me as a little bit of realism crept in.

Credit to Baz, he was a bit gutted for me as well as he knew how close I'd come to a big step up. He thought Birmingham would have been a perfect move for me and felt certain the fans would have loved me. None of which made me feel any better.

However, the next time Barry called me up out of the blue, it was no false alarm. He even got me off the golf course, which showed how serious it was. 'Jim, I've had a call about you, get off the course and get over here.'

As I walked into his office at London Road still in my golf gear, part of me was convinced this might have been a wind-up or a Birmingham-style false dawn. But it was neither. It was the real thing.

'I've got Paul Jewell on the phone on loudspeaker. He wants you at Wigan, do you want to go?'

Baz loved putting me on the spot like that.

Wigan were in the same division as us, but they were running away with the title, miles clear of everyone and it was only January. It may not have been the dream move up to the next tier of English football, but it was only a matter of time before the Latics would be promoted. Their ambition and potential was on a different level to Peterborough's so it was quite an easy decision.

'If it's going to make me a better player, I'd like to go,' I said, which was a pretty diplomatic answer for an inexperienced twenty-four-year-old.

While I was standing there, Barry resumed his conversation with Paul.

'Hello Paul, I've got Jimmy Bullard in here with me and he's threatening to hit me over the head with a four iron if I don't let him move to Wigan!'

Paul said he wanted to meet me first – rumour had it that he wouldn't sign players if he didn't think they wanted to play for him. Apparently, if Pelé wasn't up for doing things the Paul Jewell way, he'd have turned him down flat.

There was £275,000 on the table for Posh, but Barry thought I was worth way more. He wanted a million for me, but he never did the deal in the end – that was handled upstairs. If Baz had his way I might never have left. To be fair to him, he always said he would never stand in my way if a decent offer came along and, although he was gutted to see me go, he knew it was a good move for me and he was true to his word. Even if my valuation was £725,000 short of his.

So it was down to me to go up to Wigan and show Paul Jewell I was up for it.

Up for it?

My new gaffer was about to relearn the meaning of those three words.

PILLAR 5

ARGUING WITH YOUR MANAGER IS FUTILE; ESPECIALLY WHEN HE HAS YOUR HEAD SHUT IN A DOOR

'Wise men talk because they have something to say; fools, because they have to say something.' ***Plato***

I looked at the team sheet for the Chelsea game because I always checked it, not for one minute because I expected not to see my name. But when I didn't see it, my first thought was that there must have been some mistake.

But then I read down and saw that I was named there after all. As a substitute.

An instant rage built up inside me. What the fuck was going on?

Here I was playing in the Premier League with Wigan, on a run of 123 consecutive games for the club, stretching back to when I'd first joined them in the third tier. Madness, I know, and not a run I wanted to end unless I was physically unable to play. And the last time I checked, I'd trained that Friday morning and was absolutely fine.

For some ridiculous reason, Paul Jewell clearly thought it was time for a change but I wasn't having it. This was bang out of order. So I went steaming down to the gaffer's office and knocked on his door.

'What's the fucking script with me being dropped, then?'

I said as I sat down opposite him. 'Chelsea away? There's something wrong with you ain't there?'

'What do you mean?' he said, looking unimpressed with my attitude. 'I've picked the team I think will do best.'

That was like a red rag to a Bullard.

'You cannot tell me I don't deserve to be playing,' I told him.

But Paul was adamant: 'No, I think you need a rest.'

'No, I'm not having it.'

'You need a rest,' he repeated.

'Are you saying I'm not good enough to play?'

'You need a rest,' he said for the third time.

But I wasn't listening. I was livid.

'Look, you mean I've fought through a boyhood career tooth and nail, only to miss a game against Chelsea at Stamford Bridge? I don't think so. After more than 100 games in a row, go and drop me for Middlesbrough or something, not against Chelsea, the title holders.'

'I'm not playing you,' he said. 'I've already explained to you and everyone else that we've had a tough run of games and I'm going to be rotating the squad to give everyone a rest. That way, we'll have a better chance of winning the games we're more likely to win.'

I don't know the meaning of rest. That word doesn't exist in my dictionary.

Suddenly, I was back on the parks pitches as a kid after a defeat, or the West Lodge working men's club after losing at pool. But there were no tears this time, just pure anger.

I stood up and yelled, 'Fucking poxy decision that is!' and shoved my chair away, hurling it across the floor.

I grabbed the door, but I was only halfway out of the room when Paul launched himself across his desk, shouting: 'Who do you think you're fucking talking to?'

And as he said that he pushed on the door that I was pulling open, cracked my nose and shut my bloody head in it!

For a split second I was in the maddest position. The manager was holding a door shut with my head stuck in it as I looked on at Bill Green, the chief scout, who was sat at his desk, opposite the gaffer's office, watching this scene with a look on his face that could only mean: 'What the fuck is going on?'

I managed to grab Paul and he grabbed me at the same time, shoving me up against the wall in his office, yelling, 'Have a bit of respect!' as he did so.

'You've broken me fucking nose!' I screamed back.

'Have you calmed down?'

'You've broken me fucking nose!'

'Have you fucking calmed down?'

'Yes, I've fucking calmed down, now get your hands off me!'

He released his grip and I stormed out screaming, 'He's broken me nose' to anyone within earshot and muttering 'Fucking bastard' to myself until I got into my car.

I hadn't lost it like that since I was a kid and part of me immediately regretted it. Another part of me was mentally going through the boxing moves I'd learned years before that I should have used on Jewell. I'm not sure the gaffer would have appreciated that too much.

I took my place on the bench at the Bridge the next day, but not before Bill Green asked me what had happened.

I blamed it all on Paul, naturally. 'He took a right liberty, squashing my head in the door' I remember saying to him with half a grin on my face.

The gaffer was certainly over the scrap as he brought me on for the last twenty minutes at Chelsea, but we still lost – even with my added threat.

After the game, we spoke about our scrap – Paul reminded me that I was lucky to get out of his office alive – and agreed to move on. Months later, I even realised that his decision was right because that rest made me hungrier than ever.

We joke about it now whenever we see each other. I always say I still owe him one for shutting my head in a door. And Paul clearly doesn't have a problem with me as he signed me for Ipswich a few years later.

I didn't miss many more games for Wigan after that as what was turning into an amazing season continued with a run to the Carling Cup semi-finals where we were drawn against Arsenal. The first leg in January 2006 was a memorable occasion as we beat the Gunners at the JJB Stadium – except I'll always remember it for my antics when the lights went out.

I had attention deficit disorder when I was at school – I've probably still got it now – and I just couldn't help myself as I always had to be the story. If you were sitting next to me in geography, you weren't doing any work because I didn't fucking want to.

So, when the floodlights failed during a hard-fought semi-final that had been goalless to that point, I was that kid in the geography class again. I felt a need to entertain everyone – don't ask me why, this was pure adrenaline pumping right in the middle of the game. You can't just switch that off as easily as the lights.

Every other player on the pitch had stopped for a breather, but not me.

I yelled to our goalkeeper Mike Pollitt to chuck the ball to me. I realised that even though it was pitch black out there, the referee Howard Webb hadn't blown his whistle to stop play.

Polly was a bit baffled but hurled the ball to me anyway and I ran down the other end and took a shot from just outside the box, but missed the target by a good ten feet. Good job the lights were off.

'What are you doing?' said Webb, looking at me.

'You didn't blow your whistle,' I told him with a shrug and a grin.

Some of the Arsenal players found that funny and started laughing. Not a smart move as that only encouraged the schoolkid inside me.

Taking full advantage of the murky conditions and the fact that most players were doing the sensible thing and stretching to keep warm, I crept behind Arsenal's Freddie Ljungberg, yelled 'Fuck off!' and pulled his shorts down.

He'd been the star of Armani ads and I told the press afterwards that I wanted to check if he was wearing the sponsored undies underneath his shorts, but the truth is I didn't really know what I was doing. It just seemed like a fun thing to do at the time.

Luckily for me – and the rest of the Arsenal players – we left the pitch at that point and returned fifteen minutes later when the lights came back on so we could all get on with the game.

The Gunners had some decent players out that night, but

it wasn't their strongest team and we took advantage with a 1-0 win thanks to Paul Scharner's goal on his debut.

It gave us a sniff in the second leg two weeks later, although most people expected Arsenal to turn it around at home, especially when their starting line-up included all the big dogs – Sol Campbell at the back, Dennis Bergkamp and Thierry Henry up front. Make no mistake, this side was awesome, not far from the team that lost to Barcelona in the Champions League final four months later. Highbury looked amazing that night. The pitch was like a bowling green without a blade of grass out of place. I watched Henry warming up in his Nike Vapors and couldn't help but admire the bloke. Don't worry, I didn't pull his shorts down as well, but in situations like that I was almost a fan, a disbelieving little boy looking on.

Once the game got underway, Polly was inspired for us. He saved a José Reyes penalty in the first half and then stopped everything Henry threw at him. Well, almost – the bugger did score in the second half to level the tie.

My mate continued his heroics in goal as the game went into extra time. But Arsène Wenger threw on Robin van Persie and the Dutchman scored with a brilliant free kick which gave Polly no chance and Arsenal now held the overall lead. It didn't seem fair. We'd worked so hard.

Then, with a minute to go of extra time, the miracle happened. I'm not a religious man but thank God for Jason Roberts. He latched on to Graham Kavanagh's pass and steam-rollered Campbell and Philippe Senderos before scoring to put us into the final on the away goals rule.

We went mental. I was doing backflips with Leighton Baines. Everyone was jumping on top of each other. The manager was out on the pitch bear-hugging every single one of us. The fans were going bonkers. It was just unreal.

And in the middle of it all, Polly, whose heroics all night had seen us over the line, ran over to me and said 'What happens now then?'

I looked at him, thinking he was taking the piss, but his face was quite serious.

'We won on away goals,' I said.

'Oh right,' he replied. 'I wondered why we were all celebrating so much.'

What a fucking donut. The dopey bastard had no idea we'd reached the final. He thought it was going to penalties, but it's probably just as well for Arsenal that it didn't because the way Polly played that night he would have saved all five of theirs anyway. I've never seen a better goalkeeping display. Thankfully, Polly didn't use his brain when he played, just his instincts, or we'd have shipped about ten against Henry and his mates.

The club's owner Dave Whelan also joined us on the pitch to celebrate (Polly probably thought he'd come down from the stands to take a penalty) and the atmosphere in the dressing room and on the coach afterwards was unforgettable. Funnily enough, that was partly thanks to Arsenal, who gave us all the champagne that they'd had ready in their dressing room in anticipation of winning the tie. Rather than save it for another day, they gave it to us for the long journey back to Wigan.

We didn't let them down either, as we really went for it.

The gaffer was normally very strict, but that night we were pretty much given free rein to get plastered and celebrate our achievement. There was a lot of singing all the way back to Wigan, loads of us were stripping off at the back of the coach and we even got the driver to join in.

Gary Teale, Lee McCulloch, Alan Mahon and myself were right in the thick of it, but we all celebrated together, as a team.

We'd made a CD specially, which we agreed we'd play if we won. Each player had chosen their own track and that only added to the high spirits, especially when my choice, Chas and Dave's 'Rabbit' came on. The boys loved it, even the gaffer joined in, as I got into my 'old cockney geezer' character, swinging my arms and legs while chirping 'Rabbit, rabbit, rabbit, rabbit, yap yap'.

It was a special journey home. I think deep down a lot of us felt that we may never experience a moment like that in our careers again – I know I certainly did – and we had to really mark it.

A huge part of our success was how close we were as a unit.

When other teams stayed overnight at a hotel they'd get together in groups of two or three, but there were always eight or ten of us in a room together playing cards or just messing about. Of course, the fact that we enjoyed so much success during that time helped to make sure we all got on well with each other. But I know that overall squad closeness was unique, because I played for enough other clubs and saw how different it could be.

The gaffer's attitude was obviously crucial as well and he would never let us rest on our laurels. Two mornings after our greatest night we were back in for training, but the session was sloppy and Paul was disgusted with what he was seeing. He stopped us right in our tracks, with a stern look on his face and said: 'Right, get that champagne out of your system because we've got a big game on Saturday.' The focus immediately returned and we were on our way again.

A month later, we were all crowded into a plush hotel room in Cardiff the night before the Carling Cup final. Man United were waiting for us at the Millennium Stadium (I'm not saying they kipped there overnight as I'm sure they also splashed out on a hotel) but we went through our usual pre-match routine. The only difference was that this time we were staying in an incredible gaff.

After being treated like royalty, we arrived at the stadium in a bit of a daze and we never really emerged from it. It was a massive occasion for us and we all had loads of family and friends packed into the stadium.

When I'd asked the club for 130 tickets for my Bexleyheath mob they thought I was messing about, but I wasn't joking. My mum and dad organised an entire coachload to come to Cardiff and plenty of others got the train over. They all had a good day out, but it wouldn't have had anything to do with the football.

It all started to go wrong in the third minute when Polly picked up a freak injury just gathering the ball. He did his hamstring and left the pitch in tears. We were all absolutely gutted for him, but there wasn't much time to dwell on it as United were running us ragged.

They led at half time thanks to a Wayne Rooney goal and then blitzed us at the start of the second half as we tried to get back in the game. We left gaps, which they exploited as they scored three times in seven minutes. Game over. No way back.

Maybe we went a bit gung-ho in trying to get back into the game, but it was probably also a tie too far for us. We'd performed miracles and worked our nuts off to beat Arsenal, but we couldn't live with United that day. It didn't really seem like a 4-0 type of game but we couldn't have any complaints.

I was certainly not overly disappointed. I thoroughly enjoyed the experience, just not the result. I never thought I'd get to play in a final like that at any stage in my career so how could I not enjoy it? I'd have enjoyed it if we'd lost 12-0. And we'd lost to Man United with the likes of Rooney, Ronaldo, Giggs and Ferdinand. Fergie had even left Ruud van Nistelrooy on the bench – they may well have scored twelve had he played.

There was a big post-match party planned for us afterwards which we all still attended. And, to be honest, we all really went for it and got leathered. The gaffer didn't mind as he knew we were all triers and had given everything, but it just hadn't gone our way. He didn't really feel like being there as he was gutted, but I'm sure he realised how far we'd come in such a short space of time.

If you'd told me that we'd have been playing in a game like that less than three years after I first walked through the doors at the JJB, I'd have laughed you all the way to the loony bin.

But I was aware how ambitious the club were from the minute I'd first met Paul, who promised me they were going places and he wanted me to be a key part of that journey.

He'd watched me play a couple of games for Peterborough

and liked what he saw as I ran both matches, although he admitted that I started to get on his nerves because wherever the ball went, I went. I made no secret that I played the game as if I was still in the school playground.

As soon as I arrived in Wigan, I felt like I fitted in straight away – and that was despite never having spent any significant time up north. Other than away matches, I was completely unfamiliar with that part of the country, but I immediately liked what I saw. And what I saw was a 30,000-seater stadium which, with all due respect to Peterborough, shat all over London Road.

I was with my agent, Andy Evans (I'd wised up enough to get one by then), and I told him straight away that I wanted to sign. At that stage, I was only thinking about playing in the First Division (or Championship as it is now) and I was pretty confident that would be happening the following season, given how far ahead Wigan were at the top of the table.

Money didn't come into it for me, but I'm not ashamed to admit that the £2,500 per week they offered to pay me was gratefully received. I'd more than tripled my wages overnight and my career prospects had soared too.

Once I'd met Paul and proved to him how much I wanted it, the rest was a formality and I signed a three-year contract. Diane and I left our home on the outskirts of Peterborough and rented a place near Wigan. I loved it up there because everyone was so friendly. I'd go for a walk and people passing by would say, 'Hi Jim, how are you?'

I eventually came to see myself as a northerner. Hard to believe, really, as when I first arrived up there my accent meant I could barely make myself understood.

I'd go into a shop in the morning for the paper and ask for 'the Currant Bun', which most people know is rhyming slang for the *Sun*. Except in Wigan, I'd ask that and they'd send me to the bakery section. When I went fishing, I asked for some 'wrigglys' as that's what I call bait and they'd look at me like I was some kind of nut.

Most people up there were fascinated by my accent, but didn't understand my slang at all, while the really strong local accents were impossible for me to pick up – they seemed to miss out so many important words, I didn't have a clue what they were on about. At first, there was no point in me having a conversation with anyone up there.

It got easier as time went on, although occasionally one of my team-mates would say something like 'I'm just going up road to see our kid' and I'd be confused again. You what? 'I'm going out to see my brother.' Oh, right – well just say that then!

But living up there for a few years definitely affected me and I picked up words that I continued using when I moved back home. Words like 'lad' – 'Alright lad?' or 'I'm going out with the lads'. My dad wasn't happy about that at all. 'Why do you keep saying that word?' he'd say.

That whole accent thing was proof of how everything was happening so quickly for me. Four years earlier, I'd been working part-time between non-league games. I was now on the verge of playing in English football's second tier and bringing home a six-figure annual salary. I had to pinch myself to believe it and wanted to punch the air in delight.

At Wigan, I had to make sure I fitted in with my new team-mates and look like I belonged at that level, so I decided to take Del Boy's advice to Trigger, offered seconds before he fell through the bar in *Only Fools and Horses*: 'Play it nice and cool, son, nice and cool, know what I mean . . . ?'

But it turned out I didn't need to adopt Del's attitude. There were a lot of hungry bastards at Wigan who were as driven and focused as I was to succeed. They were absolutely determined to make it to the Premier League as most of them hadn't much experience of playing in the top flight; players like Lee McCulloch and Gary Teale. Andy Liddell and John Filan. Nathan Ellington and Leighton Baines. They all wanted it badly.

Go round the changing room and ask any of them what their aims were and they'd all reply: 'I want to play in the Premier League'.

There were no players who were there for the money – even though there was plenty of that thanks to Dave Whelan, the multimillionaire Latics chairman. Paul Jewell had only signed players whom he believed were hungry. And I fitted right in there.

The team was geared towards winning. If we drew, we came off the pitch with the hump. If we won 2-0 and we should have had five or six, we were equally grumpy about it. And if we lost?

Well, that didn't happen too often. After I signed, we only lost once in three months as we were promoted as champions with 100 points. We only lost four games in total that whole season.

And I received my first personal recognition in the game

as I made it into the PFA Team of the Year for the division.

Into the First Division we went and we got off to an absolute flyer. Okay, we lost our first game at Millwall, but it was plain sailing from then on as we went on a ridiculous fourteen-match unbeaten league run that saw us surge to the top of the table. It was unreal. We'd been playing third-tier football just a few months before and now the Premier League appeared to be just around the corner.

That hunger and determination in the squad continued to stand us in good stead, plus the team was full of talented players which also helps a bit.

We had Jason Roberts, Geoff Horsfield and Nathan Ellington up front (although The Horse buggered off to West Brom halfway through that season). Ellington was a phenomenal goalscorer and by that I mean he scored a lot of phenomenal goals. Have a look at his montage on YouTube – it's disgusting. I'm not kidding, it was like playing with Pelé at times. But he was a confidence player through and through. If he scored a couple of goals on a Saturday, he would be guaranteed to score again on Tuesday. If it didn't happen for him on the Saturday, it might be a couple of weeks before he found the net again.

Unsurprisingly, we found it hard to maintain that blistering start, but we kept in the play-off race all the way to the last game, where we needed to beat my old club West Ham to make the top six. Sadly, it wasn't to be as we ran out of steam and could only draw 1-1, which was our fourth game without a win – hardly the ideal end to a season.

We were probably a couple of players short of the team we needed to go up and we were still finding our feet in the new league. Deep down though, we all knew we'd had a great season. We belonged in that league at the very least and the following season we'd be able to give it a proper crack.

Personally, I couldn't have been happier. I played every game that first season – all fifty of them – and was settled up north with Diane. Everything was much closer together than London and it suited me down to the ground.

The following season we roared out of the blocks. This time we didn't bother to lose our first game, instead opening the campaign with a mad seventeen-match unbeaten run.

We refused to lose.

At one point we even refused to draw as we won six in a row. It was extraordinary and we were all loving being part of this amazing team. The spirit was still unbreakable. There were no prima donnas, no fancy-dans and no mercenaries.

Up top, Ellington and Roberts were almost unstoppable, both scoring more than twenty goals that season. Roberts's pace was extraordinary. He never wanted the ball to feet, only over the top because he was so fast. And he was so powerful, he'd run at full pelt with a defender hanging on to him, or he'd just run straight through them. On his day, he was the best striker I've played with and he packed one of the hardest shots I've ever seen.

And The Duke scored some silly goals again. There was one in a 3-3 draw at Wolves that I still don't understand to this day. John Filan took a long goal kick which was headed down by Roberts back to Ellington. He was about twenty-five yards out, to the right side of the goal, and he just unleashed a ridiculous right-foot drive which sent the ball crashing off the underside of the bar and into the net. He scored another one with his back to goal, where the ball came to him, he flicked it up, turned and volleyed it in. It shouldn't have been possible.

Then again, me playing in the Premier League shouldn't have been possible either, but it was about to happen.

We stayed with the pace even when we had the odd dip; our fast start had left us breathing space.

Shortly before the end of that season, we went away overnight for a team-bonding session in a local hotel. We weren't over the line yet, so the gaffer pulled our skipper Matt Jackson into a room to have a word with him.

'Listen, I don't want any trouble tonight,' said Paul. 'It's the back end of the season and we're going for promotion. You're responsible and you're in charge. Any trouble at all and I'll sack you.'

'No problem gaffer,' said Matt as he walked out of the room, from where he could see the front of the hotel and the car park. And I'd loved to have seen his face when he looked out there and saw me surfing on the roof of a taxi which was cruising down the hotel drive. The driver was completely unaware that I was on top of the car, some of the lads had to run alongside and tell him. So that was a good start to the gaffer's trouble-free night.

Stunts like that just relieved the pressure a little bit and it was definitely building ahead of the final game of the season, at home to Reading. Win that, and we were in the Premier League.

We had a great week's training ahead of the game, which

we cruised through. Not winning never even crossed my mind, I wanted it too badly and I know all my team-mates felt the same.

A goal each from McCulloch and Roberts set us on our way before The Duke put the icing on the cake. We won 3-1 and the celebrations were insane, on and off the pitch. To say we had a mad night out in Wigan that night doesn't really do it justice. It was time to let our hair down and do it in style.

The chairman agreed, only his idea of doing it in style was a hell of a lot better than ours. He saw our night out in Wigan and raised it with a trip to Barbados to celebrate our achievement. Whelan not only paid for all the players to go to the Caribbean, he also took the entire coaching staff out there too. It was an absolutely blinding trip.

We all played golf at the famous Green Monkey course (also at the chairman's expense) in the exclusive Sandy Lane area, where Whelan also had a holiday home that used to belong to a British monarch. It was the most astonishing, palatial house with monkeys swinging from the trees in its enormous garden which backed on to the sea. In many ways, it reminded me of the house where I'd grown up on the estate in Bexleyheath.

One night we were all having dinner around the chairman's enormously long dining room table. The drinks were flowing and everyone was merry, to say the least. Whelan was sat at the head of the table with many of the club directors alongside him while we all tucked into a barbecue. As we ate, he made a speech from his seat and began slurring the odd word. We started whispering to each other that the chairman was sozzled, as none of us had ever seen him like that.

Every time he thanked us, we replied 'No, thank you!' This carried on for a while until, before my disbelieving eyes, he fell right off his chair! He was that steaming drunk that he couldn't even sit, never mind stand.

One of the directors went to help him up, but Whelan bellowed 'Get off me! I'm a man, I'll pick myself up', before scrambling back on to his seat again.

As funny as that moment was, it epitomised the calibre of the man and made a real impression on me. From that day on, I swore that the next time I was sat at the head of an unfeasibly long table in my Barbados mansion, being waited upon hand and foot by servants, as monkeys swung through the trees in my garden and I fell off my chair because I've had one too many, I will definitely refuse any assistance and pick myself up.

Seriously though, Whelan is a legend and that Barbados trip was immense. If we weren't playing golf, we were on the beach, where we'd usually find David Hamilton, one of the scouts, water-skiing every morning, thinking he was the business. Hammy would cruise along the surf on his skis, in front of all of us, calling out, 'Alright lads!' in his Geordie accent.

One morning, there was one of those huge inflatable donuts on the back of one of the speedboats which would take four people out for a ride, then twist and turn and fling them into the water at various intervals. Whoever went on first would be thrown off first, but only a short distance of about five metres. Second on board would go a bit further and so on, until the fourth person on would be launched about twenty metres in the air and hit the water like a bag of shit.

So we hatched a plan to get on the donut with Hammy going last. He was so busy with his water-skiing, he didn't have a clue what was going to happen and would be totally unprepared for it.

Three lads climbed on first then Hammy jumped on and off they went – the driver chucked a big right, hit a wave and in went the first man. The second and third followed soon after flying about ten or fifteen metres in the air and then there was just Hammy left.

The boat pulled an enormous left into a wave and Hammy flew through the air for an age before landing on his nose and crunching into the water. After a couple of seconds, he came up again and it wasn't a pretty sight. There was claret everywhere and his nose was round his earhole. He looked startled and came up with the immortal line: 'I must have hit a turtle!'

I can't remember ever laughing as much in my life. There were tears rolling down faces – and not just Hammy's, the poor bastard.

Whelan was brilliant at bringing us all together like that and was never shy with his generosity. At the end of one season, we were sitting in the dressing room and he walked in carrying a huge leather sports bag.

'Right boys, listen up,' he said.

You could have heard a pin drop.

'You've achieved what we wanted to achieve so share this between you.'

And as he finished his sentence, he slid the bag across the floor then walked out.

We all looked at each other, thinking the same thing – there must be cash in the bag.

Our skipper Arjan de Zeeuw opened up the hold-all, peeped inside it then looked up with a smile on his face.

'It's cash, boys!'

There must have been about £250,000 in there, which we all received a cut of in our next pay packet. We knew Whelan was loaded but that was ridiculous.

He was also a man of his word, as he proved when it came to renewing my contract.

When it comes to business, I may not be Alan Sugar but I know my way around a contract renewal deal.

After two years at Wigan, it was time to sharpen my negotiating knife and talk to Whelan.

One Saturday afternoon during the promotion season, I'd been warming up on the pitch and he called me over to tell me we needed to speak because my contract was up for renewal. He also told me that he'd backdate it from that very day, which was a huge gesture.

Naturally, being the shrewd, savvy guy that I am, I played it pretty cool and about six months went by before my agent Andy and I attended a meeting with Dave and the gaffer. In my favour was the fact that, by then, Wigan had become a Premier League club, meaning my negotiating position had strengthened considerably. My delaying tactics had paid off – either that or I'd completely forgotten to go and see the chairman for all that time. Until that point, I'd been on £2,500 per week at Wigan, which was good money, but not a patch on the average Premier League wage. I'd spoken to a few of my mates who played in the top flight to see what the going rate was but when Andy and I were sitting outside Whelan's office, I said to him that I didn't have a clue what I wanted and that we should just go in there and see what he said – another sharp move.

Dave offered me £8,000 per week, which I knew wasn't enough according to my painstaking research (a couple of texts and a phone call), so I blurted out, 'Give me £12,000 per week and I'll sign now.'

To support my case, I then made a brief speech about how important I was to the club and how I'd never previously bothered him about money. A masterstroke.

Dave asked my agent and I to step outside for a minute so he could talk privately with the manager. As we sat outside the chairman's office, I felt like an *Apprentice* contestant awaiting my fate – was I about to be fired? Of course not. But you catch my drift.

After about sixty seconds of agony, we were called back into Whelan's office, where he greeted me by saying: 'Job done. Name, sign and date.'

Not just that, he backdated it six months as he'd originally promised. What a legend. (Him, not me.)

This was in stark contrast to my previous salary discussions at Peterborough. There I didn't have many dealings with the chairman as Barry Fry handled all the players' contracts himself – luckily, I was more than equipped for dealing with him. In fact, my Posh contract was the most straightforward negotiation of my life as I stood for no nonsense and Bazza had too much respect for me to start any shenanigans.

I walked into Barry's office: '£700 a week,' he barked. 'Take it or leave it.'

'Er, alright Baz,' I replied. 'But can I, er, have an extra £50 please?'

'Okay,' said Barry.

Maybe I wasn't that shrewd. But by hook or crook I was about to become a Premier League player picking up £12,000 per week for the privilege of kicking a ball around in front of thousands of people in a stadium and millions on TV.

It was the summer of 2005. In 1999, I'd been a semi-pro at Gravesend where I was paid £60 per week. Six years and 170 professional games later, I was earning 200 times that amount and playing in the biggest league in the world. Excuse my French, but it was fucking mental.

I had to take financial advisers on board because I didn't have a clue what I was doing. And I was so pleased that I did. If you start receiving that kind of money when you're young it's so easy to make bad decisions. I've seen things go wrong for team-mates – luckily, despite most of the daft stuff I used to do on and off the pitch, I always had my head screwed on, believe it or not.

Even at that stage, I was still motivated by the terror of having to go back to my old life. For four years I had to get up at 6am to go out and graft for not much money. I didn't want to do that again. That fear kept me hungry and definitely helped me progress as a player. I knew a lot of the other players I'd be playing alongside and against in the top flight didn't have that experience and I knew that made me stronger than them.

The excitement of that close season was amazing. After the Barbados break, the squad all went away and did our own thing for a couple of months, although it was hard to concentrate on anything apart from the Premier League.

I went on a family holiday in the Algarve, but I knew the date the fixtures were due out. That morning, I was like a kid at Christmas. I was up with the larks and actually sprinted to the local town centre to buy an English newspaper. And what a present I got.

Bang! We were starting at home to Chelsea.

Fucking hell.

The Premier League champions.

José Mourinho.

Get bigger than that!

I'd gone head-to-head with Frank Lampard on my first morning's training at West Ham. Now we were going to do it again, for real, on the telly.

I didn't know who to tell first. What's the Portuguese for 'Chelsea at home'?

It was 7am and I got straight on the phone to the boys back home, waking some of the fuckers up.

'Bainesy, have you seen who we've got first game? We've only got the big dogs!'

'Polly, put the kettle on, Chelsea at home! Let's go and give them a good, fucking hiding!'

I can't imagine any of the Wigan fans were more excited than me or any of the boys – the game would be shown live around the world. This is exactly what we'd worked so hard for.

We were all buzzing when we got back for pre-season. All the talk was about Chelsea. It was hard to think about anything else – sod the other thirty-seven games we had to play, Chelsea were coming to town.

The press loved the fixture too and, as it drew nearer, there were plenty of write-ups about it. Wigan had only been a league team for around thirty years and here we were in the top flight. Of course, the chairman's cash had helped us, but you've still got to do it on the pitch.

And that's exactly what we were trying to do as we took the field against Chelsea one sunny Sunday August afternoon. We were all realising a dream. We were up against the best players in the country, arguably Europe, and it felt great.

We were also up against everyone who had written us off and we were really sticking it to them as we were holding the champions to a 0-0 draw, giving as good as we got throughout. We created the better chances and probably should have won the game, but a draw would be a decent result.

Except we lost. I felt sick.

In the last seconds of the match, Hernán Crespo scored a screamer to spoil our big day. I even remember thinking, 'They're going to score here' and, to be fair, I probably should have acted upon that, but it was too late. A moment of magic had denied us and we had to take it squarely on the chin.

What might have been a flat dressing room was actually more upbeat than you'd imagine. We were gutted and felt we'd been dealt a 'Welcome to the Premier League' card at the end of the game but we'd outplayed the champions at times and proved we belonged in this league.

We just had to do that every week and we'd be fine. Except we didn't in our next match against Charlton and lost again. So that wasn't necessarily part of the plan, but we finally got going in the following game by beating Sunderland, which sparked a nine-match unbeaten run – another of our trademark form streaks that went on and on.

We even managed to win six in a row during that time and by early November we were second in the table! Only Chelsea's ridiculous start was better than ours. We had twenty-five points from eleven games, five clear of Arsenal, seven ahead of Man United. Mind-blowing.

During that run, I scored my first Premier League goal. And it wasn't just any old goal. No scrappy consolation strike for me. No, I netted the winner in injury time at West Brom. It was 1-1 and I was lurking around the edge of the box looking for a lucky break as we attacked. Bang on cue, the ball into the box ricocheted off a defender and rolled out right into my path – I love it when it comes rolling out like that.

There were a crowd of players in between me and the goal, but a tiny, unguarded corner of the net became visible and the old light bulb in my head lit up. Fortunately, it was a light bulb telling me to shoot rather than the usual one advising me to do something daft for no particular reason. I struck it with my instep. It was a low, skidding shot that whistled along the surface at lightning speed and tucked into the corner with no fuss at all.

Which was quite the opposite of my reaction as I went absolutely mental.

My first Premier League goal to win us the game in injury time. It was an unbelievable moment and it's tough to explain the buzz I got from it, but I'll give it my best shot.

The adrenaline's pumping anyway when you're playing. Then something like that happens and it goes through the roof. There's no legal way down – I was as high as a kite for hours afterwards.

First of all, I was full of it in the changing room, still

celebrating with all the lads and really milking the moment. Then I got on the coach and wanted to share the experience with friends and family.

That night, I was on the phone to my missus, my mum and dad, all my mates. I must've talked them all through the goal at least a dozen times, to the point where my team-mates on the bus actually started to get pissed off with me because I just couldn't shut up about it.

If my yakking wasn't enough, my phone was beeping and buzzing relentlessly for a good two hours all the way back, as friends got in touch to say well done. This is what it can be like being a footballer. Loads of people want to share in the successes and it feels good.

By the time I got home it was around 9pm or 10pm and I was still pumped. Diane was there to welcome me and there was only one thing I wanted to do – watch *Match of the Day*. (What were *you* thinking?)

It's moments like this that I lived for as a kid. This is why I played football on the green in front of my parents' house for hours on end. This is why I ran after my dad's car for miles when all I wanted to do was, well, absolutely anything really, except that. Because now I was about to watch *Match of the Day* in which I played a starring role. And it doesn't get better than that.

The game came on and I tried to take it all in. It was so surreal seeing it back so soon after. Luckily, when the ball came to me on the edge of the box, I stuck it in the corner again. Phew.

Best of all, the boys in the studio then had their say.

They watched the goal back, paused it, slow motion, the works. 'What a strike by Bullard,' someone said.

Was that me? Yes it was. And it was the best feeling in the world.

That unbeaten run really set us up for life in the Premier League. For such a young, relatively inexperienced team to make an impression on the toughest league in the world at that time, gave us a huge amount of confidence.

We relished playing against the best teams in the country. Nobody wanted to miss out on a touch of the ball in a game, never mind miss out on a match itself through injury or suspension. That's why I got so pissed off with the manager when he rested me for that Chelsea game. And I wasn't the only one who got the arsehole with him like that.

One Friday, during the previous season, our full-back Nicky Eaden had just found out he wasn't playing on the Saturday and he was steaming. He was in the shower in Wigan's old training ground, moaning away about Paul Jewell, completely forgetting that those showers had windows which opened out on to the corridor – the same corridor that housed the gaffer's office.

So Paul had heard Nicky and came into the changing room, but Nicky, who had shampoo and soap all over his face, was completely unaware he was there.

'What does he think he's doing dropping me? It's bollocks!' said Nicky.

We could all see Paul standing near the doorway of the showers, so someone called out: 'Why's that then, Nick?'

'He's a fucking fat, Scouse bastard!' said Nicky.

Suddenly, the gaffer piped up, 'Is that right then, Nick?'

'Oh, er, is that you Paul?' said a panicking Nicky, desperately trying to wipe the soap out of his eyes.

'Yeah, it is me.'

'No, no, what I was saying was . . .'

'Come and see me in my office,' said Paul as Nicky stuttered and mumbled, while still trying to get the soap out of his eyes. I think Paul took mercy on him, giving him a severe bollocking but nothing more.

We ended up finishing tenth in our first Premier League campaign, which was two fingers up to all the people who predicted relegation for us, but the season did end on a bizarre note in the Highbury dressing room.

Of the new recruits that the gaffer had attracted to the club for our first stab at the top flight, right-back Pascal Chimbonda definitely made the biggest impression and he was named in the PFA Premier League Team of the Year.

Paul Jewell had brought Pascal over from France and really looked after him as he got used to living in England. Several times in the first few months, I took Pascal and our new Senegalese striker Henri Camara out for the night to make them feel welcome.

We often went out on Kings Street – no, not quite the Chelsea's King's Road, but the more glamorous strip in Wigan – where they got to know some of the locals who always looked after us. We also went to Manchester a few times to some of the footballer hangouts there. I even took them to some moody bars, which they loved, but the less said about those, the better.

Back at Highbury, we'd played Arsenal in their last-ever

game at the old ground and we were all in the changing room after a 4-2 defeat – a game I didn't play in or else it would have been so different, of course.

Pascal was still in his kit as he handed Paul Jewell a card, which the manager thanked him for and walked out. Polly looked at me with a strange look on his face and whispered: 'The gaffer thinks it's a thank you card, but I think it's a transfer request.'

Seconds later, Jewell stormed back in and I was thinking Pascal's head might soon become acquainted with that dressing room door. He marched straight over to Pascal: 'You fucking prick! After everything I've done for you, you hand in a transfer now.'

He had to be pulled away from Pascal who didn't seem to understand what all the fuss was about. None of us could believe what he'd done as we all knew that you have to see the manager privately to hand in a transfer request, but Pascal had decided to do things a little differently. Perhaps he'd been badly advised. Really badly advised.

Pascal was a hell of a player and it was no surprise he wanted to leave as he clearly felt he could play for a bigger club – and he was probably fed up with my repeated attempts to grab his willy in the shower for a laugh. Tottenham eventually signed him on transfer deadline day later that summer, but only after the club had made him sweat.

My own time at Wigan had come to an end, too, but I left on better terms than Pascal. Fulham had bid £2.5 million for me, which triggered a release clause in my contract. I had to sit out the final two games of the season, including that Highbury game, and that was that.

The three years at Wigan couldn't have gone any better, but Fulham gave me the chance to return to my family in London and with my Diane pregnant it was an easy decision to make.

It was time to move on.

PILLAR 6

TO TRULY EXPERIENCE PLEASURE, ONE MUST EXPERIENCE PAIN. BLOOMIN' LOADS OF IT

'He who conquers himself is the mightiest warrior.' ***Confucius***

Imagine someone slicing your knee open then pouring boiling hot water inside it. Not the most pleasant of thoughts, but that was the feeling of red-hot pain I had to endure at St James' Park in September 2006. As it happens, because of the injury I suffered that afternoon, my knee was sliced open quite often over the following few years but at least I was out for the count then and, as far as I know, there was no boiling kettle on standby either.

I was playing for Fulham at Newcastle and everything was perfectly normal. I'd made a decent start at my new club and playing in front of 50,000 was just another buzz in what was turning into an incredible journey for me.

There was a loose ball to be won in midfield, which was perfectly normal. Scott Parker was running towards that loose ball too, which was also perfectly normal. I thought I could get to it before him. It was one of those millisecond decisions that run through your mind. You don't really make those calls during a game, it's almost automatic, intuitive, from the gut. And it happens so fast it's virtually imperceptible.

A flash of panic ran through my mind as it suddenly seemed that my body was in the wrong position. There was nothing normal about that. And there was no super slo-mo available for me to adjust my position, this was happening in real time. I stuck my right leg out to try to win the ball, but Parker got there first, nicked it away from me and his momentum carried him straight through on to my leg.

I took the full brunt of Parker's challenge off-balance. Time didn't stand still, as so many people tend to say it does in these situations. If it had, I would have moved out of the way and Parker wouldn't have got near me. In fact, it was quite the opposite. Time was on fast-forward, like a runaway express train. And the express train was Parker, who crashed straight into my outstretched right leg, folding me in half like some kind of bonkers human origami expert.

My right knee took Parker's full body weight due to the awkward position I was in and I fell forwards into a heap.

Nothing normal about this whatsoever.

My initial reaction was that my knee felt weird and uncomfortable, but that I wasn't in too much pain. Okay, maybe I'd got away with it and avoided a serious injury, something I'd managed for my whole career until that point.

So I pulled my right leg around in front of me to survey the damage.

'Oh shit,' I thought. 'This is the one.'

It's funny because you spend all your playing days living in fear of a serious, career-threatening injury. Some players may be lucky enough to never experience one, while others, like West Ham's Dean Ashton, are not so fortunate.

But when it happens to you, it isn't a huge, soap opera-style moment of drama. Instead, it's just a bit weird. And that's how I felt as I sat on the famous St James' Park turf inspecting what used to be my lovely, trusted, perfectly functioning right knee – weird.

Suddenly, the Fulham physio Jason Palmer was alongside me, talking to me, looking at my knee. I have no idea what he said but I certainly know what he did – this is the knee-slicing, boiling water moment.

The knobbly thing was dislocated, which is why my initial reaction upon inspecting it was 'Oh shit'. Not the most thorough medical diagnosis admittedly, but nonetheless an accurate one given what was to unfold for the next eighteen months.

As I lay on the pitch somewhat bewildered, Jason put my knee back in place with his hands. No general anaesthetic, no local, no nothing. Instead, just pain on a scale I'd never previously encountered.

That knee, a crucial component of my football career, which had carried me through promotions, a cup final, a few great goals and plenty of ridiculous celebrations, was now a red-hot, burning, boiling, minging mess that I wanted nothing to do with.

The pain was unbearable and nothing could stop it. Not even the St John Ambulance girl, who came to my assistance with gas and air, but couldn't get the bloody thing to work.

In my frustration I grabbed her by the neck and growled: 'All you've got to do is make the gas and air work and you can't even do that, can you?'

'Alright, alright, I'm trying!' she screamed back.

'Well fucking hurry up then,' I said.

I definitely wasn't my usual, happy-go-lucky self at this point. I was struggling to see the funny side of this one.

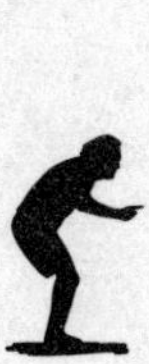

But my spirits soon lifted when my girlfriend from St John managed to get the gas and air working. 'Gooooooooood giiiiiiiiiirl . . .' I said as I drifted away with the fairies to escape the throbbing torture in the middle of my leg.

By this stage, I was surrounded by around half a dozen people, including Jason and more St John Ambulance staff. I didn't know this at the time, but while I was being treated on the pitch and manoeuvred on to a stretcher, Newcastle's manager Glenn Roeder was having a real heart-to-heart with Parker, who was absolutely devastated. The pair had their foreheads rested on each other's as Roeder attempted to convince Scotty that he'd done nothing wrong. When I left the pitch Roeder came over and put his hand on my shoulder, which was a nice touch. Literally.

He was right about Parker. It could have happened to me, it could have happened to anyone. Our paths have crossed so many times since, on the pitch and also on the golf course as we both play at The Wisley in Woking. Yet we've never talked about that incident once. I suppose it's just easier not to bring it up as it's too painful for both of us.

Football's a game where freak injuries can happen. There was absolutely no malicious intent on Scott's part and he must have felt awful. Although probably not quite as awful as me, as I was carried off the pitch on a stretcher, in tears, to a standing ovation. I'd always dreamed of leaving a pitch to the sound of 50,000 fans applauding me, but it wasn't supposed to be quite like this.

As I lay on a bed in the changing room, the drugs had really kicked in. Imagine what I'm like at the best of times; then imagine me with gas, air, morphine and whatever other powerful shit they pumped into me to ease the shock and pain. I was off my nut.

'Pass me my phone!' I yelled to anyone who'd listen as medics told me to take it easy.

'Pass me my phone!'

I was desperate to talk to my parents.

As I was handed my phone, Kieron Dyer and Peter Beardsley walked into the changing room to see how I was.

'What the fuck are they doing in here?' I thought in my hazy state. Opposition players and coaches don't come in to see you unless something serious has happened so maybe this really was a career-threatening one?

Through the cloud of painkillers, I couldn't really think straight. And that's why I rang my old man and told him I was fine. I had no idea what was going on. The drugs were certainly doing their job.

But he knew it was a bad one as he'd been following the game at home – and he also knew that I was as high as a kite on morphine. My mum, who had feared this moment since I was a kid, was shopping at Bluewater and my dad rang her to come home.

Bless her, but ever since my first injury while playing for the Bexley District team aged ten, my mum's been incredibly nervous about my football to the point where she can't actually watch me play.

It was a sliding tackle that did for me all those years before. I flew into a challenge and did my ankle ligaments. I came home and my ankle swelled up like a balloon, eventually turning all the colours of the rainbow. And it frightened her – and me.

The problem was that from then on, she found it very hard to come to my games. Other people, especially family of my team-mates, could never understand it but she just could not put herself through the terror of watching me play out of fear for what might happen to me.

She had the odd kindred spirit as Frank Lampard's late mum also suffered from the same anxiety and found it hard to watch him play.

When Mum came to see me in the Carling Cup final in Cardiff, she spent the whole game sitting in the stadium concourse talking to one of the hot dog sellers. Probably not a bad move on her part, as that afternoon never got better than the warm-up for me.

Back in Newcastle, I was taken to hospital where my knee was strapped up to secure it in place and I even managed to make it on to the plane home with my team-mates. There was plenty of sympathy flying about for me, but I was still optimistic about making a rapid recovery, which was probably down to a combination of the drugs and my naivety.

In fact, the morphine was so strong that I repeatedly hallucinated seeing Glenn Roeder, which freaked me out. He was actually at the airport and came to wish me well, but in my drugged-up state, he kept popping into my head and scaring the shit out of me. I learned so much from him while I was at West Ham but, through no fault of his own, his face was just bad news as I always associated him with being stuck in the reserves. Then I finally make it into the Premier League and my career's flying until I get struck down with a serious injury. And who's there to greet me? Glenn Roeder, the unfortunate figure of doom in my football career.

The worst injury I'd suffered previously was a broken toe at Peterborough, which didn't keep me out for long. Then at Wigan, I'd had that ridiculous streak of consecutive performances. Maybe because of that, I didn't really understand the severity of my knee injury, but by the following morning it soon became clear.

Think of the worst night's sleep you've ever had, multiply it by ten and you're probably still nowhere near how bad mine was that night.

I never realised how much I must move when I'm asleep – I must hop around almost as much as I do when I'm awake because I hardly slept a wink that night due to waking myself up every five minutes each time I shifted position. Whenever I moved, my knee moved and the pain was intense. It was killing me. It must have been the longest night of my life. It felt like a lifetime.

When I got up on the Sunday morning, I was all too aware that I was in a fair amount of trouble, but if I could avoid surgery I still had a good chance of playing in a few months.

That optimism was shattered when I scrambled off the sofa to go to the loo.

I had no strapping on my knee and, as I stood, on my left foot, peeing, I watched the lower half of my right leg dangling down from my knee. It was swinging gently from side to side and it felt like there couldn't have been more than a fag paper connecting it to the top half of my leg.

It was the weirdest, most frightening thing I'd ever seen in my life and I broke down on the spot, crying my eyes out.

Who the hell was I kidding? Not only did I need surgery, but there was a decent chance I might never play again, given that there aren't many Premier League footballers who play with the lower half of their right leg hanging off.

I thought again about how hard I'd worked to get to this point – the grafting years of laying cable, painting and decorating, playing non-league and running after my dad's car while he hooted away and I hated every minute of it. Was all that blood and guts going to end like this?

I was petrified and heartbroken.

My dad drove over to my place in Cobham where I'd moved after leaving Wigan. I didn't want him to think I'd completely lost it so as soon as he walked in I told him, 'Now I know why people do drugs', referring to my state when I'd spoken to him the day before.

He smiled and then asked me how the knee was and I broke down again.

'I think this might be it for my career,' I sobbed to him.

He tried to talk me out of it. 'You'll be back,' he said in that way of his, which gave me a bit of belief. He'd propped me up with his words since I was a kid and he wasn't going to stop now. And the state I was in, I was looking for any crumbs of comfort to keep me going.

The following morning, I went for a scan and the inevitable was confirmed.

In medical language, surgery was required as I had dislocated my knee and torn my medial collateral ligament, anterior cruciate ligament and posterior cruciate ligament. In plain English language, I was fucked. There are only four main ligaments which make the knee work and I'd wrecked three of them.

Now, here's a *really* weird thing. Three days before the

Newcastle game I was playing golf at The Wisley when I saw Jamie Redknapp walk off the course after nine holes. Jamie had a nightmare with injuries his entire career and needed twelve knee operations to keep him going.

Without really thinking, I said to him: 'You tart! What are you doing walking off after nine?' and carried on slagging him off a bit until he explained his knee was swelling up so he couldn't carry on. Oops.

Guess who received my first phone call that Monday morning after my scan? That's right, Jamie Redknapp. I wanted to know all about the knee specialist who'd saved his career when he was just twenty-six and out of options. He told me his man was Richard Steadman – or Steady to his clients – and that he was the best in the business. He'd also helped save the careers of Alan Shearer, Ruud van Nistelrooy and Craig Bellamy. He couldn't have come more highly recommended.

Steady was based in Vale, Colorado, and I was soon on a plane out there alongside my family and Jason Palmer. Fulham were superb and covered all our expenses, they couldn't have done any more.

From everything I'd heard about Steady, I was really looking forward to seeing him, but our first meeting wasn't quite what I was expecting.

Steady works in two ways. He makes his judgements based on what he sees when he goes inside the knee during surgery and also on what he feels by touching the knee. I thought I was there for surgery so when, during our first meeting, he turned off the light in the room and began feeling my knee and the area all around it, I was gripped by a bit of panic and thought 'Is this guy a bit of a weirdo or what?'

Luckily, he was not. In fact, he was as good as he was cracked up to be and I couldn't have been in better hands. Although I preferred it when the lights were on.

But, without getting all Eileen Drewery, those lights being off did represent one of the darkest times in my career as I reached my lowest point after surgery.

Steady used a pioneering new bleeding technique in which he reconnected the damaged ligaments to the bone by bleeding them into it instead of completely reconstructing the knee – unfortunately, I became something of a knee expert myself over the next few years. Even today, I could probably give Steady a run for his money.

I had to undergo two surgical procedures three months apart and each time that meant spending a few weeks in Colorado in rehab.

The first operation was in September, straight after the injury. Soon after surgery, I was sitting with Luke, an Aussie physio who I got to know quite well, as we unwrapped the heavy bandaging on my knee.

I had never seen a sight like it in my life.

It was a horror show down there. My knee was five times its normal size, there was an enormous scar stretched right across it and it was bright, bright red. I was close to tears and said to Luke: 'There's no way I'm coming back from this.'

'You will,' he tried to assure me.

'Not a chance,' I said. 'Look at the state of it.'

And then, just at the point where I was feeling like throwing the towel in, a man hopped into the room walking on what looked like two paper-thin, artificial legs. It was as if he'd been sent there especially for me.

'Have a look at him,' said Luke.

I was crying by now as I looked up and studied this bloke.

'Fuck this,' I thought as I watched the guy struggling to adjust to life with no legs. 'What am I worried about? Even if I don't play footy again, it might be really tough on me, but have a look at this bloke.'

And that proved to be a huge turning point in my mental battle to make it back to the Premier League – or any league. From then on, whenever I was experiencing difficulty in my rehab I'd think about the man with no legs. He became my mantra. Him, and Jason's 'slice of bread'. I'll explain.

Jason, who went on to become Chelsea's physio, was brilliant. He really helped me through some of the tough physical challenges. One of the most daunting aspects of the rehab was that Steady estimated I'd be playing again in about sixteen to eighteen months. That was just a monumental slice of my career gone and an inconceivable amount of time to wait to play.

But Jason helped to break it down. I just wanted to run before I could walk but he encouraged me to think of the recovery process as if we were making a slice of bread, crumb by crumb. Every day the work I'd do in the pool or on the weights would add crumbs to the slice of bread. After a week or two, we'd have the corner of the bread, by the end of the month we'd have the top crust on and so on.

Now I know I might sound like a total fruitcake with my slice of bread and man with no legs, but these are the things that kept me going and drove me to get back on a football pitch. Every weight my leg lifted I was thinking, or even saying, 'Man with no legs, slice of bread'. It helped massively.

It was especially valuable because it was tough to find inspiration in Vale, Colorado, where Steadman was based. The place was scenic, stunning and beautiful, but there wasn't a hell of a lot to do. It's a fantastic place to go skiing, for example, but skiing's not so good if you only have one knee.

Probably the most exciting thing to happen to me on my first trip there was the end of my constipation. Seriously.

After the operation, I was given an unbelievable amount of tablets to stop the pain and help my recovery. They did the job, but they also did another job of completely clogging up my insides to the point where I just could not go to the toilet for days.

One day, nature finally took its course and, without wishing to get too graphic, the whole world seemed to pour out of me and I completely blocked my hotel room toilet.

Because I could hardly move, I had to ask poor Jason to come and help but every time he flushed the chain, all the water flowed over the top and out on to the floor. Hilarious, but a total nightmare as I ended up flooding the whole floor of the hotel and the manager had to come up to sort it out. It's lucky I don't really do embarrassment, or I'd have died of it.

When I went back for the next part of the procedure three months later, it was just me and Jason as my family stayed at home. I was so bored by then that I was reading the hotel tourist information pamphlet, where I discovered that local fishing trips were available with a guide.

This was an opportunity not to be missed so I hobbled along with Jason and we went trout fishing for the day. I even managed to catch a few little ones – Jan Porter would have been so proud.

That was about as buzzing as it got out in Vale for me. Well that and doing my rehab with Owen Hargreaves.

If I thought I had it bad over those few years, that poor sod had it far worse. Every time I went out to Colorado, Owen would always be plugging away in rehab, working his socks off to get fit again.

He was a pretty quiet bloke and, apart from our hair, we didn't have a whole lot in common, but we bonded over our German connection. Owen spent the first seven years of his pro career with Bayern Munich and could have played for Germany as he had residency rights, while I'm a quarter-German – my nan on one side is German – so Owen and I got used to each other's different ways and he ended up helping me get through the rehab too.

It was a long old process and there were plenty of times where I lost patience with it. When I was back at Fulham, I used to be in the gym Portakabin watching the boys training through the window and my heart wouldn't be in the exercise regime anymore.

A couple of times, I went to see Chris Coleman and explained that my head was gone and I needed some time off. He was absolutely brilliant about it and would always tell me to come back when I was ready.

After a week or so, I was ready to go again and continued with Steady's programme, which was all based on not doing anything which caused the knee pain. Instead, I spent about five or six months fixed up to a machine which moved the knee gently – I even had to wear it while I slept.

Steady's message was that if you felt any pain, you shouldn't be doing it, but at the same time you have to work as hard as you can to get your knee moving. Which wasn't necessarily a view shared by our nutter of a fitness instructor at Fulham, Steve Nance.

Steve was a no-holds-barred, fifty-eight-year-old Australian former rugby coach. He was a proper animal, without doubt the craziest fitness coach I've ever worked with. If you thought you'd had enough, Steve had news for you – you've got another hour, boy. Even with my strict rehab programme, which he helped me through brilliantly, Steve would still insist on me doing things I wasn't certain I should do.

And he loved boxing. Once I was back playing again, he'd get the gloves out and we'd have one-on-one scraps right there in the physio room, where he'd throw jabs at you without a care in the world. Occasionally, blood was spilled and if you hit the old bloke back – as I sometimes did thanks to my boxing training as a kid – he'd just snarl and say 'Come on boy!' before digging you straight on the nose for your trouble.

Despite Steve and Jason's best efforts, nine months on from my first operation I was still feeling unstable on my knee, which was worrying me so much that I thought I was going to have to hang my boots up.

So I flew back out to Colorado again, said hello to Owen Hargreaves and saw Steady. This time he kept the lights on and asked me to remove my trousers.

He took a long, hard look at my knee while I prayed it wasn't going to be bad news. 'Jim,' he said. 'Your leg is not big enough, you've not done enough work on it. The knee is strong now so go back and build your leg up.'

And that was the last time my knee felt unstable (until the next serious injury, of course).

I returned to Fulham, to Jason and Steve, and really crunched through my exercises when I got back. I had the bit between my teeth again. As I watched the boys training through the gym window, I was focused on joining them. I even used to go out to watch them for half-an-hour to spur me on and mad Steve would always be waiting for me when I got back, making sure I finished my exercises for the day.

I brought in my own tunes to help motivate me while I was doing all my leg strengthening work. I could write a book on leg weights – a boring one, admittedly – because I had to do so much work to build up my strength again. But I was up for the challenge now, like a coiled spring, ready to explode into action. The slice of bread Jason and I had been making was almost ready to be buttered.

After the longest sixteen months of my life, I was raring to go again – probably a bit too much as I had a fight with my team-mate Chris Baird in training just a few days before my comeback.

I was pumped up and we had a little disagreement about something trivial. Words were exchanged between us, but it was pretty innocuous really as these things always are.

Except while my back was turned, Baird approached from behind and gave me a dig right in the nose – an absolute liberty. I was livid and chased him round the training pitch while the gaffer, Roy Hodgson, tried to break it all up. It was all a little bit Benny Hill as I chased Baird and Roy chased the two of us trying to calm the situation – unfortunately, there were no sexy nurses chasing all of us. The whole incident was completely bonkers and one of those things that was soon forgotten about.

A few days later, I was back in the changing room with the Fulham boys at Upton Park. Although I was only on the bench, it was an incredible feeling to finally experience a matchday atmosphere as a player again. I even got a taste of the action when I replaced Moritz Volz for the last fifteen minutes. I received a great reception from both sets of fans, which meant a lot.

I followed that up with one half against Arsenal and then a crazy 120 minutes against Bristol Rovers in an FA Cup replay, which we lost on penalties. Despite the result, I felt great that night, back to my old self and Roy Hodgson heaped a shitload of praise on me after the game.

After another away appearance at Bolton, I was finally ready to make my first home start for almost a year-and-a-half against Aston Villa and it couldn't have gone any better. I enjoyed one of those dream games I used to read about in *Roy of the Rovers* – at least I would've read about it if my nose hadn't been stuck in *Angling Times*.

Not only did I get through another ninety minutes completely unscathed, but we claimed our first victory for three months and I scored the winner with a blinding twenty-five-yard free kick with five minutes to go. Now, *that's* a comeback.

The goal celebration was insane. I went even more mental than I normally do, if that's possible. I was completely overwhelmed and still celebrating the goal at the final whistle. So much so, that I went up to the referee Chris Foy and, instead of shaking his hand like most players normally do, I gave him a celebratory hug.

It was one of those moments where I just got carried away,

but I knew Chris well as he used to train at Wigan occasionally. And he'd also been the ref when I got injured at Newcastle. It was an emotional moment and I just grabbed him and said: 'Chrissy boy, come here you big bastard!' and gave him a good old cuddle.

Next up, I was interviewed by Geoff Shreeves live on Sky after the game. I was so pumped I was like a boxer who had just won a fight and then has a microphone stuck in his face so talks a load of nonsense because of all the adrenaline flying around.

Never mind cloud nine, I was on cloud eleven or twelve. He asked me the first question about the goal and I just replied: 'Alright Geoff, how are you?'

He was interviewing *me* and I was asking *him* the questions.

He looked at me as if to say, 'You're off your head, son', and he was right. I was as high as a kite and started rambling into the mic.

'Eighteen months out!' I shouted to nobody in particular. 'I've not been back playing for so long and I've scored the winner, Geoff.'

He nodded.

'Geoff! I've scored the winner!'

I think the producers must have cut to an ad break because it was only a matter of time before I would've sworn or hugged him or something. Some of my mates said to me afterwards, 'Er, Jim – that interview?' But there was no way they would've understood what I was experiencing at the time.

In my overexcited state after such a long time out, hugging the ref and losing the plot during a TV interview both seemed like perfectly normal things to do. And they still do. Because you have to make the most of it when the going's good. And I'm glad I did because it wasn't long before I was laid up again.

Almost a year to the day after that Villa game, I made my debut for Hull City after a £5 million move – no pressure then.

I was Hull's record signing and they pulled out all the stops to make me their player, including a thorough medical with particular attention placed on my knee.

I'd been playing without any problems for the previous year; in fact I was probably playing the best football of my career as I'd helped save Fulham from the drop and was then called up to the England squad at the start of the following season.

I was desperate to make a good impression at Hull, who were enjoying their first Premier League season and had ambitions to stay there permanently, because they'd paid a lot of money for me and were paying me a load of cash as well.

We were playing West Ham in an evening kick-off in late January and I'd been suffering from flu; it was that time of year where everyone picks something up. The gaffer Phil Brown asked me how I felt and I said I was really bogged down with it but agreed to go on the bench although I was probably only about twenty per cent fit.

But by the time the game came along that night, the matchday adrenaline meant I'd soon forgotten all about the illness and was desperate to get on the pitch, especially as we were losing and I wanted to help.

I got my chance early in the second half when I was sent on to replace Geovanni. It always takes a little while to catch up with the game when you come off the bench, but I was soon flying about all over the place and felt good.

Scott Parker had moved to West Ham by that stage and we had a good old midfield scrap. He threw himself into a challenge, which I hurdled and glided along the grass as I landed. Given that it was January, the pitch was rock hard but wet, so gliding wasn't a problem but I stopped abruptly and felt a sharp crunch in my right knee. *That* knee.

'You've got to be kidding me,' I thought.

I felt no pain, which was reassuring, as was the Hull physio Simon Maltby, who came on to the pitch to check me out and told me I was fine to continue. I finished the game with no further problems, other than the fact that we lost, and I didn't really think about my knee again.

Until the following morning.

I got out of bed the next day and fell straight over. Unless I'd been drinking in my sleep, there was something seriously wrong. I looked down at my knee and nearly fell over again. It had swelled up like a football, at least three times its normal size.

Now and again, since the first operation, I used to get fluid on my knee, which was part and parcel of the recovery process, but this was more like a bowl of soup on my knee.

I rang Simon immediately and he told me to come straight in so he could have a look at it. I was close to breaking down again then and there. Without anyone examining me, I knew that I was facing another long stretch out of the game. I felt especially sick as this was the last thing the Hull chairman Paul Duffen needed after all the money the club had paid for me.

He'd moved heaven and earth to get me up there only to see me crocked after thirty-seven minutes of action – not exactly value for money.

Duffen and Phil Brown both came to see me after Simon had told me I needed a scan and I could see the genuine concern on their faces – they looked like I felt on the inside.

I wanted to go out to Colorado and see Steady again but, given the circumstances, I couldn't really expect Hull to foot the bill so I insisted on covering it. It was the least I could do and there was no way I was going to put my knee in anyone else's hands.

So off I went to Vale again with my family and another Hull physio, Liam McGarry, with all kinds of questions racing through my mind as Steady turned the lights out and felt my knee.

How long was I going to be out for? Would I ever get back to my best? Would I ever play again? When was he going to turn the lights back on so it didn't feel so spooky?

Steady's verdict was that the knee felt loose – I could've told him that myself with the lights on – and that it would need surgery to fix it. The anterior cruciate ligament had come away from the bone and needed sorting out.

When he opened up my knee, he found that there was a ninety per cent tear of the ACL, much looser than he thought, which meant replacing my dodgy ligament with a dead man's fully functioning ACL. I hoped he might use George Best's, but no such luck.

Steady told me this time I was looking at nine months out. I was devastated. Even though it was less than the first time, psychologically I wasn't prepared for it. I'd accepted the first one as the kind of thing that can happen to anyone once in their career; I was not expecting this.

But, once I'd got my head round it, it seemed obvious to me that my knee could never have been as strong again after that first injury. In a way, the knee is like an elastic band and once it's been snapped, it will never be as strong (I told you I learned loads about knees). One of the theories is that you build your leg up to be twice as strong to support the knee, hence all those bloody leg weight drills. But, even with all that, I can't believe the ligaments would ever be the same.

And that's why I was back in rehab in freezing cold, mid-winter Colorado. I walked in and look who's there – Owen Hargreaves.

'Hello mate, how are you doing?'

Obviously not so good given that he was now renting a place and living out there. He'd done both his knees, the poor sod, but he put a hell of a lot of graft in, trying to save his career.

Looking at him, I suppose I was lucky to have one good knee and had a much better chance of making a good recovery. But I was so worried about whether I'd be able to perform like a £5 million Premier League player even if I did make it back.

It was time to reacquaint myself with my old friends: the man with no legs and the slice of bread.

Back at Hull, the recovery process felt much harder than

at Fulham, where I'd known a lot more of the players and staff. I'd only been on the pitch for half an hour at Hull so hadn't really had time to make friends with anyone, and there I was stuck in the gym with Liam and Simon.

I didn't even have Diane and my family up there with me permanently as they divided their time between Humberside and Cobham. When it was just me up there on my own trying to do the rehab, I experienced some of the lowest moments of my career. I'm no good on my own at the best of times, but in that situation I was awful.

Simon and Liam were brilliant though and really helped get me through it, although we had our disagreements. I'd often refuse to do any exercises which caused my knee too much pain, remembering Steady's advice from the first time. But the physios were employed by the club and their job was to get me back on the pitch as soon as possible. Especially when I was costing the club about £45,000 a week. My concern was for my body – I'd rather take an extra few weeks and make sure that I was completely ready than come back too early and do myself more damage, and that was surely in everyone's long-term interests. And given how much of an impact I made when I returned from sixteen months out for Fulham, I like to think I was right to err on the side of caution again.

I felt ready by October, which also happened to be nine months on from my disastrous debut. This time, the *Roy of the Rovers* bit happened in a reserve game I played against Bolton as part of my recovery.

It was a freezing night with a howling wind blowing across the pitch and I was wearing tights, gloves and a snood. I didn't care what I looked like as I was taking no chances with my recent track record.

We won an indirect free kick about twenty-five yards out and I really fancied it so I told one of my team-mates to roll the ball back to me. I flicked it up and volleyed it first time with the wind, sending the ball dipping over the keeper, who barely moved, and straight into the net. Maybe I did have George Best's ligament after all?

I wouldn't put myself in the same bracket as him or Matt Le Tissier, but they'd both done that trick and now I had as well – no matter that mine was in a reserve game, they all count.

The incredible thing was that about a month after that glorious reserve match moment, I was playing for the first team in a Premier League game in front of a packed KC Stadium when we won a free kick in a similar position.

There were 30,000 pairs of eyes on me as I stood over the ball with our full-back Andy Dawson, who had a fantastic left foot on him and would definitely have fancied his chances.

'Roll it back to me and I'll try to volley it,' I said to him.

'Jim, we haven't practised it, we can't do it,' he replied.

'I don't care, it'll go in. We'll catch them off guard,' I insisted.

'No, I'm not doing it!' said Dawson.

The risk was all mine. All I was asking him to do was roll the ball back to me. Finally, after what seemed like about five minutes of intense negotiations, I made him realise that and we were all set.

The pressure was even greater after that standoff, but that didn't bother me. I was supremely confident – I had Bestie's ligament after all.

Dawson rolled the ball back, I flicked it up and smashed it straight in.

To the fortieth row of the stand behind the goal.

Some you win, some you lose.

One of the essential qualities a footballer needs is a big pair of bollocks to try things like that. You cannot be afraid of making an idiot of yourself.

As it happens, that was a mere blip on my comeback trail. I'd made my first appearance a few weeks earlier as a substitute against my old side Fulham and followed that up with a decent run as we took five points from three games.

Coming off the bench against Fulham was weird. There was no sympathy that it was my first game for nine months from any of my old fans, but that was to be expected. Instead, they started up a chorus of 'There's only one greedy bastard!' It took me a few minutes to work out what they were singing. Once I did, I could hear it loud and clear and thought, 'Oh, here we go, it's about me!'

I had no problem with that either as, in the version of events they'd been told, I had been a greedy bastard. They just didn't know the full story – but more about that later.

Soon after I came on, Diomansy Kamara barged into me and sent me tumbling to the ground – that produced the biggest cheer of the game, but I just got on with it. What else could I do?

Things improved massively in my next match against Stoke when their goalkeeper Thomas Sørensen couldn't hold my shot and Jan Vennegoor of Hesselink slammed in the rebound to hand us the three points.

We then drew with West Ham, a game in which I scored

a penalty, and I scored from the spot again the following match as we grabbed a fantastic draw at Man City – and followed it up with *that* goal celebration.

Things couldn't have been going better as a few days later I found out that I'd been named the Premier League player of the month for November – the man with no legs and the slice of bread had done the business again.

The next match was away at Villa and we started badly, going a goal down early on. Soon after, I went up for an aerial challenge with James Milner and ended up going right over the top of him, landing on the ground with a double thud as my back and legs hit the deck.

I was badly winded and struggling for breath so Simon the physio helped me off the pitch. But as I was walking off I felt something wobbling inside my left knee and knew instantly it was my medial ligament – as I keep telling you, all the time spent with Steady had turned me into a leading authority on knees.

Once I'd got my breath back, I tried to carry on playing. I ran back on to the pitch but felt the same looseness in my knee. I tried to run again but my knee wouldn't let me.

Enough was enough.

I was royally pissed off.

I sat down in the middle of the Villa Park pitch and had a huge tantrum. If I'd had a pram with toys in, I would've hurled them across the pitch. As it was, I only had my boots so I took them off and chucked them across the turf instead.

Even when I landed on my back, I had still somehow managed to smash my knee up.

I'd been playing for less than two months since my second

serious injury and here I was again, back at sodding square one. I left the pitch in tears again. I just couldn't take any more of this. My right knee twice and now my left knee – I was starting to think I'd been spending too much time with Owen Hargreaves.

I told Simon my diagnosis and he could see there was little point in disagreeing with me as my head was completely gone. I just needed to get out of the ground and back to my loved ones as soon as possible, so someone from Villa called me a cab which took me all the way back to Cobham. My team-mates were ringing me nonstop but I just wasn't in the mood to speak.

Once I'd calmed down, I was able to think a little more rationally about the whole thing. I knew I had to see Steady again, but this time Hull tried to persuade me to go elsewhere. I stood firm though because, despite the ongoing problems, I knew my man in Colorado was the best in the world and I kept faith in him.

So I flew back out to what was fast becoming my second home. The lights went out, Steady did his thing, no surgery required, phew, 'Hello Owen, how are you doing?' and I was back home as quick as a flash.

It wasn't all plain sailing though as I still had three months of rehab ahead of me to recover from the injury. Just because there was no surgery didn't mean there was no hard work.

Out came the man with no legs, the breadcrumbs and crusts and all that – it felt like they'd hardly been away – as I hit the leg weights. Groundhog Day!

Compared to the previous two injuries, three months didn't

seem like a long time and I was ready for action again by late February. But the fact is, it was still a third of a season out, and when you add that to a nine-month layoff and a sixteen-month break that's pretty much two-and-a-half years without football.

A football career is not that long, especially if you have to come through non-league and work your way up the football pyramid, and that's a massive chunk of time out of it which, not only would I never get back, but also had a massive impact on my ability.

Most of what I learned on my journey from Dartford to the Premier League was the improved skill level required, which I only achieved through practice. By playing 123 straight, games for Wigan, I was able to get better and better. Sadly for me, the reverse was true. Being out of the game and not being able to practise the skills required to play at the highest level meant that I was always going to be losing ability to some extent. If I wasn't playing, I was certainly not getting any better and the chances were I was getting worse.

On top of that, I was now playing with fifty per cent of one knee gone and twenty per cent off the other so, inevitably, I found it that much harder to manoeuvre my body the way I used to. The slightest tweak caused by an awkward movement on the pitch would cause me huge pain.

And then there was the mental side of it. If you think I approached games after my injuries in the same way as I did before, you'd be mistaken. In the back of my mind, there was always that self-preservation instinct, stopping me from going into tackles in a one hundred per cent full-blooded way. Show me a player with similar injuries who says otherwise, I'll show you a liar. The knees might take the physical damage but the mind takes a huge psychological hit from those injuries too.

That's not to say I didn't give my all in every game I played in. Knowing there was that little something missing from my game, I tried my best to make up for it in other ways by using my experience, but I never felt like I truly got back to where I was at my peak.

But there were still plenty of amazing moments – one of my comeback games (yes, another one) against my old club Fulham being another good example. Because one of the great joys of being injured is playing again. If anything, you appreciate that incredible buzz even more. I'd loved every second of every game after my journey to make it as a pro, but those matches where I'd fought back from career-threatening injuries were even more special.

Hull were in desperate trouble near the bottom of the league when I was fit enough to play again, but I still relished the opportunity even though we were up against it on the pitch. That game against Fulham gave us some rare hope as we won and I opened the scoring from the penalty spot.

It was a weird game because it felt a bit like a training session to me as I was up against so many of my former team-mates. At one point, Simon Davies clattered into me with a heavy tackle and I said, 'You bastard, you did that on purpose!' He looked at me and nodded his head to confirm that's exactly what he'd done.

Because I was so familiar with everyone on the pitch, I felt a lot more relaxed, which helped me play better and, when our striker Jozy Altidore was brought down in the box by Chris Smalling, I grabbed the ball to take the spot-kick.

I loved Fulham but I was a Hull player and I had no qualms about celebrating after I smashed that ball into the net past my old mate Mark Schwarzer to give us the lead.

I've seen loads of players score against their former clubs then ham it up by giving it the old stone arms and legs and push their team-mates away as they refuse to celebrate the goal. I don't really get it, especially if they've chosen to take a penalty. If they're that bothered about it, don't take the penalty in the first place.

I wasn't that fussed and I ran off to celebrate as I always did, but perhaps with a bit more emotion than usual as this was soon after returning to full fitness – which probably explains why I ended up celebrating in front of the Fulham fans. Oops. Mind you, I usually go to all four corners of the ground when I score if time (and the ref) allows so I was always going to end up in front of them at some point.

Even if I did go over the top, after the frustration I had put up with I couldn't help it. Any footballer will tell you how short their career is. For the sake of the man with no legs and Owen Hargreaves (the man with no knees), I had to make the most of the good times.

PILLAR 7

LOVE YOUR COUNTRY AND IT WILL LOVE YOU BACK

'At the centre of your being you have the answer; you know who you are and you know what you want.' ***Lao Tzu***

I was walking down the corridor of The Grove, one of the nicest hotels I've ever been in, looking for my room. Across my arms I had some England training kit and sticking out of my hand was the key card to get into my room.

Looking back on it now, I was a bit like the *Gavin & Stacey* character Smithy played by James Corden in that Comic Relief sketch when he stumbles upon the England squad. Except the important difference was that I was actually *in* the England squad. The painter and decorator from Bexleyheath had hit the big time.

If I could only have found my sodding room, I'd have been in business.

I walked up and down the corridor, 292, 294 . . . Aha, got it!

Room 296. The temporary abode of England footballer Jimmy Bullard. It felt good saying it, never mind writing it.

I was still a bit overwhelmed by the whole experience, but I was trying to do my best impression of someone who wasn't a bit overwhelmed by the whole experience.

I wiggled my key card into the door and turned the handle but nothing happened. No green light. No electronic whirring. Not a bloody thing.

So I did it again. And again. And again.

If I had to go back to reception carrying all this gear because I can't get into my room, I might not even make it out on to the training pitch because they'd probably throw me out for being too blinking thick.

I gave it another go and, as I wiggled the card in the slot again, I heard someone coming down the corridor – hopefully a member of hotel staff who could get me into my room.

I looked down the corridor but couldn't make out who it was from a distance, although it wasn't anyone from the hotel as they were also carrying gear so it must be another player.

The figure finally emerged from the shadows of the hotel corridor and my heart skipped a beat when I realised it was David Beckham. Goldenballs! He was going to think I was a right spanner.

'I've heard about you,' said Becks as he got close enough for me to hear him. 'I suppose that's my room, is it?'

'Naah, no, no . . .' I replied, but before I could say anymore, Becks looked up at the door number and down to the envelope for his key card and said: 'It *is* my room!'

I looked down at my envelope and saw that it said 269, not 296.

What a total donut. To make matters worse, I immediately felt guilty for no reason: 'I know you think I was going to do something in there, but I wasn't, honestly,' I kind of pleaded.

Becks grinned at me and replied: 'Go on, hop it you!'

I was so embarrassed, completely mortified.

As I went off towards my real room I kept thinking, 'He's

never going to believe that I wasn't trying to pull some kind of prank.'

The problem was that Becks and I had a little bit of previous which would certainly have raised his suspicions. So not only did he now think I was trying to break into his room, he also knew I had a history of practical jokes and wasn't afraid to ask him questions about his private life.

It all stemmed back to a pre-season trip I'd been on with Fulham a couple of years before.

I'd just joined the club from Wigan and we were on a tour of Austria and Germany. We were staying in the same plush hotel as Real Madrid, who Becks was still playing for, as we were playing them in a friendly.

Although I hadn't been at Fulham for long, I'd bonded pretty quickly with a few players, including Michael Brown, and I let him in on a little plot I'd worked up since we arrived at the hotel. When we checked in, I was stood behind our gaffer Chris 'Cookie' Coleman and I clocked his room number, 206. 'Right,' I thought. 'This will be a classic.'

I have no idea why I did it, other than that I just thought it would be really funny, but for the entire six days we stayed there, I put everything on Cookie's room. Actually, I do know why I did it. It was because I didn't want to pay for anything myself.

Apart from Brownie, my roommate, none of the other lads knew what I was up to. So when we went to play golf and I said to them, 'Don't worry boys, I'll get this and you can all have buggies too', there were a few quizzical looks. But most of them thought I was just trying to make a generous gesture as I was new to the team. That all went on Room 206 as did

the new Vokey pitching wedge and a load of golf gloves I ordered for myself.

Later on, we were all in the bar and so were quite a few of the Madrid lads, including Becks and Raúl. 'Right lads, what are you all drinking?' I said as I proceeded to order one of the most enormous rounds of drinks in history. Beckham and his team-mates were staring at me with, 'Who is this madman?' looks written across their faces, but we all had a drink, courtesy of Cookie.

Feeling pretty pleased with myself, I called Becks over for a chat, although my team-mates were all reluctant as if they were somehow scared of him, or of an embarrassing situation developing: 'No Jim, don't get him over,' said a couple of them as they scarpered.

But they were soon back in the thick of the action when I asked the England captain about the rumours that he'd had an affair with the Beckhams' former nanny Rebecca Loos.

'What's happening with Loosy and all that then?' I said to him. 'Come on, open up!'

He started to laugh.

'To be honest, she fancied Victoria, not me!' was his reply.

We all started to laugh.

'That's a great "Get Out of Jail Free" card, that is, Becks,' I said. 'Don't give me that, what's the true story?'

But he told us he was being serious – we laughed even more. What a great lad.

That was the highlight of the Cookie room card scam, which went on all week until we checked out of the hotel and the gaffer had a look at the extras on his bill – £5,500 worth of extras to be precise. As soon as he saw that, he yelled, 'Bulllllaaaaaaaard!'

'How did you know it was me?' I said. I didn't bother trying to protest my innocence, and luckily it didn't matter anyway as he had no intention of making me pay him back – and that's just one of many reasons why Cookie was the nicest manager I ever played for.

Anyway, back at The Grove, I finally made it to my correct room and lay my England training kit and tracksuit on the bed, still struggling to believe that I was really part of the national squad. I stopped for a moment and thought to myself: 'I'm here now. I've got to show people what I can do.'

From then on, I was less overwhelmed and more focused, full of belief that I belonged with England's finest.

I had received my call-up a few days earlier, via a phone call from the FA. I'd been playing really well for Fulham since my comeback from injury at the beginning of the year (2008) but I didn't have the slightest inkling that I might be anywhere near the England squad.

A lovely woman from the FA called to tell me that Fabio Capello was considering involving me in the squad and I was on a list of thirty players for the World Cup qualifiers against Andorra and Croatia, which would be cut to twenty-four by the weekend.

I was helped a little by the circumstances as three midfielders were injured – Steven Gerrard, Michael Carrick and my old mate Owen Hargreaves – but even without those three, I was still surprised to be so close to the squad. Then again, it was obviously no coincidence that Mr Capello, a lover of art and the finer things in life, was also a fan of mine.

As exciting as the recognition was, I played it right down to avoid disappointment. My attitude was that it was already an enormous achievement to be included in a squad of thirty and I could at least tell all my mates that. I was ninety-five per cent certain that I wouldn't make the final twenty-four, but still held that little bit of hope that I might.

The lovely woman from the FA told me that she would try to contact me before the final squad was confirmed, but that it might be announced on TV first as they had so many calls to make.

Someone else might have taken it all in their stride, but I couldn't possibly have done that. For all the acting I was doing pretending this was a perfectly ordinary few days as I waited to find out whether I'd made the final squad, I could think of nothing else.

Finally, Sunday lunchtime arrived and I sat in front of the telly with my phone right next to me and Diane and my boy, Archie, not much further away.

Over in Crayford, my parents had invited a load of mates to their pub for a drink, hoping to see my name included in the England squad. No pressure then.

They put the telly on at The One Bell and we were watching *Sky Sports News* in Cobham.

On the stroke of twelve noon, a list of names who had made the squad appeared at the bottom of the screen. My phone hadn't rung and my heart was sinking until there, right on the telly in front of me, was my name – BULLARD.

Unmistakably, one hundred per cent my name in great big capital letters.

But was this the final twenty-four? Diane and I started

counting the names to see if there was a total of twenty-four. That way, I could be certain I'd made it.

I don't think we'd got further than twelve or thirteen when my phone rang. It was the even lovelier woman from the FA, confirming that I was in the squad, I'd be travelling to Andorra and Croatia and that she'd be in touch with further details.

I could've kissed her. Instead I kissed my missus, which was far more appropriate. The Bullard household went absolutely crazy. Over at The One Bell, the party was in full swing, too. Apparently, a huge roar went up in the pub when my name appeared on the screen and many glasses were raised.

I felt like celebrating myself, but turning up drunk to my first England squad gathering might not have impressed Mr Capello too much even though he was my new biggest fan. My phone didn't stop ringing, beeping and buzzing after that as friends and family got in touch to congratulate me.

It's hard to explain how much this meant to me. It was the pinnacle of my career and I don't think I've ever had a higher footballing high. It all came from out of nowhere as well, which made it all the more amazing. I often think I'm still celebrating that call-up now and I don't think I'll ever stop.

My ambition as a boy was to play at as high a level as I possibly could. When I was playing non-league I thought to myself that if I really gave it a hundred per cent and made it to the lower professional leagues or even the Championship, then I'd have had a great career. Most boys playing non-league would have given their right leg for that . . . although they wouldn't have been able to play then, but you know what I mean.

When I progressed to the lower leagues and Championship I thought how chuffed I'd be to make it to the Premier League and it happened for me. But that wasn't enough. Somehow, I now had an England call-up too and I was thinking, 'How much higher can I go now? Imagine if I get on the pitch and get an England cap . . .'

These thoughts were racing through my mind as I headed off to The Grove to join the rest of the squad. My head was spinning with excitement, but I was still quite nervous when I met everyone for the first time.

Players like Rio Ferdinand, Frank Lampard, Wayne Rooney and Becks were my idols so, even though they knew what I could be like as they'd have seen me playing the fool on *Soccer AM* or on the pitch, I was hardly going to arrive in that environment and be straight in everyone's faces: 'Waaaaaaaahhhhhh, Jimmy's here!'

I don't think so. Instead I played it cool by trying to break into Beckham's room by mistake. Nice start, Jim.

My first training session with England was an unforgettable experience. A bus took us over to nearby London Colney and as it parked up, I could see that Rooney was itching to get off. The door opened and he flew out of it like a dog that had just been let off its leash. He pegged it straight over to one of the goals, picked a few balls out of the net and started shelling them at the crossbar, hitting it every single time.

While he was doing that, the rest of us were stretching and loosening up and I just couldn't help thinking how weird it was to be doing that alongside all those huge names.

'Wayne!' screamed Capello, snapping me out of my daydreaming. 'You'll pull a muscle!'

'Behave Fab, I've not pulled a muscle since I was thirteen,' said Rooney, or something like that anyway. Nothing stopped that boy from playing football, certainly not warming up.

Before long, David Bentley had joined him too and there was only so long I could stay out of the action before I had to get involved.

Soon after, everyone had the balls out for passing drills and I felt like I'd entered a different planet altogether. The pace of the training was at least twice as quick as I was used to at Fulham – and bear in mind that I was training with a load of internationals there on a daily basis.

England was a class above that and what struck me the most was that all those players knew they were the governors and that they belonged there. They didn't have to do anything special as their normal game was so bloody good.

We started with a five versus five keep-ball session in an area that seemed not much bigger than the average table-cloth. At Fulham, we would've done that in a space twice as big. With England, you barely had room to move, never mind pass. We might as well have been playing keep-ball in a lift.

Yet the ball was still pinging about like a pinball machine as pass after pass was completed. It was a fucking joke (in a good way), the talent was unreal and I immediately thought, 'I really don't belong here.' The ball was getting spanked around twice as hard as I was used to and players like Becks, Rooney and Rio knew exactly where it was going before it had even reached them – they even read the random ricochets.

As I was wondering what I was doing there, the ball bounced off my leg and happened to find its way to a team-mate. 'Oh yeah,' I thought, 'I can play one-touch with the best of them!'

After taking part in a training drill like that, I couldn't believe that England would ever get slagged off by the pundits for not being able to pass the ball. Maybe, our problem is that we need to play internationals on pitches the size of tablecloths.

Another myth that was put to bed after my first England training session was that Becks was all about the looks and didn't have much ability. Utter nonsense. You can't get anywhere in football without ability, no matter how good-looking you are – and I should know!

Watching him train that day made me realise just how talented the bloke was. He had the sickest strike of a ball I'd ever seen and his vision was an absolute joke (again, in a good way). He'd played around the world's best players for so long, which definitely takes you to another level as I found out. At each stage of my career I was learning more from playing with better players. After only a couple of weeks with the England squad, I returned to Fulham a better player. My team-mates even commented they could see the difference – unless they were taking the piss, of course.

The trick is staying on top of it. I couldn't train with England the whole time and then it wears off. But it's definitely the players around you who make you the player you are. For example, if you took a sixteen-year-old parks player and made him train with the world's best players for five years, by the age of twenty-one, I guarantee you he'd be among the best in the world himself.

I'd imagine that was what Capello was hoping for me, but

I never really found out. There was something of the schoolteacher about him, which made him difficult to warm to let alone talk to. He was a real disciplinarian, a very stern, strict man.

Having said that, I do remember having two very in-depth conversations with him.

The first time was after one training session where we'd been playing on a pitch that was a third of the size of a normal one and I hadn't really done as much as I'd have liked.

He approached me after the game and said: 'Jimmy, why aren't you getting on the ball more?'

'I'm much better on a bigger pitch,' I explained. 'If I've got more space to run into then I'll get on the ball more.'

'Oh.'

And that was the end of that one.

The other one was when we were playing golf at The Grove. There's a half-decent nine-hole course there and we were all set to tee off. Fabio walked up to me and said: 'One handicap, huh?'

'Yeah,' I replied with a smile. 'One handicap.'

And he marched off to talk to someone else.

He ran a tight ship and was big on rules. Punctuality was crucial – you could not be late for any meal, training session or team meeting. Mobile phones were banned from mealtimes, room service was banned and we all had to dress appropriately.

The whole squad always had to eat together but we had supper at 7pm, the same time my kids have it. That was never going to last me until the following morning. If I was at home and I got peckish later in the evening, I'd go to the fridge and have a bite to eat. But with room service off limits, Fabio left us to starve until breakfast.

That was way too strict for my liking. It would get to about 9pm or 10pm every night and I'd be starving. Something had to be done. So I paid a visit to David Bentley's room.

Bents was a great lad. Don't get me wrong, the bloke is an absolute wrong 'un, make no mistake about that, but a lot of fun nonetheless. He was always laughing and I mean, *always* laughing. It wasn't necessary for anything funny to actually happen, Bents would just laugh for the hell of it. That's what he was like. I once went on a night out with him and he laughed all night. It got to the point where I ended up laughing along with him and even *I* didn't know what we were laughing about.

I stepped out of my hotel room – my one this time, not David Beckham's – and walked towards Bentley's. There was always heavy security surrounding the England team and I noticed there was a bouncer at both ends of the corridor. I had no idea how we were going to get food in there, but it had to be done because I was starving.

I knocked on Bentley's door which he immediately opened and he burst out laughing: 'Wa-ha-ha-ha-ha-ha-ha-ha!'

'Bents,' I said, 'I haven't even said anything.'

'Wa-ha-ha-ha-ha-ha-ha-ha!'

'Listen Bents, I'm starving. I've got to eat something.'

'Wa-ha-ha-ha-ha-ha-ha-ha! Funny you should say that. So am I.'

'How can we eat something?' I asked him.

'Leave it to me,' he said as he grabbed his phone and called a mate of his.

Within half-an-hour, there was a knock at the door and Bentley's mate was standing there with a large McDonald's brown paper bag full of Big Macs and chips. You fucking beauty!

Bents stuck his head out of the door in the direction of one of the huge security men at the end of the corridor. 'Cheers boy!' he called out as the bouncer nodded back. The nutcase had the security blokes on tap, didn't he?

I don't think I've ever enjoyed a Big Mac as much as that one and, given that McDonald's were an FA sponsor, it's what both parties would have wanted.

Bentley was also my partner in crime when it came to taking the piss out of Mr Capello. I remember looking at the gaffer on my first day and thinking, 'I can't believe how much he looks like Postman Pat; it's him!' The only thing that was missing was the black and white cat.

Because I was new to that whole environment, I didn't want to make too much of my discovery so I did it on the sly and used it as an icebreaker, letting some of the boys know that we had a TV personality running the show.

Bentley obviously loved it – 'Wa-ha-ha-ha-ha-ha-ha-ha!' – and when we were on the team coach, we sat at the back and started singing the *Postman Pat* theme tune. A few of the boys joined in – I think Rio, Ashley Cole and Jermaine Jenas might have had a quiet little sing-along – but most of the other dry lunches weren't really up for it.

Another daft scheme Bents and I came up with was seeing who could say 'Postman Pat' as loud as possible within earshot of the gaffer. It was based on a game I used to play at school with my mates where we'd have to say something louder and louder in front of a teacher and the winner was the person who didn't bottle it.

I can safely say that I was the bottler on this occasion because Bents was an utter lunatic. I'd walk past Capello and say 'Postman Pat' out of the corner of my mouth, but Bentley took it to another level when he would walk straight up to the boss and scream 'Postman Pat!' in his face before adding 'And his black and white cat!' for good measure.

I had an idea to borrow a black and white cat, give it to Fabio and say 'Hold this for five minutes, would you?' but I didn't dare share that with Bents because he would've been on the phone to his mates sorting it out.

Bentley had just as much front on the training pitch. Capello set up a training exercise in which he sent three players out wide to put crosses into the penalty area. He asked David Beckham, Stewart Downing and Joe Cole to do the honours but Bents just followed them to the far side of the pitch.

'No,' Capello shouted to Bentley. 'Just three, you come back.'

But Bentley was having none of it.

'Leave it out, send one of *them* back,' he told Capello. 'This is my game. I'm one of the best crossers in the country!'

The pair of us weren't involved on the pitch as we won the two qualifiers against Andorra and Croatia, but all was not right with that squad.

I travelled with them for both games and the England fans got right on the team's backs as they struggled to break down a very poor side. England were booed off at half time which I totally understood, but we're not always going to smash six or seven past teams like Andorra.

However, I never felt that Fabio gave the boys a lot of direction. For starters, his English was poor and it was very difficult to understand what he was going on about most of the time.

The only thing he said that stuck was: 'Let's all attack together, let's all defend together.' Not terrible advice, but when I remembered that this was international football, the pinnacle of the game, I thought it was just a little bit basic. To be frank, I'd had better coaching when I was playing non-league.

The other problem was that the man-management side of things didn't really exist in that England set-up either. When I first arrived at The Grove, at no point did Fabio put his arm around me or welcome me into the fold. I never felt particularly loved and he just seemed harsh and standoffish. A few times he mentioned to me that I shouldn't run beyond play and that I should sit back and provide a supporting role instead. But, other than that, he never really asked me to play in any particular position or style. From the coaching side of things, it was ever so slightly disappointing.

Naturally, Fabio was never going to be overjoyed with that stuttering performance against Andorra, so he was much happier with the Croatia win, in which Theo Walcott scored a hat-trick. I watched that from the stands in Zagreb and I've still got a picture of me with Wayne Bridge and Bents in our England suits at the game.

And then it was suddenly back to the real world of Fulham and the Premier League.

If the whole England experience had seemed like a bit of a dream, that was confirmed a month later when Postman

Pat named his squad for the next two qualifiers and my name was not included, no matter how hard I looked. That bloody selfish Steven Gerrard had got himself fit again so there was no room for me.

I don't think I could really complain about that too much and it was more of the same the following month when twenty-three players were chosen to go over to Berlin for a friendly against Germany but I wasn't one of them. With one of my grandparents being German that would've been lovely, but it wasn't to be.

Or was it?

Three days before the game, I got a call from the lovely woman at the FA to tell me that I was going to fly out to Germany with the squad after all. Turns out that Gerrard had realised how out of order he'd been and had been ruled out of the game with a knock so I was in through the back door.

I headed back to The Grove to meet up with the boys, not feeling like such a fish out of water this time and the following day we flew to Berlin.

Germany v England. This was what it was all about. And as it was a friendly, I might have even had a small chance of getting on to the pitch because we were allowed to name eleven substitutes.

I took my place on the bench and from the very first minute I was absolutely desperate to get on that pitch and play for my country. Every time Capello turned around, I'd do everything I could to catch his eye and make sure he had no choice but to think about me as an option.

Half time came and went, during which he made two changes, but I remained benched.

I was getting desperate now and, as the clock kept ticking, I started to perform the most overelaborate stretches anyone can possibly do while seated, in a bid to get the gaffer's attention. Anyone watching would've thought there was something wrong with me.

Peter Crouch was pissing himself laughing as I waved my arms around and started to put my shin pads on in the most exaggerated way imaginable. I had to let Capello know I was ready to play as I kept thinking that this could be the last time I ever got picked. It's only a friendly, he had to put me on, surely?

With thirteen minutes left, he turned round to make a change and I was doing everything but wave my hand in his face and screaming 'Put me on!' He nodded to Ashley Young who stripped off and got straight on to that pitch – the pitch I would've killed someone to get on at that moment.

Desperate times call for desperate measures and I considered going up to Capello and asking him for a game – 'Oi Fabs, I might not get in the squad again – any chance?' – but I decided against such drastic action. He wouldn't have liked that and it would certainly have ruled out any chance I might have had of getting another call-up.

Then, as we went into stoppage time, Capello turned round again to make another change. 'Please, please, please be me,' I thought at the exact same moment as Crouch, who I'd been keeping entertained with my ludicrous efforts at getting Capello's attention, got up, took his tracksuit off and had a two-minute run around on the pitch. Another bloody cap for him then.

As we made our way back to the dressing room, I was

gutted while everyone else around me was buzzing as we'd won the game 2-1.

I cheered up pretty quickly on the outside as I didn't want to dampen the mood and, as I started to get changed, the gaffer came up to me and we had our longest conversation yet:

'Jimmy, I'm so sorry. I've just been told you haven't got a cap.'

'No,' I said. 'That's why I was doing the crazy warming up.'

'I didn't see,' he replied. 'My mind was on the game.'

'No problem,' I said, although deep down I now felt even more gutted. 'But next game, put me on, eh?'

'Yes, ahem, yes,' he coughed and spluttered as he walked off.

And that was the end of my England career. The next time Capello had a squad to select I was hobbling around in Colorado, trying not to block any more toilets. Out of sight, out of mind and all that.

To this day, I still wish I had approached him on the touchline and asked him to bring me on during that Germany match. I know it's not the done thing, but if it had meant I'd got an England cap then it would've been well worth it.

But it wasn't all in vain as I learned from that experience. A few years later, I was sitting on the bench for Ipswich in a pre-season friendly against Southend, towards the end of my time at Portman Road. I'd been struggling to get into the side and was desperate for a chance to show the manager, Paul Jewell, what I could do. With what had happened with England weighing heavy on my mind, I decided to take matters into my own hands.

There were fifteen or twenty minutes left when I got up off the bench to talk to our assistant manager Chris Hutchings. 'Who's making the subs here?' I asked him. 'I need to go on!'

He looked at me as if I was mad and pointed to the gaffer up in the stands.

I looked up at him, but decided against running up thirty rows to where he was sitting – it wasn't like I'd just won Wimbledon. But I must have made something happen, because ten minutes later I was on the pitch, doing my thing.

I may not have won an England cap, but I played in that Southend friendly – nobody could ever take that away from me.

At the next Ipswich training session, the gaffer pulled me to one side.

'I can't believe you asked to come on,' he said to me.

'Let me tell you a story,' I replied. And I proceeded to tell him what had happened when I'd been on the bench for England against Germany, how much I regretted not asking Capello to bring me on and how I wasn't going to let that happen twice.

Paul listened carefully, staring at me all the while and when I'd finished, he said: 'You're mad.'

'I didn't mean to be rude,' I explained. 'I was just showing you how much I wanted to play.'

He wasn't having any of it, but it made perfect sense to me. If I was a manager and a player said that to me, I'd put them straight on to the pitch because they were hungry. But then nobody thinks like me.

Paul definitely didn't, because the club let me go a few weeks later.

I had no regrets then, and looking back on my England

experience, other than that friendly fiasco, I've got to be happy that I was involved with the squad at all. Of course, it would have been amazing to get that cap but it wasn't to be.

I was invited back to Wembley for England's final World Cup 2010 qualifying game against Belarus as the FA had decided to ask everyone involved in the whole campaign to join in with the celebrations as England had made it to South Africa. Except it wasn't the sort of knees-up that I was used to.

We had a sit-down meal before the game and a glass of champagne in the dressing room afterwards. In terms of celebrations, I don't remember it that well, but I'm fairly sure my first birthday party was wilder than that.

But that's part of the story with the England team. It lacks that relaxed club atmosphere where most team-mates are comfortable in each other's company. With England, there's a lot of awkwardness as, in my experience, most of the players are not that close. It was nowhere near as together as I expected it to be. Apart from pulling on the Three Lions and being bonded together by that shared cause, there was very little in the way of team spirit.

Having said that, there was one bizarre situation before a team meeting where a few of us were crowded round a laptop watching a funny video. Out of nowhere, someone flicked on some porn. There we were, several England players about to go to an important tactical meeting, watching a porno like a bunch of teenagers. All of a sudden, Fabio walked in and someone flung the computer on the floor while the rest of us instantly dispersed. We acted like kids, perhaps because Capello made us feel like kids.

Those little moments of daft rebellion were never enough though, because when you spend a week or two at a time with people whom you're not that close to, it can be mentally tough. I loved the training, but certainly didn't enjoy being cooped up in a hotel for days and weeks at a time.

The most senior England players never get a break from that goldfish-bowl pressure either as there always seems to be a tournament coming round and that means no summer holiday – unless it's an odd year. So they can go two years straight without a proper, long break, which can't be good for them, or the national team.

I'm not saying I didn't enjoy the England experience because I really did. It was beyond my wildest dreams to be part of the squad and, without a doubt, it was the best moment of my career.

But I might never have got that England experience at all, had a phone call from Barry Fry been followed up. While I was at Peterborough, he rang me to ask if I had any Irish relatives. I told him I didn't have any that I was aware of, but I'd look into it. He liked the sound of that and told me that Brian Kerr, who was the Republic of Ireland manager at the time, was struggling for players and would be in touch with me to discuss it.

Of course, this was Bazza and nothing whatsoever materialised. He never mentioned it again and Brian Kerr sure as hell didn't phone me. I'm sure if I looked hard enough I might have found some Irish connection somewhere; judging by some of the non-Irishmen who have turned out for them over the years, it can't be that hard.

What I did have, however, was a German nan and my agent

Andy Evans was keen to exploit that as he was convinced I might be able to play for them.

'Fuck off, Andy,' I told him. 'I don't want to play for Germany.'

He made sure the story got into the press anyway, as it was in the run-up to the 2006 World Cup, and I was even asked about it in interviews. Unsurprisingly, Jürgen Klinsmann never called me.

The truth is I would've played for any country that wanted me as playing international football was another huge honour. It was first come, first served, and England got there first. Unfortunately, old Postman Pat hadn't read the full script though, had he?

PILLAR 8

WHO IS A MAN? HE WHO CAN LAUGH AT HIMSELF AND HIS TEAM-MATES. MOSTLY HIS TEAM-MATES

'Seek not the favour of the multitude; it is seldom got by honest and lawful means. But seek the testimony of few; and number not voices, but weigh them.' ***Immanuel Kant***

Big Papa Bouba Diop was lying with his head down in the face-hole part of the massage table, getting a good rubdown. And I just couldn't resist.

It was the day after a game and the Fulham lads had come in for a warm-down and a stretch and most of us were in the changing rooms. Michael Brown was usually my partner in crime although he never actually did anything himself, he just encouraged me and I always got reeled in. And now he was egging me on to get little Jimmy out and stick him through that hole into Pap's face. Juvenile? Absolutely. Funny? Bloody hilarious if you were in that dressing room.

I approached the bench. The massage bench that is. It was going to be far too difficult to manoeuvre myself into that space so I made a spur-of-the-moment decision and put my nuts on top of his head instead.

He was still mid-massage so I said something like, 'How does that feel, Pap?' and the boys started wetting themselves laughing. Pap was the only one not laughing. He was also the only one springing off the massage table and chasing me round the dressing room.

Now Papa Bouba Diop is a big man. A very big man. So when you place your nuts on a bloke who's six-feet-five tall and fourteen stone of muscle, you'd better make sure you can run because, if my experience was anything to go by, he will not be happy.

You'll notice by the fact I'm writing this book that Pap didn't actually kill me for doing that. But he came quite close to it, as he spent a couple of days dragging me around by the scruff of my neck. But all in all, he was quite good about it and didn't take it too seriously, just saying, 'Not again Jimmy, not again.'

Not a chance, big man. I know when I've got away with one and I got away with one then. The problem was, that I just couldn't help myself sometimes and I blame my dad because he wanted me to learn my trade at West Ham. I'm not sure he meant that I should be schooled in the art of dressing-room daftness, but that's exactly what happened.

When you learn from the old school, players like Razor and Ian Wright, you're only going to end up a bit of a nutcase yourself. What I did to Pap was exactly the kind of thing that Moncur would've done to Razor. And it was also the sort of thing that helped me settle into my new club because, believe it or not, I was missing my Wigan boys.

After three years of playing with a really close-knit squad who'd enjoyed so much success, I'd built up a lot of friendships with those lads and it was a wrench to leave them. It was obviously fantastic to be back in London close to all my family again, but I'd lived up north for so long that it had started to feel like home for me. It was only when I moved to Cobham that I realised how much I missed Wigan, which is probably not a sentence I ever thought I'd write.

It was the dressing room more than anything else that I missed because I would never have that kind of close bond with an entire team again. From a football point of view, it had worked out brilliantly for me. I'd joined Wigan in the third tier and left them in the Premier League after a cup final. My career had changed forever there but it was time to move on – I had to be a man about the whole thing as nothing lasts forever.

Fulham manager Chris Coleman had big plans for me and the team so it seemed like the right move. They were a more established Premier League side and Cookie wanted to take them on to the next level. When we met up with my agent he told me he wanted to give me the licence to play in a free role where I would just go out and make things happen as if I was playing in the school playground. Given the Bouba Diop incident and my abuse of the manager's hotel room number during that first epic pre-season, I probably took his back-to-school vision a bit too literally.

First stop that summer was a trip to Devon where we stayed at Woodbury Park, Nigel Mansell's hotel and golf resort. Myself and big Pap got a little carried away, though, as we continued playing golf back in the hotel and cracked the glass door of the lift in the process.

But that was nothing compared to our second trip, which was that mini tour of Germany and Austria where we played a couple of friendlies and were allowed to let our hair down now and again, mostly courtesy of Cookie's room tab.

One night, me and a few of my new team-mates were sat in our hotel's canal-side bar, having a drink. It was about 11pm when the manager popped his head round the corner to tell us we needed to be in our rooms by midnight at the latest. Given the fact that it was pre-season, we thought we might be able to stretch that a bit. And when I say a bit, I mean quite a lot because by 2am, we were still there, downing vodka shots and making merry.

While we were in full flow, Chris and his assistant, Steve Kean, came down the stairs and into the bar. We all froze.

'Don't worry,' said Cookie. 'We'll join you.'

What a legend that man was. In the blink of an eye, it was 4am, we'd had several more shots and goodness knows what else and we were all smashed, obliterated and pie-eyed. Call it what you like, we were definitely very drunk.

Which probably explains why I thought it was a good idea to nick one of the assistant manager's flip-flops and throw it into the canal alongside the bar. Quite why he thought it was acceptable to come down to the bar in his flip-flops is another matter, sadly not up for discussion right here.

Kean went mental with me. 'Go and get it!' he ordered.

'You go and get it,' I replied, which was the best I could do in my state.

That carried on for a bit, until Kean got up to have a look at where his flip-flop was in the canal. As he stood there bent over the canal, drunkenly searching for his flip-flop in the dark, I was talking to our goalkeeper, Mark Crossley, discussing how funny it might be were I to rugby tackle Kean straight into the water.

'Go on then,' said Crossley, egging me on.

I didn't need a second invitation.

I leapt over the long table we'd been sitting at and launched myself full length at our assistant manager, dropping the pair of us straight into the canal.

Bosh!

Splash!

I'd only been at the club for two months and suddenly I was roaring drunk in a German canal with my new assistant manager who was trying to kill me.

We had a bit of a struggle in the water as Kean started throwing right-handers at me while I was trying to clamber out of the canal. All this time, Cookie and the rest of the lads were looking on and laughing so hard that it was difficult not to join in with them, and I would've done were it not for the fact that Kean was all over me like a wild dog.

I eventually scrambled out of the water, followed by Kean, who then chased me through the park that was next to the canal. That went on for some time, until my new mate Brownie smuggled me away into the safety of his room. By the time I'd dried off and stopped laughing it was morning and I was desperate for a kip.

A few hours later, I came downstairs in the hotel lift in search of some breakfast. As the doors opened to the lobby, guess who was standing right there, waiting to get in?

None other than Mr Steven Kean, assistant manager of Fulham FC and my new synchronised swimming partner.

'Hi Steve,' I smiled. 'How are you doing?'

'Blinding night last night,' he replied, giving me a wink and getting into the lift, and showing me straight away that he was as decent a man as Coleman.

I can't think of any manager/assistant manager combo who would've presided over a night like that. But that was Cookie's relaxed management style, possibly down to the fact he was still a player at heart. He had moved into management after his career ended early when he broke his leg badly in a car crash aged thirty, but he still seemed like one of us.

For that reason, there seemed like there was a good spirit about the place, with the added bonus that Fulham was a great opportunity for me to advance my career. On top of that, my wages had been doubled.

I was now earning somewhere in the region of about £25,000 per week, which was mind-blowing. Whenever I made a leap in my pay bracket like that, I always thought back to my non-league days. Madness, utter madness.

And I spent the whole of that pre-season trying to get my head around the transfer fee of £2.5 million that Fulham had paid Wigan to trigger my contract release clause. I was a seven-figure player who wasn't afraid to put his testicles on the line – or on a team-mate's head – for the cause.

When I wasn't larking around, I was determined to hit the ground running at my new club. One Friday after training, I was working on my free kicks. Ask any player about set pieces and they'll all say the same thing: practise, practise, practise.

Ever since I'd been at Peterborough, I wasn't afraid to put the hours in after training and I'd spend many afternoons whacking free kicks into the net – or not far from it – until I was kicked off the pitch by an irate member of the groundsman's team.

To me, it was like being back on the green in front of my

parents' house, where I would just keep going until it was dark. I loved it and I wanted to be the best I possibly could.

That particular Friday, I was practising at the Cottage end of my new home ground on my own because I'd worn the goalkeepers out. I lined the ball up on the same spot, about twenty-five yards from goal, and aimed for the top left corner. A couple of steps and bang! In it went. Except it didn't. I must've taken about eighty or ninety free kicks during the hour or so I was out there and missed most of them. I hit the post, the bar or missed by miles. But I kept going anyway.

I'd taken that many that a little bit of the grass was starting to get worn out where I was standing and that was the Fulham groundsman's cue to get the arsehole with me and throw me off the pitch. Groundsmen don't tend to like me very much, but we were at home to Sheffield United the next day so I could see his point. The git.

Twenty-four hours later, the match was goalless when we won a free kick in exactly the same spot I'd been hitting them from the day before. I could even see the marks in the grass that the groundsman had been getting pissed off about.

I placed the ball down as I had done the day before and as I stepped back, I looked up and knew I was going to score. It was a weird feeling but I just thought 'goal'. I knew it was going in. I had 18,000 in the ground behind me and the adrenaline was pumping – which was exactly what had been missing the day before.

As soon as the ball left my foot, I was ready to run off and celebrate, but just in case my gut feeling was wrong, I hung about and watched it arrow into the top left corner – exactly what I couldn't make it do the previous day.

And then I was off, all the drama and excitement of the moment came screaming out of me as I got mobbed by my new team-mates. I could see my old man watching on in the stands and I saluted him. In those seconds of joy, every bit of hard work I'd done to get to that moment came pouring out of me and the hairs on the back of my neck stood to attention.

Once I'd finished celebrating with my team-mates, I tried to take it all in and acknowledge the fans, but Graham Poll, who was refereeing that day, was having none of it and asked me to get back into my own half so we could get on with the game. I hated that. This is the bit I worked so hard for all week and now some killjoy was telling me to cut the celebrations short.

The way I celebrated that goal, you'd have thought it was my first for the club and first for an age. But the funny thing was that I'd also scored three days before when I stuck in a last-minute penalty to get us a point against Bolton. Always make the most of it . . .

I also smacked the post later on in that Sheffield United game, which we went on to win thanks to my goal. I'd had a great game and Cookie was brilliant afterwards as he told the press that I was the best two million quid he'd ever spent. I had to do loads of interviews after the match as I'd scored the only goal, which meant *Match of the Day*, radio and newspapers, but I didn't mind that one bit.

I played with a lot of players who hated doing interviews and would try to shirk them, which I could never understand because I was always up for it. It was a chance to talk to the world, let people know a bit more about who you are and possibly even open up new opportunities off the pitch if you were half-decent in front of the camera.

A few of the boys I played with were very guarded and were just worried about saying the wrong thing in an interview, like slagging off the club or another player by mistake. Not me. I had nothing to hide and would always say it how it is, which seemed to work for me.

But I hadn't said much the previous weekend when I made my Fulham debut at Manchester United. No matter how many teams I was a part of that got beat at Man United during my career, I never tired of playing at Old Trafford. What a place that is.

I think the problem was I used to spend too much time floating around in a dream-like state when I played there so it was like my teams were playing with ten men. And it's hard enough to play a team like Man United when it's eleven v eleven.

Six months earlier I'd been part of the Wigan team that was walloped by United in the Carling Cup final and there I was making my first start for my new club and it was déjà vu all over again, to coin a phrase.

Just nineteen minutes into the game, and we were four down. The match was being televised at home and all over the world. I don't think I could have been more humiliated if we'd been forced to play the game naked. But this is what a team like that can do to you. For all the dreams I had as a kid of playing against Man United, the reality was very different.

Cookie didn't go too crazy in the dressing room afterwards though. It was the first game of the season and we'd played

Man United. Obviously, it wasn't acceptable but that can happen in the Premier League.

We bounced back well and things were going brilliantly for me, until we played Newcastle and I busted my knee. Throughout that frustrating time, I still managed to keep my spirits up thanks to some of my new team-mates and a few more Bouba-Diop-style pranks.

Like all walks of life, footballers come in all shapes and sizes but tend to laugh and joke at the same kind of things. But, occasionally, you'll meet a player who's unlike anyone you've ever played with before. Step forward Moritz Volz, Fulham's proud-to-be-strange right-back.

Don't get me wrong, he was a great lad to be around and very funny too. But he relished being different. He prided himself on that oddness and played on it in the same way as I played on my reputation as a joker.

Every day, we'd all drive into the players' car park in our flash motors and get out of them thinking we were the bollocks. By then, my Fiesta had become a Range Rover, mainly because I could fit all my golf and fishing gear in there. I'd park that, get out of the car and then Volzy would turn up on his bike with a basket on the front containing fresh bread he'd just bought for his missus. I can't think of anyone who does that, let alone a footballer.

He'd park his bike next to all our cars and stroll into the training ground changing room as if it was the most normal thing in the world. He'd have cycled all the way through London to the training ground and should have been knackered before we'd even started training – but he'd still perform way above most other people's levels because he was an absolute animal.

He was one of those defenders who would throw themselves in front of a bomb, like Newcastle's Steven Taylor but twice as hard. Although, one morning, he hurled himself in front of a shot of mine which folded his hand in half and busted all the ligaments in his wrist.

I would've felt bad for him, but it was really Volzy's fault for thinking he was a goalkeeper. If you chuck yourself in front of everything, you're going to get hurt. I was never in any danger of suffering like that as I was a 'back bloke' – the only place I was taking a shot was straight in the back.

Another of Volzy's standard oddball lines was to always say that he'd scored three Premier League goals and then let you in on the fact that two of them were own goals. For a German, he was a very funny bloke. And so was Danny Murphy, who arrived at the club about a year after I did, although he wasn't actually German.

Danny and I got on very well, which was lucky because we played in central midfield together too, so a good understanding was crucial. Once I was fit again, we worked out a pretty good relationship on the pitch where he'd let me go wherever I fancied. As a central midfielder I wasn't really supposed to overlap the right winger and put a cross in, but that was the way I played and Danny would help me out by sitting a bit deeper and allowing me to run around like a lunatic.

He had always taken free kicks at his previous clubs, but when he saw me taking them for Fulham he didn't even try to suggest he should have a go. I was the free-kick governor there, so I let Danny have penalties instead. If I'm being really honest, and this hurts, he was probably a better penalty-taker than me.

Danny was a hell of a player and he became a good friend off the pitch too as he's a sensible bloke with a good head on his shoulders, the exact opposite of me. If we were playing away, as soon as we got to the hotel, Danny's would be the first door I'd knock on for a quick chat – and I'd still be there at one in the morning.

One of my biggest problems with being a footballer was that I hated being on my own, and on those away trips I'd often be given my own room because nobody wanted to share with me. I mean absolutely *nobody* was interested in sharing with me because I'd drive my team-mates mad and keep them up all night. It was just my way. I had loads of nervous energy and no idea what to do with it.

So the lads all avoided me like the plague and I was on my own – unless, of course, one of the youth team or a trialist was on the trip with us. On those occasions, I'd grab my unsuspecting victim before they had a chance to work out what was going on and say, 'You're rooming with me!'

The next day the poor sod would be walking around like a bleary-eyed wreck of his former self. And the rest of the lads would point, laugh and say, 'He's been rooming with Jimmy.'

One of my good mates, Michael Weirs, always tells a story about how bad I am on my own. He was staying with me up in Hull when my family were in London. He heard me calling him into my bedroom.

'Weirsy! Weirsy! Come in, come in!'

'What is it?' he called back.

'Come in!'

So he came into my bedroom and found me taking a shit on my en-suite loo. He looked startled and puzzled.

'Talk to me,' I said. 'I don't like being on my own.'

But for all the times they avoided rooming with me, the boys still enjoyed a good crack and I never let them down on that front.

One of the many fire extinguisher incidents I was involved in was particularly memorable and planned to perfection. The A-Team couldn't have done it any better.

Fulham had these plush old marble-floored corridors inside the training ground that didn't look like they'd be too hospitable to anyone who tried to walk on them wearing studs or football boots. So, in the interests of science, I decided to find out what would happen in those very circumstances.

I went into the changing room and started slapping Clint Dempsey and a few of the other boys, saying, 'Come on then. Who wants it?' and generally acting like a tool. There's only so much of that behaviour that the average footballer can tolerate before they take the bait and, sure enough, Clint and a few others had had enough of me and got up to throw some digs in the general direction of my face.

I bolted it out of the changing room, on to that marble-floored corridor where I had the fire extinguisher waiting, and they followed me out there, still in their football boots.

Oh dear.

I pressed the nozzle on the fire extinguisher and unloaded jets of water right in their faces, and all over the floor. The resulting scene was like watching a cartoon as, one after the other, they slipped on the wet, marble floor and fell arse over tit on top of each other. What a scene that was.

They all saw the funny side of it too – eventually, after weeks trying to kill me – but the club didn't find it that amusing. They were furious that the floor had been sullied in that way and made me pay for it to be cleaned. And that's why if you look at my payslip that month (not that I'll ever let you see any of my payslips) you'll see about £80 deducted from it with the words 'fire extinguisher' alongside it.

In total I incurred around £500 worth of fire extinguisher-related fines while at Fulham – I even became known as 'The Extinguisher' for a while there before the usual swearing and name-calling resumed.

Those were meticulously planned ruses, but a more spontaneous act of lunacy at Fulham occurred the day I decided to fill TJ Moncur's car up with water for no particular reason.

TJ was a young player who'd come up through the youth and reserve teams and was knocking on the door of the first team. One morning he pulled up at the training ground in a new Peugeot 206 convertible, which got me thinking.

Once he'd cleared off, I grabbed a huge wheelie bin, filled it with water and poured it straight into his car. Which was quite funny, but not as funny as a convertible car with two wheelie bins full of water in it. I soon rectified that situation.

Little did I know, but there was CCTV in the training ground car park and, after training, TJ and a few of the boys were gathered round a screen in the club office watching footage of me pouring water into his car.

I walked into the office, saw a crowd around the monitor and innocently asked what everyone was watching. Big mistake.

'Was that you in the car park, Jim?' someone asked me.

'Errrr, no.'

They had me bang to rights.

'You bastard!' said TJ.

Luckily, there was a decent spell of warm weather around which helped dry the car out and I sorted it all out with TJ. Served him right for turning up in a convertible when he wasn't long out of nappies.

While all that was going off, it was musical chairs time in the Fulham manager's hotseat, which was an unusual experience for me. At my previous clubs, the managers who signed me were still there when I'd moved on. Fulham was very different. Managers came and went so frequently that there was even one for whom I never actually played a game.

It all started with Cookie's departure, which we were all absolutely gutted about as we had so much respect for the bloke. Problems in his personal life coincided with the team going seven matches without a win and the club sacked him. It was harsh in my opinion as we weren't doing that badly in the league. We were four points above the relegation zone with five games to play, but the club didn't like the direction we were heading in.

It was doubly frustrating for me as I couldn't do anything to help because I was still recovering from my knee injury. It was my Diane who broke the news to me as she'd seen it on the telly; I hadn't even been told. Being the man he is, Cookie wanted to say goodbye to all of us and he even did that with a smile on his face.

The week before his sacking, the papers had run a story about how his wife had bugged his car as she suspected him of having an affair, so he came into the changing room to say goodbye to about thirty of us, looking a bit shifty.

'Boys, you know what's been in the papers about the missus bugging me,' he said, but stopped suddenly and started looking around the room as if he was checking that it wasn't also bugged. He got a big laugh for that one.

He said his farewells to every one of us, which was great because my team-mates were saying how most managers usually just do one and don't bother saying goodbye.

Coleman was replaced by Lawrie Sanchez, and I'm not entirely sure he would have needed to clear his desk by the time he was given his marching orders, because he wouldn't have had much time to put anything in it.

He arrived in April but was gone before Christmas, during which time I was still doing my rehab. Lawrie was always very good to me and showed me plenty of understanding regarding my knee and I can safely say that he was the best manager I've never played for.

By the time he left we were in a right old relegation scrap and that's when Roy Hodgson arrived to steady the ship. His appearance coincided with my return to fitness and that beautiful moment when I scored the winner against Villa.

I'd heard about Roy's achievements at other clubs, but I didn't know him at all as a person. Let's just say he was a completely different man to Chris Coleman. They were on two opposite ends of the scale and I'd originally come to Fulham to play for Cookie.

The truth is that Roy and I never clicked because I was far too outgoing for his liking and I had to rein that in when I was in front of him (not that it stopped me letting off the odd fire extinguisher).

On the pitch, there were no problems as I gave my all for

him, as I would've done for any manager, and played a big part in helping Fulham avoid relegation that season. We just never had that special relationship I'd enjoyed with Cookie and Paul Jewell at Wigan. He never really opened up to me and let me know what he was thinking like they had, but he's not that type of manager. He was far more like a school-teacher-style gaffer who you couldn't get close to. The English Capello, if you like.

Funnily enough, the only time Roy loosened up a bit was when the chairman Mohamed Al-Fayed visited the training ground.

Al-Fayed was actually a really down-to-earth normal bloke – for a billionaire. When I first signed for the club, the deal was agreed before the end of the season so I wasn't allowed to play. But they invited me to watch a game so I went along to Craven Cottage with my mum, and Al-Fayed spotted me in the bar and came over to talk to us.

He was really warm and friendly, although my mum was a bit miffed that she didn't get a Harrods discount off of him. Whenever he came to visit the training ground, the word would go round that the big dog was coming and an air of expectancy would rise over the place.

Socks would be pulled up, floors would be cleaned and we'd all brush our teeth . . . okay, that last bit was a joke. In fact, the whole act was a bit of a joke because from what I could tell Al-Fayed wouldn't have cared about any of that as he just wanted to have a bit of banter with his players.

And that's why the gaffer had no choice but to laugh along with the chairman, who was actually quite open and crude with us. He'd tell us what he'd been up to on the weekend, go into details on any mishaps he'd had and generally try to be a bit of a lad.

If Hodgson had heard any of us talking like that, I'm sure he would have done his usual headmaster routine and said: 'Oi, you! Curb it!'

But in front of the chairman, he'd have to laugh along with all his chatter. We were all too aware how awkward Roy found that, which made us love it even more.

The one thing everyone knew about Roy was his inability to pronounce his Rs properly and that wasn't something that a group of players were going to let pass without comment. I developed a bit of a reputation for doing a 'Woy' impression, as did several of my team-mates. I was certain that the gaffer would've heard us doing it, and it even made the papers.

So we took the piss a bit, but there was no doubting Roy's coaching know-how and ability to attract top players. Especially Scandinavians. Within a month of turning up, he'd signed Brede Hangeland, a top-quality Norwegian defender who most people in this country had never heard of, Erik Nevland, a Norwegian striker and Jari Litmanen, a former European Cup winner, who'd played for Ajax, Liverpool and Barcelona.

Unfortunately, the latter signing didn't work out. Jari didn't manage to make it on to the pitch during his time with us, but if football was judged on stretching alone, he'd be the greatest player in the history of the game. He stretched so much that I honestly thought there was something wrong with the bloke. Whenever we were out on the training pitch, it always seemed to be a cold morning and he'd have his tracksuit bottoms on doing stretches. Those groins and hamstrings must have taken a battering over the years judging by the way he worked on them.

The manager would turn up and Jari would be straight on his toes, doing little sprints up and down on the spot before going back to the stretching. I'd look at him and think, 'Is this fella alright or what?'

One day I looked over at Danny Murphy, tilted my head towards the permanently stretched Jari and said, 'What the fuck's he doing?'

Danny had a bemused look on this face, but he just said: 'Do you know how good he is?' and I replied: 'No, I don't even watch football.'

All the while, Jari was still stretching away – he'd even do it in the middle of a training drill or a match – but I could never approach him. In the rules of football banter, I wasn't officially permitted to question him because the bloke's a legend. If I'd asked him what the hell he was doing, he could've just replied, 'Barça. What have you done?' and I'd have nothing to say except, er, 'Wigan'.

Putting the stretching to one side – which is hard because that's all he ever did – when we did ball work in training, you could see straight away what a class player Jari was even if his pace was gone. His touch and vision were amazing, a class above anything I'd seen up close – apart from some of the Premier League's finest talents I was now coming up against on a weekly basis.

Sometimes, I had to do double-takes on a football pitch and actually say 'Wow' out loud, such was the quality of some of the players out there. I'd say I was sharing a pitch with them, but in terms of the football they played, we weren't even in the same universe. There are three occasions which spring to mind when I just had to concede that some of these boys were playing a different game to me.

The first time was when I was playing for Wigan at Arsenal in the Carling Cup semi-final and Thierry Henry gave me an education. I really wanted to see just how fast he was and early on in the game I was running alongside him trying to close him down as he had the ball.

He was going so fast I could barely keep up, and then he'd just stop. In a split second. Then start again. I have no idea how he did it. He showed me a fake shimmy, stopped and carried on in the same direction and in the meantime, I'd already headed off five yards in the opposite direction.

And he did it all so bloody fast. He was like shit off a shovel. I looked at my midfield team-mate Graham Kavanagh and said, 'You can mark him.'

The second time was in the subsequent final against Man United, where I was chasing a ball that looked like it was going off the pitch and Cristiano Ronaldo was in front of me. The section of the crowd I was running towards happened to contain my parents, family and friends, who had come to watch me play.

Ronaldo managed to control the ball that was supposedly going off the pitch, kept it in and then, with the same touch, he caressed the ball with his foot for a second or two as I ran towards him, before slipping it through my legs and running towards goal.

Excuse me, could you run that one by me again please?

I had no idea what the hell had happened, but I knew it

had happened in front of everyone who was watching me. So I did the only thing I could in that situation, which was chase after the bastard and try to hack him down. Even then, he was still dancing around me with the ball as I fouled him three or four times, but incredibly the referee didn't blow his whistle. I even came away with the ball in the end, but the victory was all his.

The third jaw-dropping moment was playing for Fulham against Man United. An attack of theirs had just broken down and there was nobody within a mile of me, so our keeper Mark Schwarzer bowled the ball out to where I was near the halfway line.

The closest player to me when the ball left Mark's hands was Wayne Rooney, but he was at least twenty-five yards away so there was no danger there. Yet, as the ball dropped and I was about to control it, I could feel Rooney's breath on my shoulder and he went straight through me with a tackle that was the equivalent of a runaway roller coaster smashing me over.

What he did was impossible. Actually impossible. To this day, like the Ronaldo bit of skill, I still think somebody must have helped him. It's not just because of those miraculous things, but those three opponents were in a class of their own.

When I was called up to the England squad in 2008 and had the chance to train with Rooney, he didn't disappoint. He was definitely capable of doing things that no other players could do.

At that point, it was the start of the 2008/09 season and my form for Fulham going back to the start of the year had been recognised. It was definitely the pinnacle of my career, which is why I would never have believed anyone who would've told me then, that I'd be a Hull player by January.

But this is football and anything can happen, both on and off the pitch. Things like the future manager of England playing golf instead of turning up to a meeting with me to discuss the possible extension of my contract.

Having suffered that horrible knee injury, I was worried that the sixteen months left on my Fulham deal would not cover me sufficiently if it should happen again. So I asked the club if they would consider giving me a new, longer deal to make me feel more secure. I was playing well and I'd had the England recognition so I really didn't envisage any stumbling blocks with this one.

A meeting was set up between me, my agent, the Fulham chief executive Alistair Mackintosh and Roy Hodgson. I was hoping that it wouldn't take too long so I could just get on with focusing on my football, but it didn't quite pan out like that.

Andy Evans and I met up with the chief exec, but there was no sign of Roy. Alistair was a bit confused by that and called him, only to find out he was playing golf and wouldn't be coming. Talk about an awkward situation – that was the end of that meeting.

I thought it was bang out of order. It doesn't matter if you're the chairman, owner or manager, you have to treat people with respect and that's pretty much what I told Roy to his face the next time I saw him. I asked him where he'd been when we were supposed to have had a meeting and I told him it showed me and my agent a lack of respect. Perhaps

I shouldn't have been so hostile towards him, but his decision not to attend that meeting spoke volumes.

We clashed from that day on and, despite several attempts to set up another meeting, it never happened because, in my opinion, Roy didn't want it to happen. I think he felt that I was holding the club to ransom when all I wanted was to sort out my future. He certainly didn't want to address the issue, which proved to me that neither he, nor the club, wanted me. If they did, they had a very odd way of showing it. Finally, Alistair told us that if it was down to him he would've signed me on a new, longer contract but it had to be a joint decision between the manager and chairman and, given that wasn't happening, I was free to talk to other clubs.

So there I was with sixteen months remaining on my contract and the distinct possibility that I could be out of work at the end of it, especially if my knees were to disintegrate again.

I never understood why Fulham weren't more upfront about telling me they didn't want me. I'm sure it was because of my knee and I guess they didn't want to say anything like that officially in case it would scupper the chance of another club signing me, taking me off their payroll and handing them a nice transfer fee in the process.

This wasn't football, this was business and once again my eyes were opened up to the fact I was just a valuable asset to them rather than a player.

Fortunately, a number of clubs *were* interested in me despite my knee, but Hull backed up their inquiry about my availability with a brilliant offer and a load of ambition to boot.

Sadly, Fulham put stories out which suggested that I'd just upped and left for the money, which was clearly not the case, but in football, whenever a player's version of events differs from a club's, everyone seems to believe the club.

I had to take that on the chin, but the blow was softened as Hull were providing the financial security I'd been seeking and, equally importantly, manager Phil Brown really wanted me to play in his side. Like Chris Coleman, he wanted to put me in the free role I loved so I could entertain the fans in the process.

That was music to my ears, but not to my right knee, which clearly had ideas of its own.

PILLAR 9

REMEMBER THE OLD ADAGE: FAME IS TEMPORARY, CLASS IS PERMANENT. OR SOMETHING ALONG THOSE LINES . . .

'If your happiness depends on money, you will never be happy with yourself. Be content with what you have; rejoice in the way things are. When you realise there is nothing lacking, the whole world belongs to you.' ***Lao Tzu***

If you're ever at Chester Races, my advice to you is never bump into a drunken Duncan Ferguson. Especially, if you've recently offered him out in the tunnel after a game.

That's exactly the predicament I was in a few weeks after Wigan had played Everton, and I was shitting myself. I'd been drinking with my team-mates at the races and we were all having a blinding time, when someone spotted Big Dunc in the room, sipping champagne and smoking a cigar.

Immediately, the boys were on at me, telling me how he was going to batter me or worse – everything you'd expect to hear from your mates. My heart was racing faster than the drinks were being downed, my face went red and I started to sweat.

It had all started with an incident which had been seen by almost every football fan in the country, thanks to *Soccer AM*. The video of it had become an instant YouTube classic and is probably the moment that most people mention within seconds of meeting me.

On the video, you see Duncan Ferguson about to be sent off for Everton after punching my team-mate Paul Scharner. As he's standing there with hands on hips, you see me sidle up to him and look him straight in the eyes, talk to him, then think better of it. My facial expression, as I look towards a team-mate, is an absolute picture as I have no idea whether I should be laughing or really crapping myself.

To fill in a few gaps, what actually happened that night was that Big Dunc had been brought on by David Moyes as a substitute with the match level at 1-1. There were about twenty minutes left and the idea was that Ferguson would cause us a few problems up front, given the fact he's an enormous presence at six feet four – I was glad I wasn't one of our defenders that evening, especially poor Scharner who was marking him at corners.

He certainly caused us problems, but not in a footballing sense, as seven minutes after coming on, he showed us why they called him Duncan Disorderly when he gave Scharner a belting right-hander in the stomach in an off-the-ball incident, seen by almost everyone including the ref Mike Dean. He absolutely walloped him and Paul went down like a sack of shit in the penalty area.

I couldn't believe what I'd seen so I instinctively went over to Big Dunc to see what had gotten into him, but I took one look at him and that's when I did my double-take, that weird look that the cameras picked up.

I'd never seen anything like the look on his face that night. His eyes were deranged, wild and angry. He looked like he wanted to kill everyone on that pitch, probably his own team-mates included.

Not too keen on the vibes he was giving off, I called over his team-mate, James McFadden, who I kind of knew from seeing him out and about, and said: 'Is he alright him or what?'

But McFadden just straight-batted that one back at me: 'I'm having nothing to do with this.'

'Fucking hell,' I thought. 'I'm in a bit deep here.'

I looked back up at the big man and said: 'Dunc? You alright, son?'

It was probably the most stupid question I'd ever asked in my life. Even more stupid than when I asked my teacher if spelling counted in the school spelling test. Of course, he wasn't alright. How many people that are alright punch a man in the stomach for practically no reason? His response, although unsurprising, certainly made me back off.

'Do you fucking one want as well, pal?' said Dunc.

'Nah, you're alright son,' I replied, quickly backing off as Mike Dean approached to show him the inevitable red card, which happened to be the eighth and last of his Premier League career – so it was a bit of an honour for me to be present at such a landmark moment.

I should have left it there. Most people would definitely have left it there. But I can be a cocky bastard and, once Dunc was a safe twenty metres away, I called out: 'See you in the tunnel, Dunc!'

My team-mates looked at me as if I was as mad as him, and who could blame them? It was pure theatre and bravado on my part. At roughly the same time, Dunc stripped off his shirt and flexed his muscles for the benefit of the two benches as he walked straight off the pitch to the changing room.

I did not want to be seeing him anywhere for a long while, never mind in the tunnel at the JJB straight after the game.

I managed to avoid him after the match as I made sure I took as long as possible to get ready – this hair does not look after itself, let me tell you.

Dunc's reputation was not just made on the pitch, he had a pretty good track record off it too. I've heard stories about him fighting off burglars. Once, two blokes broke into his house while he was sitting on the sofa and he greeted them by saying, 'Alright boys, I think you've picked the wrong fucking house.' Those poor burglars. One ran off, but he sat on the other one until the police came.

Another time, he found a bloke about to nick loads of crates of whisky and champagne from his storage house. That daft sod received a firm wallop around his chops (in self-defence of course) and spent two hours in hospital once the old bill came to arrest him.

Back at Chester races, I was thinking about those burglars as my team-mates continued to wind me up. And things soon took a turn for the worse, when these so-called mates literally picked me up in the air, carried me over to where Dunc was quaffing his champers and sucking on his cigar, and just dumped me right in front of him. I might have missed him in the tunnel after the game, but there was no missing him right now.

Deal with that.

He looked me up and down, drank a bit more champagne then lunged towards me.

Shit!

But instead of the expected Glasgow kiss, Dunc gave me a big hug.

'Hello, wee man!' he said. 'Here, come and have a drink with me.' And as he said that, he handed me his bottle of champagne, then walked off, chomping on his cigar.

I never saw him again.

I couldn't have been more relieved and yet, across the room, the Wigan boys couldn't have been more disappointed. 'How the fuck have you got away with that?' they asked as I rejoined them.

The mad bastards fully expected me to get a hiding from Big Dunc and they wouldn't have done a thing to stop it. Just as well he was on the champers as that must have chilled him right out. Moyes should have stuck some in Dunc's water bottle before bringing him off the bench – and they say I wouldn't make a good manager.

Dunc wasn't the only player to scare me on the pitch, although he was the only one who made me fear for my life. Paul Scholes and Steven Gerrard were also hard bastards to play against in midfield.

Scholes tackled like a battering ram, I would dread going anywhere near the bloke. The first time I played Man United, he must have fouled me about five times in the first twenty minutes alone.

And there was no harder tackler in the game than Gerrard. I don't think I ever saw him shirk a challenge on the pitch. When he tackled me, he used to clump me so hard my knees would knock.

The same can be said for Big Dunc, but the challenges he tended not to shirk on the pitch were the ones that involved him dishing out a pasting to someone. But I have to hand it to the big man because if it wasn't for him, it's possible the other side of my career may never have taken off as my whole public image changed once that clip aired on *Soccer AM*.

It's funny how often people mention that show to me as if I was one of the presenters or something. The truth is I've only been on it three times, yet it's one of the first things random punters will say to me in the street. But I understand how I somehow became synonymous with the programme and that, without it, I may not have become as well-known.

Reaching the Premier League with Wigan opened a lot of doors to me as I was on the telly a lot more and I started to get recognised more when I was out and about. I know I'm not David Beckham, but don't believe anyone who tells you it's hard to be in the public eye because it's not. It's bloody brilliant. I will never tire of people who I've never met in my life, recognising me and talking to me about football.

I'm pretty certain that if I'd stuck to painting and decorating, not many people would have approached me in the street and asked me about that cracking off-white finish I'd done in the top floor flat two streets away.

I relished the attention then as much as I relish it now. Plus, I get bored very easily so it's nice to know that people will come and talk to me even if I'm on my own.

Playing in the top flight meant being asked to do more media interviews and that's when *Soccer AM* came along. I think they saw me as a happy-go-lucky kind of bloke, especially when random videos of me started appearing on the internet, backing that up.

There were a couple that were filmed when I was at Peterborough, including one where I interrupted a website interview with Bradley Allen and Andy Edwards.

I saw the two of them chatting away to the camera while sat on a bench so I just wandered over to have a look what was going on – then I had to get involved. Within a few seconds, I joined them for the interview and started answering the questions myself. It was one of those 'dish the dirt' type features where you have to shop your team-mates, but I wasn't really up to speed on any of that. So when they asked us who was the smelliest player, I didn't realise it had to be one of our team-mates so I started banging on about how much Olivier Bernard stank when we played Newcastle in the cup, which was very funny, but probably a little bit unfair on the geezer. He did reek when we played them though, honestly.

The other clip from Peterborough which went big on the internet was when I was doing an interview about our win at Northampton, but couldn't keep a straight face. Someone farted at the beginning of the interview which set me off laughing and, before I knew it, I was in crackdown mode and could not recover. Every time I was asked a question by the interviewer, I laughed like David Bentley and we required about a dozen attempts to get past the first question.

It's a bit like one of those *It'll Be Alright on the Night* clips, except it's with me, not a professional actor – but people liked it and *Soccer AM* showed it when they invited me on for the first time.

I always felt comfortable there from the minute I sat on that sofa. I just had the feeling that I could never mess up when I was on there as it all felt natural, like I was having a bit of a laugh with my mates in front of the cameras.

That's not always the way for a lot of footballers and I've seen plenty of players freeze on the telly and make right berks

of themselves. The funniest one I've ever seen was when former West Ham goalkeeper Stephen Bywater was on *Goals on Sunday* with Chris Kamara and Clare Tomlinson.

He was trying to describe the swear word someone had called him but knew he wasn't allowed to use that word on the show so he spelt it out instead and said something like: 'Yeah, he called me a C-U-N-T!' What a donut! I laughed so hard at that and poor Kammy had no idea what to do.

Fortunately, I managed to avoid any moments like that when I was on the box and that's probably because the *Soccer AM* guys made me feel so relaxed. I used to go for a drink with them all after the show, too, as I was always open to doing things like that. My attitude was that you never know what these things will end up bringing to your life.

For one thing, the show brought me a lot closer to the fans than I'd ever been before. It was as if loads of them really felt that they knew me once I'd been on the show for the first time. And the amusing videos they kept showing of me, even when I wasn't on the sofa, certainly helped my relationship with supporters all over the country. Apart from one.

I'm no Joey Barton or El-Hadji Diouf so I'd never had a problem with the fans before until the time I was playing for Wigan at Norwich.

We won a corner and, as I went over to take it, a section of home fans started to get on my back by yelling offensive things like 'Gypo' and throwing me loads of wanker signs with their hands. That was all pretty standard abuse so I just yelled 'Bollocks!' at them with a smile on my face and they all loved it and showed their appreciation.

That's always been my philosophy for dealing with the fans.

There's absolutely no point going all Eric Cantona and getting aggressive with supporters who are winding you up. You're never going to beat ten thousand people, and getting really wound up about it is just embarrassing yourself. Taking it all with a pinch of salt just seems a lot more sensible and has always worked for me.

Except that wasn't good enough for one ginger-bearded Norwich fan who was standing around ten yards from me as I was about to take the corner. He just went psycho-aggressive and started calling me every name under the sun.

'You fucking arsehole, Bullard! You fucking wanker!'

He looked so angry I honestly thought he might come on to the pitch and chin me, so I hurried up with the corner and got the hell out of there.

I didn't really think about the incident again and just got on with my usual post-match routine of showering, changing, speaking to the press if required and then hopping on to the coach and heading home.

But, as I was about to board the bus, there were a few fans dotted around asking players for autographs, including one very familiar-looking bloke with a ginger beard. I could not believe it. An hour before he wanted to kill me and now he was asking me to sign an autograph for him.

'You're some kind of prick aren't you?' I said to him. 'I've seen you slagging me off when I took the corner!'

'H-how did you know it was me?' he mumbled, sounding like he was shitting himself.

I had to laugh. With a mob behind him, he was the hardest, most intimidating bloke I'd ever seen. Now, with one man and his dog, he was no-one.

But that's what football fans are like. They're just normal people who have a drink and get carried away by the atmosphere and passion of a game. I always knew that most of them didn't mean any harm, mainly because I usually enjoyed such a good relationship with them.

Once I'd been on *Soccer AM* the first time, the floodgates opened and more or less anything I did – or had ever done – on or near a football pitch was liable to make it on to the internet and subsequently on to the telly.

For example, during that Wigan game against Everton – the Duncan Ferguson one – there wasn't a great deal happening and I was desperate to be involved and force the issue a bit. We were on the attack and there was a bit of a goalmouth scramble as the ball came across. A couple of our players were trying to get on the end of the loose ball, while a few Everton bodies tried to clear it and goalkeeper Richard Wright attempted to pounce on it.

'This looks interesting,' I thought to myself so I started sprinting towards the penalty area, firmly believing there could be something in this for me. By the time I got into the box at full pelt, there was just a huge pile of players on top of each other with Wright at the bottom of it with his hands on the ball. Nothing doing here whatsoever.

But I couldn't stop so I just thought 'Fuck it' and carried on running, leapfrogging over Tim Cahill's back and diving straight over the pile of players, for absolutely no reason. I then got back up with a little smirk on my face and ran back towards the halfway line.

To this day I have absolutely no idea why I did it or what the hell I was thinking. It was just one of those spontaneous moments where I was a little bit too keen to be part of the action. Afterwards my team-mates asked me what I was doing and I just shrugged. I watched it back and was thinking, 'Is that actually me?'

My brother John, who's definitely a bit of a wrong 'un by the way, loves that clip, especially the way I just trot back afterwards as if nothing out of the ordinary has happened. And it was one of those moments which loads of fans seem to love, certainly judging by how many of them have asked me about it over the years.

I suppose the appeal for fans is that they wouldn't have seen players like David Beckham or Alan Shearer larking around like that during a match, which made me seem a bit more real to them, probably a bit more like them. Just a normal bloke who happened to be a footballer – that's what people would say to me.

They certainly would never have seen Beckham or Shearer's naked antics in the changing room, but that's exactly what happened to me after someone posted a video online of my Wigan team-mates and I messing around.

A few of us were bored after training so we decided to recreate a Roman chariot race using the big kit bins. In theory, there were going to be two of us in separate kit bins, having a pretend sword fight. Three of my mates had already been in the bin and had a go, but surprise, surprise, it was my turn that ended up on YouTube.

When it was my go, I climbed into the bin without a stitch of clothing on bar the Y-fronts which were on my head and a couple of my mates pushed me across the dressing room, but there was no second chariot to meet me, despite me waving my imaginary sword and chanting 'Yeah, yeah, yeah'. Instead, I just crashed straight into the bench at the opposite end of the changing room.

And that was it – not something that I would find that interesting, but plenty of others did as the video got something like half a million hits, which is just mind-blowing.

It's a shame there was nobody filming on the previous occasion I'd been in that kit bin as that was a true classic that probably would've broken the whole internet in one fell swoop.

Wigan had a kit man called Joe. I think he was about seventy-eight, and we used to love winding him up – but he was old so we had to be careful. Not that we were.

I decided to hide in the kit bin in the changing room one day, shortly before he was due to come in and pick it up. The boys helped cover me up with a load of laundry and when Joe came in, I leapt up from inside the bin and screamed. Poor Joe nearly popped his clogs on the spot. He absolutely shat himself.

Better still was the time when Joe flew to Barbados with us for Dave Whelan's promotion party. Spirits were very high on the flight as you can imagine. We'd just been promoted to the Premier League, we were on our way to a few days of luxury courtesy of the chairman and we were in the mood to celebrate.

Joe was sitting behind me, snoring away with his mouth wide open, making a right racket. A few of the boys were sitting with me as I started fiddling around with a packet of Maltesers and thinking evil thoughts.

'You wouldn't do that!' said one of them.

Never say things like that to me.

I took a Malteser and threw it straight into poor Joe's wide open gob. Time stood still for Joe as he seemed to pause for a few seconds before he opened his eyes and started breathing as fast as he possibly could, making all kinds of noises at the back of his throat, trying to come to terms with the mysterious invasion of the Malteser.

Everyone on the plane was crying with laughter as Joe eventually calmed down and started breathing normally again. 'You could've killed me!' he said to me once he'd got his breath back.

Thinking about it, it was probably just as well that nobody filmed that one or I'd have been done for attempted murder. My problem was that I just couldn't resist a prank, no matter how daft. It's a combination of the kid in me, boredom and a need to entertain people.

Some people used to accuse me of being immature for doing silly things in the pressurised environment of football. They were probably right in some instances as the sort of things I did were really childish, especially when I look back at them. But what people don't understand is that when you're there at the time, these stupid things are funny and actually help relieve the pressure sometimes.

And it wasn't just me dishing it out – I'd often get done by team-mates, too. It's been said many times, but a dressing room with a good spirit where players aren't afraid to take the piss out of each other and lark about, is more likely to produce a successful team than a serious, miserable set-up.

At Wigan, the spirit was fantastic and there was all sorts of nonsense going on, from naked chariot racing to attempted murder of the kit man, and we were successful on the pitch. There were times during my spell at Hull, where the spirit wasn't great in the dressing room and there was no unity among the players. Squabbles were common and we didn't all socialise together on a regular basis. I'm not saying this is a foolproof theory but that disharmony coincided with a pretty lean period on the pitch including a relegation, followed by a struggle in the Championship.

I suppose it would be the same in any place of work – if you and your workmates get on well, you'll produce better results whatever you do – even if you're all messing around, leaving Deep Heat in each other's pants.

Okay, you might not do that because your workplace doesn't necessarily require you to get naked on a regular basis. Thank your lucky stars, because I was left in that vulnerable position every day and once suffered the Deep Heat experience.

It wasn't pleasant down below and as soon as I felt the burning sensation on my meat and two veg, I yelled but ripped those pants off in record time. The problem for those boys was they had no idea who they were toying with. When I used to show them the level I was prepared to go to, I never heard from them again.

Their first mistake was the amateur desire for instant revenge. If someone had pranked them they'd try to get them back immediately, which was the worst possible time to strike as your victim would be most alert to a retaliatory hit.

I was different. I would wait two or three weeks, by which time whoever I was targeting would have probably forgotten what they'd done to me in the first place.

Take the Deep-Heat-in-my-underpants example. That was the handiwork of my Fulham team-mate Michael Brown. The last thing he would have imagined when he was putting on his face moisturiser three weeks later, was that I'd filled it with Ralgex. And that's because he'd forgotten about what he'd done to my pants and his guard was down.

And what he certainly wasn't expecting after having to deal with his burning, red-raw face was experiencing even worse in his mouth. That's because he had no idea that I'd got hold of his toothpaste, squeezed a bit out and filled it with Ralgex before carefully refilling it with a bit of toothpaste at the top. So the second or third time he brushed his teeth, he got a very nasty shock. His mouth was on fire for hours afterwards. He wouldn't be messing around with my underwear again after that.

And it wasn't just me that my team-mates had to deal with. If they thought I was mad, sometimes they'd have to handle my mates, like on one night out with the Wigan boys.

I was the kind of bloke who'd bring my mates along to almost anything – I drew the line at bringing them out on to the pitch to play with me although I must admit the thought did occur to me more than once. But I've turned up at weddings before with mates who clearly weren't invited and I don't see a problem with that as long as they behave themselves.

That's why it seemed perfectly reasonable to me that if any of my old mates were in town visiting me, they could come out with my team-mates. As long as they behaved themselves.

And, if behaving involves threatening to kill someone, they did just that.

We were out in Warrington and there must've been at least a dozen of us from the club and my mad mate, who I can't name for national security reasons, all sat round a table. He's the sort of character that you think you've seen in a film. He is an absolute, out and out wrong 'un. A complete nutcase. But I've known him since we were kids, so what can I do?

We'd been out for most of the day and our keeper Mike Pollitt had been giving my mate a bit of stick and wound him up a bit – mainly because after a few drinks, he'd had been getting on everyone's case. Polly's jibes would've been fine if it was the sort of thing that was being said between us team-mates, but not so fine when it's my mad mate because he wasn't a footballer, he didn't understand our relationship and he wasn't very good at taking any kind of good-natured ribbing like that.

Actually, he wasn't very good at being on the receiving end of any kind of piss-taking – even I played it cool in front of him.

My mad mate said something stupid and, from the other end of the table, Polly piped up with: 'Shut up you donut!' which drew a few laughs that definitely didn't help the situation.

Clutching a fork tightly, my mad mate informed my team-mates Arjan de Zeeuw, Matt Jackson and Lee McCulloch who were all sitting near him: 'Sorry lads, I don't know any of you, but that prick at the end of the table . . . Polly, are you listening to me?'

'Yes,' replied the keeper.

My mad mate walked towards Polly at the other end of this long table, still holding the fork and looking like he meant business.

'Pick a window,' he ordered Polly once he'd arrived next to him.

The keeper had a puzzled look on his face – reminiscent of the time when he realised we'd reached the Carling Cup final about five minutes after the rest of us – but pointed to a window on his right anyway.

'That one,' said Polly.

'If you don't fucking shut up, you're going straight out of that window, goalkeeper or no goalkeeper.'

Nobody was saying a word now. Polly looked at me for help, as if to ask if my mad mate was actually being serious, hoping that I'd burst out laughing to break the tension. No such luck.

'He will do it Polly,' I told him.

'Do I make myself clear, Polly?'

'Yes. I won't talk to you again,' said the keeper.

'Thank you,' said my mad mate, before walking back to his seat and carrying on as if nothing unusual had happened.

I'm still not sure that Polly realised just how lucky he was with that particular incident. Had he not taken my mad mate seriously at that moment, or said the wrong thing at any time for the rest of the night, he would've ended up with a fork in his neck, or going straight through the window. And that was by no means the end of the nutcase's antics for the night either. If anything, he was just getting warmed up.

A few hours later, he had de Zeeuw in a headlock and I didn't know where to look. Arjan was a huge presence; more than 6ft tall, a strong leader on the pitch and a real colossus of a man, but there he was in the vice-like grip of a total nutcase, who was screaming 'It's Arjan de Zeeuw! Arjan!' as if he was his biggest fan.

The longer I looked away, the longer my mad mate seemed to keep hold of de Zeeuw. Some of the boys were pleading with me to call him off, but there was nothing I could do. He pays as much attention to me as he does to anyone else – which is not one fucking bit.

Eventually, he let go of him and, not long after, we managed to sneak off and leave my mad mate to his own devices. There was only so much apologising I was prepared to do and there would've been trouble if we'd stuck around with him any longer. So, one by one, we each pretended we were going to the loo, but instead headed straight out of the bar and legged it down the street, pissing ourselves laughing.

After a stint at another bar in Wigan, I finally got back home at about two in the morning and, to my horror, there was my mad mate – who would've had no idea where I lived – sitting on my sofa with three empty Champagne bottles surrounding him, and my Diane looking utterly pissed off. He'd been driving her mad for hours and my phone must have died so she couldn't get hold of me.

A few days later, there was a knock at the door and it was my next-door neighbour asking me if I'd seen the aerial from his new BMW 7 Series which had gone missing. I had no idea what he was talking about so told him I couldn't help him, but when I stopped to think about it, I knew it had to be connected to you-know-who.

I did some investigating and found out that my mad mate had kept my address on a piece of paper in his sock that night which explained how he'd found my place. When he'd first tried knocking, Diane hadn't answered the door and he couldn't get in. Naturally, he decided that breaking in was the best option and, in order to do that, he'd better snap off my neighbour's brand new car aerial to pick my lock. I also discovered a load of 2p and 50p coins underneath all the big, sash windows outside my house as he'd been using them to try to force one open.

Fortunately for Diane, Polly, de Zeeuw and all the Wigan boys, he never visited the north west again – at least not to my knowledge anyway – so they never had to deal with him. But they still had to deal with me and any number of non-life threatening, daft japes. Away trips were usually primed for that kind of nonsense and everyone got involved.

Standard fare included finding out the room numbers of your team-mates just before dinner, then waiting outside their room with a bucket of water. As soon as they opened the door, all ready for their din-dins, bosh! That bucket of water goes all over them.

Better still, we'd burst into someone's room when they were still in bed and muller them with a bucket right there. Try sleeping in a soaking wet bed. Hotel housekeeping staff hated us, but we always left them decent tips to make up for the carnage. Alternatively, we would wait by an open first-floor window, below which everyone was walking to dinner, and then soak them with a bin full of water.

If you weren't getting drenched, there were other more old-school, low-rent wind-ups that went on. Filling trainers with water – or worse, wee – happened a fair bit: 'Bit squelchy in there is it, boy? You didn't check that!' And if you did remember to check the inside of your shoes, you'd probably have missed the fact that your laces had been cut to pieces and you couldn't tie them up. Either that, or the toes would have been cut off your socks so you put your foot straight through them.

I always found mealtimes particularly boring and we were often left to our own devices so I took full advantage by doing childish things like hiding under the table as the poor waitress was coming with food, and then leaping out like a dog, barking, and pretending to bite her arm. The food would always go everywhere, except on the table.

One of my favourite away trip pranks was buying a Pritt Stick and then covering someone's bathroom towel with glue. When they tried to dry themselves after a shower, they would become covered in sticky white fluff, which was really hard to remove. A few hours later, we'd all be getting changed before the game and we could all see the Pritt Stick victim straight away: 'He's been Pritt Sticked; he looks like a fucking sheep!'

That was funny, but not a patch on the time my Wigan team-mate Alan Mahon suffered a very smelly night's sleep, thanks to the handiwork of me and Michael Flynn. We, ahem, had a crap into a bag, which we then slipped underneath Alan's pillowcase. Horrible. But hilarious.

'Someone's had a shit in my room and whoever's done it has not flushed the chain properly,' he complained to everyone the next morning, as Flynny and I started wetting ourselves.

'You wanna check your pillowcase son,' was all I could say in between my fits of laughter.

I would also do stupid things on matchdays, which was quite daft looking back on it now. Once, at Wigan, I chucked all of Polly's gear in the team bath and turned the shower on. Kit, boots, gloves – the works.

He was standing in front of his changing area half-naked, looking around for all his stuff. 'Where's my kit?' he yelled.

'I think it's in the shower!' was my instant reply, as if it had a mind of its own and had innocently wandered in there.

'Fuck off Jim, you can't do that,' he said.

Even the gaffer, Paul Jewell, who would normally stay out of all the nonsense that went on between the players, was pissed off with me but I explained that I was getting Polly back for something he'd done to me.

'Have you got spare kit?' the gaffer asked Polly.

'No, I've done that as well,' I answered immediately before Polly had even had a chance to work out where it might be. 'I'm not that soppy!'

From the moment I turned up at West Ham's training ground in my dad's Granada Ghia, everyone knew I was a bit different. You need the confidence to deal with the abuse you're going to get for that and I had it. And if you can show you're prepared to give as good as you get (or, in my case, way more than you get), most people will leave you alone. If not, you will get picked on and you'll always have squelchy shoes, a wet bed and socks with holes in.

It sounds ridiculous for grown men to behave like that, but that's what the football environment is like. I didn't make the rules, but because I was prepared to go the extra mile when it came to the daft stuff, I made sure I was never that victim.

In football, your reputation goes a long way. Once I'd established myself as that bloke who would go to any lengths, the

stories travelled round and became embellished. Then I would turn up at a new club and there would be an instant respect for me.

'Did you set fire to a player's car?' my new team-mates would ask me, referring to TJ Moncur's motor that I filled with water.

'Yeah, I did,' I'd reply. 'You don't want to fuck with me, I'll take your wheels off.'

And, just like that, I'd be left alone.

There was one time when one of my pranks backfired spectacularly. I'd discovered one of those numbers you could ring up, where an automated voice answers and waits for you to respond which triggers it to talk again. I was on the Wigan team bus when I called a mate, connected them to this prank number then listened in.

'Hello,' said my mate.

'What do you think you've been doing messing around with my wife!' says the automatic hard man's voice.

'You what?' said my mate.

'I know what you've been up to; my missus has told me everything.'

'What you on about, I've not been doing anything,' said my mate, starting to panic as me and a couple of the Wigan boys pissed ourselves laughing.

And so it went on, until my mate realised he was being wound up.

It worked so well that I thought I'd try it again on my brother John, although this time I was on my own as my team-mates had fallen asleep or something. No staying power, those boys.

It was the same scenario as the voice started to wind my brother up, except he continued to believe it was real.

'Look mate, I've not been shagging your wife,' he said.

'Don't come the innocent with me, I know what you've been up to,' said the voice.

'It wasn't me, I swear to you,' said my brother.

'I've seen you at it,' said the voice.

I was cracking up again on the bus, until my brother said: 'Look mate, it wasn't me because I'm gay! G-A-Y, gay!'

Bloody hell. My brother had come out to an automatic prank answerphone and I heard it all. I didn't try that gag again in a hurry. I was in complete shock although on reflection it didn't come as a massive surprise. Over the years, a few of my mates had mentioned that they'd seen my brother hanging out with an alternative crowd but I didn't really think much of it. It didn't bother me at all as I'm all about live and let live, but I never really discussed it with John until recently, as our family don't tend to talk about things like that so openly and I also felt quite bad about that phone call. John wasn't that fussed about it though and that was that.

There was one phone call I received which I was convinced was a prank, but turned out to be completely genuine – yet to this day it remains the most bizarre phone conversation I've ever had.

It all started when I went to Wimbledon to watch some tennis and I bumped into this bloke who told me he was Alastair Campbell's son and we had a bit of a laugh. It was while I was playing for Fulham, probably at the peak of my career and his old man was still a bigwig in the Labour party.

A couple of weeks later my phone rang, and it was a bloke telling me he was Alastair Campbell. I would've fallen off my chair in surprise if I had been sitting on one at the time.

I thought it was a joke at first, but it was definitely him and he started telling me how his boy had met me at the tennis and how it would be good for the two of us to meet up one day.

'What the fuck's going on?' was the thought going through my head, but I just went along with it.

'Yeah, that would be good,' I said, and that was the end of the conversation.

And I never heard from him again.

Eh?

Thinking about it, it wasn't far off an election and I reckon he was trying to tap me up to 'come out' as a Labour party supporter. He loved his football, he'd probably seen me messing around on *Soccer AM* – his kid certainly had – and he might have thought I'd be a good person to have on board. But me and politics? I don't think so.

I didn't need to get involved with that as I was far more comfortable making a fool of myself in the football world where I'd built up a reputation and continued to play on it.

And that's why when the Sky cameras turned up at Hull one pre-season to film us, there was no way they were leaving without another set of outtakes of me being a dick for *Soccer AM*, YouTube and who knows where else.

They turned up one Monday morning to film those bits you see when they do the team line-ups before a game, and all the players take a few steps towards the camera, looking all serious and professional.

I must admit I was feeling a bit lively that morning as I'd had a couple of coffees so I was buzzing about and acting up for the cameras – business as usual, really. When it was my turn, I stood with my back to camera in front of the green screen they use to film these things, turned around and strolled up to the camera doing a bit of a funny walk and grinning like a buffoon.

The boys behind the camera loved it and I saw that as my opportunity to entertain them. For the next take, I hiked my shorts right up past my waist, halfway up my torso and tucked my shirt in too for good measure. I then walked up to the camera like a total donut, playing it as straight as I could while the Sky crew in the room fell about laughing.

Take three and it was time to perfect the hard man routine I'd been developing just in case Hollywood ever came calling – if Vinnie Jones can do it, why can't I?

So I walked up to the camera in a slow, deliberate and menacing way, full of swagger, with an expression on my face which said I was the don, a no-nonsense, mean son of a bitch, not to be messed with. Once again, everyone was in stitches.

Finally, fourth time lucky, I managed to play it straight but even then I still had a big, cheesy grin on my face and had to work so hard not to completely lose the plot laughing. When they called cut, I broke out into some of my best dancefloor moves by way of a celebration. Job done.

Footage of my entire performance made it on to *Soccer AM* the following weekend and was all over the internet straight after that. Even now, I still get the odd person coming up to me with their shorts or trousers hiked right up yelling, 'Jimbo, wahey!'

People were clearly into this sort of larking around, especially on the internet and, a while later, some bright spark at the shampoo brand Wash & Go called me up and asked me if I wanted to make an advert for them.

I was well up for it and told them a telly advert would suit me right down to the ground.

'No Jim,' they said. 'It's not on the telly, it's a viral.'

'What the fuck's that?'

A viral didn't sound like a good thing to me but they explained that it was a short ad designed to be spread around the internet.

This was definitely the next best thing to being the Milkybar Kid. And where was that bloke now, eh?

It was a full day's filming, but when I turned up early one morning expecting that I'd have to dress up a bit and wash my hair in front of one camera, I couldn't have been more wrong. There must have been about ten cameras and fifty people in the room.

'Oh shit,' I thought. 'I'd better do this properly.'

So I started following all their instructions really conscientiously, doing everything I was told and taking it all really seriously. But it didn't seem to be going so well, judging from the muted reaction I was getting. The director pulled me over to one side to have a word.

'Er, Jim, we've got you here to mess about!'

'Gotcha!'

What a dope I was. The only reason they wanted me there was to play the fool. But it wasn't so easy to walk into a room full of strangers and start being funny. I wasn't a stand-up comedian. I bet the Milkybar Kid never had to tell jokes.

Anyway, we bonded a bit over a cup of tea and a bite to eat, I started to loosen up and we were away. I think it ended up being pretty funny and I enjoyed doing it, but it was a hell of a long day. I was in there from 7am until 8pm to film a one-minute ad. I definitely made the right call being a footballer – ninety minutes and you're done.

The ad itself was to celebrate the shampoo's twenty-first birthday and saw me sporting a variety of retro hairstyles before having my hair done in a ridiculous, salon-fresh style and parading around a locker room, shaking it all over the place in a deliberately cheesy way.

Half a million hits on YouTube later, it's still going strong; that's one virus nobody can shake off. There was also some great coverage of the ad in the papers at the time so I was happy enough. That, coupled with the rest of the tomfoolery, were more small steps in my evil plot to take over the internet and make those Milkybar Kid ad people rue the day they spurned me.

But for all those internet hits and pranks, the Spanish police will always be able to lay claim to pulling the ultimate scam on me.

Polly, me and a few others had gone on holiday to Marbella for a long weekend during the close season, to live it up and get right on it. We had a suitably mad one which started badly for Polly when his case didn't come through from Manchester so he had to spend the whole trip begging us for clothes and toiletries. But much worse was to come for me.

We'd done our partying and were walking back through Malaga airport to catch our flight home. Polly was in front of me in the passport control queue and when he walked through, it was my turn.

I looked at the official, flashed him a smile and worked the old Bullard magic, but then I saw a red light flashing on his screen and a worried look appeared on his face. He kept looking at my passport then looking at me and, each time, his face grew more concerned.

Suddenly, he got up and opened the door of his little booth, grabbed my hands and said: 'You must wait here.'

There was a slope leading up to where the passport control booths were and suddenly I could see a few policemen running up it, heading towards me although I kept thinking and hoping that they'd go straight past because they were after someone else.

What the fuck was going on and what the fuck had I done while I was out there?

One of the policemen called out 'Mr Bullard!' and then I really started to panic.

'Polly!' I called to my mate. 'Come back through!'

He'd been watching the scene from a distance and tried to help. 'What's going on?' he asked the old bill. 'We've got a flight to catch.'

'He will not be getting on the flight with you,' replied one of the policemen. 'You must go.'

He pleaded with them but it was no use as they forced him to leave us alone and move towards the departure gate.

As he walked off, I was handcuffed and marched off to a nearby police station where I was put in a cell. I was in there for three hours, shitting myself, with no idea what was going to happen to me or why I was there. Even though I knew I'd done nothing wrong, I was bricking it because I'd heard so many stories about people getting stitched up abroad by bent coppers.

Finally, after a thoroughly unpleasant ordeal, I was pulled out of the cell and interviewed by the police. Which went something like this:

'So Mr Bullard, have you had face surgery?'

'What?'

'You had face surgery, yes?'

'I don't know what you're fucking on about, mate.'

One of the coppers pulled out my passport, except instead of *my* photo, there was a picture of a bloke who looked a bit like my dad but with darker hair and far scarier.

He pointed to the picture and said: 'You surgery.'

'Are you fucking mental?'

While this surreal interview was going on, Polly had landed back in Manchester and was straight on the phone to my old man and our agent (we shared the same one) letting them know what had happened. Which wasn't much, as he didn't really know what had happened and neither did I. My old man phoned him every few minutes to find out if he'd heard anything and became so frustrated and agitated that he started driving to the airport to fly out to my rescue.

Back in Spain, my suitcase turned up in the interview room and the police started rummaging through it. I was terrified, certain they were going to plant something on me and pretend they'd found it in my case.

All that time, they didn't say a word.

Then, I had my fingerprints taken and I was convinced I was never going back home.

Finally, after an agonising wait, one of the coppers came back in and said, 'You can go now, wrong man.'

Thank fuck for that.

I couldn't get out of there quick enough. It turned out somebody they wanted to speak to had forged my passport and was pretending to be me. Which probably explained some of my dodgy performances at the end of the previous season.

The only place I'd ever left my passport for safekeeping was in a hotel in The Algarve, and the picture of the bruiser they showed me in the fake passport did look Portuguese. So I'd been done like a kipper – but I was free to leave.

After calling everyone at home and telling them to cancel the protest marches and the boycott of all Spanish goods, I went back to the airport and was about to buy my new ticket home when I realised I'd left my passport (the real one) back at the police station. By the time I went back to get it, I'd missed the last flight to England so I was stuck in Spain for another night.

But at least my prison nightmare was over – which is another line I never thought I'd have to write.

PILLAR 10

IT IS NOT THE WINNING THAT COUNTS. WHICH IS CONVENIENT IF YOU HAPPEN TO GET RELEGATED

'Be careful when you fight monsters, because you may become one.'
Friedrich Nietzsche

Picture the scene.

It was a beautiful spring Monday morning on Humberside. The Humber Bridge glistened in the sunlight. The sound of birdsong filled the air, blossom was starting to fall from trees and there was a feeling of hope among all those lucky enough to be outdoors on that glorious day.

Around a hundred members of the local Women's Institute were lucky enough to be out and about that particular morning, as they'd planned a march across the bridge. As they strolled along, they took in those beautiful sights and sounds.

The sun's rays bouncing off the river.

The larks whistling to one another.

And myself and Nick Barmby rolling around on the grass, yelling things like 'Fucking arsehole' and throwing punches at each other.

That was probably the most ridiculous situation I've ever been in as a footballer, and I say that having had my head shut in a door by Paul Jewell. If you're ever going to have a fight with someone, I would highly recommend not doing it in front of a hundred old age pensioners.

But it had to be done because I was absolutely furious with Nick, and the scrap just happened to take place in the car park by the Humber Bridge because the gaffer had decided that's where we were going to have our warm-down that morning.

It was the day after we'd been hammered by Everton live on telly in my first game back after my third knee injury. Not the ideal return, especially when you consider I had also had a stand-up row with Nick in the dressing room at half time. And, as is always the case with these football flashpoints, it had started over something so stupid.

We went a goal down that day after Mikel Arteta managed to run on to a deep, back-post cross, unchallenged. Nick was supposed to have picked him up, but was yards behind him when he volleyed the ball in. Nick was normally a fantastic presence at the back post, very good in the air and always covered danger thanks to his good positional sense. But, for whatever reason, he'd gone AWOL. Not a disaster as there was only seventeen minutes gone.

The BBC's match report read: 'Yakubu delivered a hanging cross from the left and Arteta volleyed home superbly at the back post, although some slack defending from Everton old boy Barmby allowed the Spaniard all the time in the world.'

Personally, I think my version was a little better than that, but then I have inside information.

During a break in play, I ran past Barmby and said: 'I thought you were comfortable at the back post there, Nick?'

'Fucking comfortable!' came his angry reply. 'You fucking cheeky bastard!'

Whoah! I really hadn't meant that much by the comment, other than expressing my disappointment because he was usually so good at the back post in those situations. He obviously felt like I was digging him out, but that's football and these things happen. So I attempted to diffuse the situation: 'Hang on a minute, all I said was that I thought you were comfortable on the back stick. We're still in the game, it doesn't matter.'

But he was still muttering away at me, and clearly not in a complimentary way. We eventually came back into the changing room at half time 2-1 down, still very much in the game, but Nick wasn't interested in that.

He was standing there waiting for me when I got in and, in front of the whole team and management, he lost the plot and crossed a line. Instead of sticking to what happened on the pitch, he took the incredible step of bringing money, and specifically my Hull contract, into it. I could not believe what I was hearing.

'This football club paid £5 million for you and pays you £45,000 a week,' he was ranting, as if to say I needed to be doing more to justify my wages.

I was incensed. How on earth had he gone from being pissed off about me having a go at him on the pitch to talking about my contract? I was more aware than anyone of how much I owed the club seeing as I was only playing my seventh game for Hull in more than a year, because of two serious knee injuries. But I certainly didn't need him discussing my personal business in the middle of the dressing room at half-time of a crucial match.

I was raging inside as I'd never been spoken to like that

before. I could see some of the other boys were shaking their heads implying that Nick was out of order but what I didn't get, and still don't to this day, is why Phil Brown or any of the management team never got involved.

'Don't worry,' I said, fuming. 'You've obviously got a bee in your bonnet about me. It's not about money where I'm from. We've let a goal in and now you're digging out my contract. We'll sort it out tomorrow morning.'

'Anytime, anywhere,' was his reply as we all stormed back out on the pitch to concede three more goals and get pasted. No surprise there.

I always had difficulty kipping after a game because of the adrenaline, but that night, I couldn't sleep a wink because I was so angry. I wanted to kill Nick Barmby and that's all I could think about. I tossed and turned all night until it was time to go to the training ground for the warm-down.

But that Monday morning, the gaffer had decided we'd have our warm-down session out by the Humber Bridge, rather than pore over hours of video analysis of our drubbing the day before.

We'd been out there before, it's a mile-and-a-half each way during which we'd do walking and jogging, then it would be back to the club for ice baths and massages. Which was great, because I would certainly need cooling down when we got back to base.

I travelled over to the bridge in my team-mate Richard Garcia's car and he sensed something was up.

'You're not right from the game still, are you Jim?' he said.

'No,' I replied. 'There's definitely going to be a fight here.'

'Bloody hell, you are raging!' he said.

But I barely noticed because I was focused on nothing other than Barmby.

Richard parked the car and, as we got out, I spotted my nemesis and the red mist fully descended.

'Come here you,' I said. 'We've got to have a word, haven't we?'

As Nick walked towards me, I reached out to grab him and he threw a punch at my head straight away. Within seconds we were having a proper ding-dong, rolling around on the ground, trying to belt the crap out of each other.

We were both throwing punches, but none really seemed to land. I was so full of anger and adrenaline that I probably wouldn't have felt it if Nick had landed one in any case.

I'd love to be able to say that I sorted him out, but the truth is that it was little more than explosive grappling for a few seconds. As the gaffer said later, it was hardly Ali-Frazier.

We both ended up lying on a bush with no real leverage to get out of it so loads of the boys dived in to split us up. Steve Parkin, the assistant manager, grabbed me by the arm and walked me down the path, while the rest of the lads took Nick and headed off in the opposite direction to make sure we were as far apart as possible . . . Except nobody realised that this particular path was circular, meaning that after a few minutes we all met up again!

Parkin kept telling me to calm down, but I was still livid and, as soon as I saw Barmby again, I shrugged Steve's arm away and launched myself at Nick. But this time, Barmby was protected by Amr Zaki and Kamil Zayatte, who stood in my path like two blocks of flats. I just bounced off them and had to call it a day.

Just when it seemed like things couldn't have got any worse, I returned to the training ground and they did too. The gaffer had started receiving complaints from members of the WI, who had called into the club and the local radio station, appalled by what they'd seen – and I don't mean our wild (and wildly ineffective) fighting styles, which they would have had every right to criticise.

I was completely unaware that there had been any spectators because I was so zoned in on righting what I perceived to be a wrong. Had they stuck up a pop-up arena and put us in a boxing ring in the middle of the fight, I probably wouldn't have noticed.

This was not what Brownie needed with the club in the relegation zone and the pressure only increasing after our performance the previous day; Barmby and I were summoned to his office to sort the whole thing out, like a pair of naughty schoolchildren – as if the whole morning hadn't been humiliating enough.

But even then, after everything that had happened, neither of us was prepared to climb down. I was still seething with anger and I'm certain Nick felt exactly the same. We were both big characters at the club, stubborn as mules and, crucially for the gaffer, essential to Hull's chances of staying up. As Brownie said, he wanted his strong characters to be fighting for the cause, not each other.

He had to have us working together if we were going to have any chance of survival – and he was going to have any chance of keeping his job. But the stand-off continued for hours until the gaffer threatened to get rid of both of us if we couldn't sort it out. A very smart move.

I realised that fighting in public like that while representing the club was a sackable offence, while Nick was Mr Hull City and there was no way he could have given that up for anything. Eventually, Hull skipper Ian Ashbee joined us in the room to help sort it all out and we all shook hands, agreeing to put it behind us.

Which was easily said, but even when I was shaking Barmby's hand I had to ask him where all the contract stuff had come from, because it still didn't make any sense to me.

'Well,' he said. 'It was something that Neville Southall once said to me.'

Oh, right. Well, that's okay then. The legendary goalkeeper had once had a pop at Nick when he was a young player at Everton, so he now had every right to use that one against me. It made perfect sense. If only he'd explained that to me the day before, we needn't have had that fight in front of a bunch of old women.

Of course, I realised we shouldn't have fought like that in public or private, but what Nick had said to me had grown out of all proportion in my mind and I felt really hurt and disrespected. For all the japes and jokes, I'd never been that rude to anyone and never would be.

I had to stand up for myself, because Nick was highly regarded. He was Hull through and through and went on to manage the club so I had to back my corner or other people in that dressing room might have thought it was acceptable to speak to me like that.

And it worked, because from that day on, he never spoke or acted in that way to me ever again. I've been heavily criticised for fighting in public like that, but I believe I earned respect from Nick for what I did as he would never say anything like that again.

The fallout from the incident continued all week. The papers had a field day, there were radio phone-ins about it on the local station and poor Brownie was having to offer apologies to everyone for his players' behaviour. The only person not to get an apology was me as I still felt the gaffer had let me down by not condemning what Barmby had said in the first place, and I told him that, too.

My team-mate George Boateng, who wasn't at the Humber Bridge with us, did nothing to help calm the situation either, although I had to laugh when I heard he told the press: 'I'm sorry, because I missed it. I wasn't there. I would have paid to watch it!'

Probably the worst bit about it was that within a week Brownie had been sacked, which I was gutted about. We'd actually played really well in our next match, which was at home to Arsenal – just what we needed after such a traumatic week.

They'd taken an early lead but we were awarded a penalty when Jan Vennegoor of Hesselink was clattered by Sol Campbell. I grabbed the ball and absolutely leathered it into the top left corner past Manuel Almunia. Unstoppable.

I ran across to the crowd and punched the air twice – a completely unintentional reference to what had happened a few days before. But, as it happened, they were two far better right-handers than any I'd thrown at Nick.

We were looking good for a decent point, but then Arsenal went and scored in injury time and that was it for us. And that was it for Phil Brown too as he was shown the door soon after.

I felt exactly the same way when Chris Coleman was sacked

by Fulham. First and foremost, I was gutted for Brownie because he was absolutely devastated about it. Hull was his whole world. He loved that football club so much and he'd taken them into the top flight.

He called us all in to tell us the club were getting rid of him, and I could see just how hurt he was. Admittedly, he had upset a few of the lads, especially with the Man City on-pitch team talk the season before. Some of the boys never forgave him for that. If I'd been there at the time I really don't think it would have continued to bother me for that long, but many footballers are like sheep – and not just because I've Pritt Sticked their towels – they hear an opinion in the dressing room and loads of them immediately adopt it as their own without thinking for themselves.

There was a mixed reaction to Brownie's departure. Some of us like myself and the skipper Ian Ashbee counted him as a friend and were upset for him; others like Boateng shed no tears. In a passionate TV interview after we'd been relegated, he told the watching millions that the team had never recovered from that on-pitch dressing down, and that if Brown had been sacked earlier in the season we might have stayed up. Harsh, but that was his opinion.

In terms of the football, I wasn't sure he deserved to get the boot as he was just having a bad year, which can happen. Yes, we were in the relegation zone at that time, but there were still nine games left and we were only three points from safety. We'd done it by the skin of our teeth the season before and I felt we could do it again.

Like when Cookie left Fulham, I thought about myself and no player is going to be happy about the manager who signed him being dismissed. It left me feeling slightly insecure. When Cookie signed me at Fulham, I went to play for him as he'd sold me a vision of how he wanted me to play and I was bang up for it. I'm not sure Roy Hodgson had the same vision for me and things went a bit sour.

At Hull, Brownie had also promised me the free role that I craved. I could go out on the pitch and pretty much do what I liked as long as I made things happen for the team. He'd also impressed me massively with his belief and ambition for the club.

When I signed on the dotted line for Hull, I didn't do it purely for the money. Don't get me wrong, a £5 million transfer and £45,000 per week wages were clearly extremely attractive, but there were other clubs also interested in signing me from Fulham.

Before I'd put pen to paper, I was in a restaurant with Mark Curtis, a football agent. He put me on the phone to Sam Allardyce, who was the Blackburn Rovers manager at the time and we had a chat about what I was looking for in terms of wages and length of contract. I told him I felt a bit weird discussing it on the phone and that it would be better if we all met up, face to face. I never heard from him again, but that's the random nature of football.

The extra incentive to join Hull – other than the fact that they actually wanted me – was provided by Brown, who, alongside the club's chairman, Paul Duffen, was probably the most ambitious person I ever met in football. He'd already signed players like Geovanni and Boateng, and was determined to make sure Hull became an established Premier League team.

Brownie had a massive amount of self-belief, which some

people confused with arrogance. He wanted to manage the best teams in the Premier League and maybe even manage his country one day. I admired that, because you have to have a dream and you need belief. If I hadn't believed, I'd have probably still been playing non-league.

The club wanted to give it a massive effort in the Premier League and it almost worked. Don't forget, when I joined they were halfway through their first-ever season in the English top flight and they managed to survive, which itself was a decent achievement.

Unfortunately, getting injured in my first game for Hull was definitely not part of all those big plans for the club or myself. By the time I was playing again, the highs of staying up the previous season were a distant memory as it became clear that another relegation scrap was on the cards.

One thing I'll never forget though was the gaffer's celebrations when Hull stayed up.

Although I was out of action doing my rehab, I was still at the KC Stadium on the last day of the season in 2009 when all we had to do was beat Man United to stay up. If only football was that simple.

United had actually done us a favour by naming an under-strength starting line-up for the game because they were due to play Barcelona in the Champions League final a few days later. I was sitting a few rows behind the bench with Ian Ashbee and our job was to keep the gaffer updated with the scores from the other games which could affect us. Newcastle were our main threat and were playing at Aston Villa, while Middlesbrough stood an outside chance of catching us if they could beat West Ham.

We were on a poor run of ten games without a win and it showed as we didn't play very well at all. Darron Gibson put United ahead and for fourteen minutes, we were going down. I could hardly watch as the thought of returning to the Championship after injury was not exactly appealing.

But then Newcastle went a goal down at Villa and a huge roar went around the stadium. There was no need for me to tell Brownie anything. He knew.

The last ten or fifteen minutes were agonising as we were relying on Newcastle not scoring at Villa to stay up. They didn't let us down and, even though we also lost, we were going to be back in the Premier League the following season. And that was a major relief to everyone – especially the manager and chairman.

The gaffer congratulated all the players and sent them off to the changing room, where Ian and I also went to join in the celebrations – and share the relief.

There was a great atmosphere in there, but someone was missing. We looked around and nobody knew where Brownie was, but we could hear a noise coming from the PA system in the stadium. Incredibly, none of the fans had left and the gaffer was on the pitch, microphone in hand, leading a sing-along.

First up, he started chanting 'We are staying up!' and everyone joined in. Then he went for the Hull fans' version of the Beach Boys' song 'Sloop John B', which saw him yelling, 'Don't wanna go hooooome, this is the best trip I've ever been on!' causing the local stray dogs to all start howling in unison.

Maybe that was a bit harsh, because I thought he deserved his moment. A lot of people might look at it and think, 'What on earth is this lunatic up to?' but Brownie had worked miracles to get the club into the Premier League and keep them there.

Afterwards, I couldn't resist asking him what his thinking was behind the stunt and he told me that the fans had been singing at him all season so he thought it was only fair to sing back to them.

He got absolutely slaughtered by the media for it, which I thought was out of order. So what if he did that? Who gives a shit? It's not like he's grabbed a fan by the neck or something. Yes, he's a bit nuts and a bit out there, but so what?

I got on well with the gaffer as he realised I was a bit, er, 'special'. Once I was up and about again after my injury, he could see what I was like and let me go fishing or for a round of golf, as he knew I needed to do something if I wasn't playing football. He understood my frustration at being part of the England set-up one moment, and then lying on a treatment table the next. He could also see that I was a bit of a freak. He was watching us play darts in the dressing room one day, and I banged in a 180 – he looked at me as if to say, 'That can't be right.'

But then he didn't know about my childhood at West Lodge – which was why soon after that 180, I was knocking up sixty or seventy breaks when we all played snooker, too. You never lose those abilities you learn as a kid.

'You're not wired right, are you?' he'd often say to me.

'No, not really,' I'd shrug back.

Within a couple of days of Brown's departure, Iain Dowie was appointed gaffer until the end of the season and it didn't start well for him or us, as we let slip a lead with two minutes left at Portsmouth, and ended up losing by the odd goal in five. It all boiled down to a crucial home game against

Sunderland where we had to win to have any chance of staying up – even if we had done so, there were still two games left after that one to negotiate.

The afternoon started badly when Darren Bent put Sunderland ahead after just seven minutes and it never got any better. In fact, for me, it would become a whole lot worse.

Later in the first half, we were handed a lifeline when our former player Michael Turner fouled Geovanni in the box and the ref gave us a penalty. As usual, I took the ball, but something wasn't quite right.

I'd never taken a penalty and thought I was going to miss at any point in my career. Of course, I'd missed the odd spot-kick before but I always backed myself to score.

Until that moment.

I stepped up having scored all four of my previous penalties for Hull. The problem was, Sunderland had Craig Gordon in goal, an absolute beast of a man, who must've been about seven feet tall – or so I thought.

As I placed the ball on the spot, he stood a couple of yards off the goal line and spread out his arms as wide as possible.

Oh God.

I looked up and there might as well have been a flipping T-Rex in goal. I couldn't see the net or the posts he was so big. I told myself the only chance I had of scoring was to stick it right in the corner and even then there were no guarantees.

Gordon moved back on to his line as I ran up to take the pen, but it made no difference to my mental state. I'd been defeated before I'd even started my run-up so it was no surprise when I saw the ball cannon off the outside of the post and away to safety. I had doubted myself and that was my undoing.

Even worse, the fans were slightly disappointed. Which is the understatement of the century. They absolutely slaughtered and hounded me for the rest of the half until Dowie took pity on me and subbed me at half time.

Injuries aside, I can't think of a worse experience I've had on a football pitch – and I include the countless times I was mistaken for a girl while playing parks football as a kid. I then had to come back out to watch us struggle through the second half to no avail as we lost 1-0 to confirm our fate.

We were down. For the first time in my career, I experienced relegation and it didn't taste particularly good.

The weird thing about relegation is that it is such a gradual experience. It's not like someone burst into the dressing room one day and informed us out of the blue that we were being relegated, so it didn't knock us sideways with shock. We had all been aware that it was on the cards. When it finally happened, it was quite tough to handle, especially for the boys like Ian Ashbee and Andy Dawson, who had worked so hard to climb up the leagues with Hull and get them to their Promised Land. Andy, one of the hardest blokes I've ever played with, was in tears while Ian and Paul McShane were both devastated. I just wanted to get out of there as soon as possible.

I didn't know it then, but I'd played my last Premier League game. After all the hard work to get there, it was over after five years and three serious knee injuries. And what a way to go out – missing a penalty and getting jeered by your own fans. Fortunately, I had some other decent memories tucked away.

None of that was on my mind at the time, though. What I was actually thinking was that it wasn't the end of the world. We were all still footballers, we would still be playing at a decent level in the Championship in front of thousands of supporters every week. Someone had to go down and it was us – now we had to work hard to get back into the Premier League, which was where we all wanted to be.

Unfortunately, the club didn't quite see it the same way. They didn't want a £45,000 per week player on their payroll in the Championship. That was made quite clear to me by the new chairman Adam Pearson, who told me he would prefer it if I went out on loan to help ease the financial burden of relegation.

I understood where he was coming from so I told him I'd be happy to do that as long as the move suited me and my family. Diane was pregnant again so it was important to me that we'd be settled somewhere that didn't necessarily involve travelling here, there and everywhere. He seemed to understand my needs and I went off on holiday to the Algarve before pre-season was due to start.

While I was there, Pearson phoned me to tip me off that I should expect a call from Celtic manager Neil Lennon. That was certainly a bolt from the blue, but I went with it. Neil duly got in touch to invite me over to his villa as he also happened to be holidaying nearby. Think you can ever get away from football? No chance.

So I went over to Neil's place – lovely gaff, by the way – and he asked me if I'd like to play for Celtic on loan.

Neil filled me in on the details. It turned out that Hull had made an agreement with Celtic behind my back where both clubs would pay part of my wages, although that total amount was short of the sum my contract clearly stated I should be paid. That set the alarm bells ringing straight away. I couldn't understand how they could have come to this arrangement without me.

I told Neil that I'd love to come and play for him, but that I would need to have a proper look at the contract first. I wanted to buy myself a bit of time to make sure I wasn't getting stitched up. I also told Neil that it wouldn't be solely my decision as I had a family and another child on the way.

When I returned to Hull for pre-season, the new manager Nigel Pearson (no relation to Adam) told me I should go up to Glasgow, have a look around at the set-up and then make a decision on whether I wanted to move. So off I went to Scotland for a few days. Everything about the club was amazing and if I had been a single man, I wouldn't have had to think very hard; I would've signed the day I got there.

But I had other responsibilities so I wanted to take my time. Celtic had kindly got me tickets to the Scottish Open golf tournament which was being played nearby at Loch Lomond, so I spent two days there watching the golf, feeling right at home.

And while I was there, I came to a decision and that was to return to Hull, for a variety of reasons.

The most appealing reason to join Celtic would've been the possibility of playing Champions League football. That would have been amazing. But I had no interest in playing in the Scottish Premier League every week.

On top of that, I didn't want to leave England because of my family situation at the time. I'd already become a dad to Archie and my daughter, Beau, was about to join us – being a parent made me think differently about big career decisions. Plus, there was also the fact that I was going to be worse off financially. I don't know anyone who would've taken that lying down.

I got back to Hull and that decision went down like a shit sandwich, with extra shit on the side. The chairman went mental and told me that I'd led Hull and Celtic on by spending four days up there and then not signing for them. Which was nonsense because the gaffer had told me to take my time.

Adam Pearson was quite rude to me, but I gave as good as I got – I had to leave the whole football thing to one side for a minute, because I wouldn't have anybody talking to me the way he had. I thought they were taking advantage of me and warned him not to mistake my kindness for a weakness.

It wasn't really about the money in any case. If the move had been right, I would've taken the hit on a few grand a week. I just didn't want to move to Celtic at that stage of my career and life.

Hull really didn't like it, but my attitude was simple; they signed me to play for them, but now they didn't want me. There was little point having a go at me about that and pressurising me. That was only making the situation worse.

Looking back on it, I massively regret not joining Celtic as it was such a fantastic opportunity, but I had so many other things going on at the time that I couldn't see the wood for the trees.

Unfortunately, the whole episode triggered the unhappiest few months of my career as the club decided to take a harsh stand against me because I wouldn't bow to their pressure.

Instead of rubbishing my name and making me look really bad in the press, what I didn't get is why nobody from the club tried to renegotiate my contract with me if it was such a major burden for them? That would have been the sensible thing to do if you were running a football club.

But I didn't think Adam Pearson ran that club particularly well, especially when it came to paying me.

For three months after we got relegated, all the players were on a thirty per cent deferral of wages each month to help the club out after relegation. After those three months, everyone got paid in full. Well everyone, that is, except me. I stayed on a deferral for a couple of months extra, purely due to the size of my contract, which was completely unjust.

I had a meeting with the chairman and the financial consultant who had been brought in to advise Pearson on dealing with relegation, and both of them admitted they'd been wrong to do that, yet nothing was subsequently done about it.

At that point, I was completely fed up with football. The only person from the club who offered to help me was Ian Ashbee, who gave me a couple of people to phone for advice. Apart from him, not a soul did a thing and I lost all respect for the chairman and Nigel Pearson, who was being really weird with me.

When I came back from Scotland, I'd asked Nigel if I'd be able to play, but he said it would be quite difficult and my best option would be to try to get out on loan. So I asked him what would happen if the season started and I couldn't get out on loan. He said that we'd see.

What he meant by that was that I wouldn't be anywhere near the team, because every time I stepped on to the pitch Hull were contractually obliged to pay me £5,000 – at least that was my interpretation of it anyway.

Not only was I not playing, I was also made to train with the reserves and youth team to make me feel even less wanted. There was a clear message coming from the club. I'd heard about these kind of things happening to other players and now it was happening to me.

The season back in the second tier started badly for Hull as they took four points from their first five games. Believe it or not, the fans who had booed me on that awful day back in April, were now calling for me to play. And I thought I was playing in one match when I saw my name at the bottom of the squad sheet which was posted on the notice board one Friday.

I was pleasantly surprised and really looking forward to it as I'd been itching to get on the pitch. For all the shenanigans that had been going on off the pitch, all I wanted to do was go and do my thing on the pitch. I'd missed enough games through injury, and now I was missing them when I was one hundred per cent fit, which made the whole situation twice as frustrating.

So I turned up at the KC in my club tracksuit the following day at 1.45pm, which is when we always arrived for a 3pm kick-off. I walked into the stadium and was about to go into the changing room but Nigel Pearson was standing by the door.

'What are you doing?' he asked me.

'I saw my name was on the squad list . . .' I replied.

'No, you're not in it today.'

Perfect. Just what I needed. There was absolutely no need for me to suffer that indignity on top of everything else. I stayed to watch the game and lend my support to the boys, but I didn't hang around afterwards.

Then, a couple of weeks later, I saw my name on the list for a midweek home game against Derby. 'Here we go again,' I thought when I arrived at the ground for the match.

But this time, I walked straight into the changing room and was told I was starting the game. I couldn't wait to get out there and didn't let the opportunity slip as I played pretty well in a solid home win. Out of nowhere, without so much as a single word about it from the gaffer, I was back in the team for the next few games and then, just as mysteriously, I was out of it. Not on the bench, just completely frozen out.

Once again, I had to sit tight and bite my lip. I'd almost worn straight through it by the time I was next called into action two months later for a Boxing Day game at Sheffield United.

This time, I was on the bench and came on to score an injury-time winner. The lads were all buzzing when we got back into the changing room and so was I as it had been a while since I scored – I'd almost forgotten how to celebrate.

Nigel Pearson came into the room and the buzz quietened down as he spoke to us about the game. He picked out a couple of boys for praise and then he turned to me and said: 'I think you could work a bit harder on the pitch, you need to run a bit more.'

Blimey. I was only on the pitch for about half-an-hour and I scored the winning goal. There was no need for the gaffer to criticise me like that in front of all the boys. It just felt so spiteful.

Despite that run-in, I was given a few more appearances as we moved into the new year, which was Hull's way of showing other clubs I was fit and available to be taken on loan. It always boiled down to money. If Hull could get me off their wage bill, someone upstairs would get a pat on the back for doing a good job for the business. Make no mistake, that's why I was back in the squad again.

When you grow up being taught that football is all about the team and then you make it as a pro to find out that business comes first, it can leave you with a bit of an empty, horrible feeling.

I must have around 200 numbers in my phone of all the people I've met through football and would be happy to have a drink with. But how many of them do I actually trust? I doubt there's more than a dozen. And that's because we were all ships that passed in the night as the game became more and more money driven. We were just the pawns in that game, albeit pawns who earned a lot of cash.

It's hard to complain when I was lucky enough to do so well out of the game. But it's also hard to explain what football can be like sometimes – at Hull, I was treated with no respect or decency and feelings like that can linger longest.

Luckily, I'm a happy-go-lucky old sod so I didn't spend too much time moping around. Instead, I got my head down and got on with it, waiting for my fairy godmother – or Paul Jewell, as he's better known – to come and save me.

PILLAR 11

MAKE THE MOST OF YOUR DOWNTIME; WHY GO ON ONE NIGHT OUT WHEN YOU CAN GO ON TWO?

'Even the finest sword plunged into salt water will eventually rust.' ***Sun Tzu***

I grabbed the ball for the free kick, feeling as confident as usual about scoring. Just because I was thirty-three, playing on two dodgy knees and in the twilight of my career, didn't mean I'd lost any of my on-pitch swagger. You'd have had to wrestle me to the ground to nick the ball from me for any set piece – but my Ipswich team-mate Keith Andrews didn't fancy a tussle.

We were comfortably beating Coventry in a televised match when we won the free kick about twenty-five yards from goal. Keith also fancied himself in those situations, so he'd come over to stake his claim.

He was very much like me as a player in that he wanted to do everything on the pitch and had no interest in sharing the workload. Taking it in turns doesn't really tend to work for free kicks in any case because ideally you only want one player to be responsible for them so that man can get his eye in, get a feel for it in each game and gain more confidence.

'I want this one,' I told him straight away.

'Nah, nah,' he said, doing his best impression of a kid making an ambulance noise.

'No, I want it,' I insisted.

'Come on then, let's do rock, paper, scissors for it,' he said.

Whoah, hang on a minute. We're professional footballers, in the middle of a televised match and he wants to play a daft children's game to decide who should take a free kick?

After a second's reflection, I decided it was a great idea.

'You're on.'

One, two, three . . . Bang!

My rock crushed his scissors.

I was taking the free kick.

And I missed it.

By miles.

But it didn't matter too much as we won the game comfortably. Except the TV cameras had caught us playing our little game and the touchline reporter asked the gaffer Paul Jewell about it afterwards.

'It's a waste of time me doing free kicks and corners if they want to do their own thing,' he told them, which was a slightly softer version of what he told us afterwards.

'You two fucking about with rock, paper, scissors – that ain't the done thing, is it?' he said. 'You made us look like a pub team.'

But Paul knew what I was like from years before when we were at Wigan together. For all the planning he'd do in training and team meetings before games, I'd often go off and do my own thing, which drove him round the bend – at times, he told me, he wanted to kill me.

He still signed me again, though, so I couldn't have been that bad, could I?

And thank goodness he did come in for me again because

I was just about done with football after my career had gone completely off the rails at Hull.

I'd been in and out of the team under Nigel Pearson and the club were still desperate to get me off the payroll. Out of the blue, I got a phone call from the chairman Adam Pearson, telling me that Paul Jewell was interested in taking me on loan to Ipswich for the rest of the season.

Hallelujah.

Not only would I escape my Hull nightmare, I'd be playing regular football again and I'd be reunited with my old Wigan gaffer.

The phone call with Paul was one of the easiest conversations I've ever had in my life.

'Do you want to come and play for Ipswich on loan?' Paul asked me.

'Fucking right I do!' I replied. 'I'm not playing here and they don't like me. Of course I want to come.'

I raced down to Portman Road and couldn't wait to get started. I could tell from the minute I arrived that the place needed a lift so I took it upon myself to get the boys buzzing again – not that I needed much encouragement.

Paul had only been in the hotseat there for a couple of weeks when I turned up. He'd come in to replace Roy Keane, with the club sixth from bottom. And as I got to know my new team-mates, I realised that Keane had made quite an impact at Ipswich but not necessarily in the right way.

Not to put too fine a point on it, but Keane had scared the living shit out of those boys. It was such a quiet dressing room because the former gaffer had ruled with fear and an iron fist. That lot wouldn't have said boo to a goose so it

took a while for some of them to come out of their shells and realise it was fine to mess about a bit after training and enjoy their football again.

And as they all relaxed, they started to share some of their favourite Keane stories with me – blimey, it was almost like I was their football shrink or something. After hearing all their stories, it occurred to me I'd arrived there at just the right time as the bloke sounded like a proper, full-blown nutcase.

Once, after a match they'd lost, Keane had the whole team sitting in the dressing room and he was talking to them while doing his tie up in the mirror.

'Tactics,' he said. 'Everyone goes on about formation and tactics.'

He turned round for a moment, pointed to the tactics board in the changing room and asked one of his coaches to set it up, before continuing his rant about tactics while fiddling with his tie in the mirror.

After a minute, with absolutely no warning, he turned around from the mirror and launched himself two-footed into the tactics board, smashing it to pieces as his stunned team looked on with mouths wide open.

'That's what tactics mean,' he said, surveying the wreckage of the board. 'Fuck all in this game.'

But, by far my favourite Keane story was told to me by new team-mate Damien Delaney. Unsurprisingly, it came after another defeat when the gaffer was going off on one in the dressing room. This was all taking place in front of an old boy, who was stood at the door because he had to keep an eye on one of the players who was supposed to be doing a drugs test after the game.

When the drugs boys come along after the match, they have to stick with you until you can piss for them – which is why they're known as the 'piss fellas'.

So Keane was ranting and raving when he turned to one player and said, 'And you, if you carry on like that . . .' – he turned and pointed to the old piss fella at the door – '. . . you'll be taking the piss for the rest of your life like him!'

The place erupted. Even the innocent piss fella couldn't escape the fury of that man.

But that dressing room was soon alive and kicking again as we set about the business of moving away from the relegation zone. I was absolutely raring to go as I'd missed so much football, almost half the season. But my fitness was never in question and I hit the ground running in the first game I played, away to Derby, where I scored on my debut.

We were losing when the ball popped up to me about thirty yards from goal. I volleyed it first time and it thundered into the net via a bounce over goalkeeper Stephen Bywater, who probably should have saved it. What a C-U- . . . no actually, let's not go there.

That sparked a great run for me and the club as we finished the season well, moving into mid-table – I also banged in a few belting goals along the way, including two in a win at Cardiff. The first I smashed in from the far corner of the box into the opposite corner of the goal, and the other was a free kick, which I celebrated with an in-joke from Ipswich training sessions.

During our extremely lengthy warm-up and warm-down sessions with fitness coach Andy Liddell, the boys would always complain: 'Fucking hell, this is killing me!' So I developed this

daft way of running where I would lower my back a bit and take really silly stride lengths, a little bit like a chicken – I christened it the 'Energy Saver'. When they were all moaning, I would run about like a chicken and say, 'This ain't bothering me boys, I'm on the energy saver. You should really try this, lads, you can save so much energy.'

I'd only ever done it in training, but I gave it a spontaneous public airing after that goal, which the boys liked while nobody else would have had a clue what it meant. Nice one, Jim.

It was really just about enjoying the moment because it doesn't matter if you're twenty-three or thirty-three, you're always going to enjoy moments like those. The Ipswich fans were also loving it and they'd always sing this chant about me (it's to the tune of 'I Love You Baby' if you want to join in):

Oh Jimmy Bullard,
You're the love of my life,
Oh Jimmy Bullard,
I'd let you shag my wife,
Oh Jimmy Bullard,
I want curly hair too.

I'd heard it sung about other players too over the years, but it was still fantastic to hear it from a new set of fans when I'd only been at the club for about five minutes. The fans at Fulham also had a great chant about me (before they started singing that I was a greedy bastard – they literally changed their tune pretty quickly, didn't they?) which was a piss-take of the Liverpool song about Steven Gerrard to the tune of 'Que Sera Sera':

Jim Bullard, Bullard,
He's better than Steve Gerrard,
He's thinner than Frank Lampard,
Jim Bullard, Bullard.

It's always a weird feeling to hear a chant about yourself. At first, you don't really have a clue what's being sung as you're too wrapped up in the game, but after a while it occurs to you that's your name you keep hearing, or someone else might give you a nudge and tell you the fans are singing about you.

The giveaway that the fans haven't really got a specific chant for you was always 'There's only one Jimmy Bullard', which they used to sing to me at Peterborough.

But I certainly preferred hearing that than being jeered by Hull fans years later, and that whole experience seemed to be a distant memory when I was awarded the Ipswich Player of the Year trophy. I was gobsmacked as I'd only been there for sixteen games so I wasn't even sure if that was right. But I'd scored five goals in that time and played really well, so who was I to argue? Another one for the mantelpiece.

Sadly, that was to be my last really consistent, sustained run of good form.

Even though it had gone so well at Ipswich, when the season ended I was left in a sort of limbo as my loan was over and I was technically still a Hull player. Luckily, my form at Ipswich had helped spark a bit of interest in me from other clubs and there were a few approaches over the summer, with one of them happening at a rather unfortunate time.

I was on holiday in Ibiza with all my old mates. I have

football mates from all the teams I've played with; I've got golf mates from over the years; and the same with fishing too. I also have my old mates, the blokes I've known since I was at school, most of whom are lunatics. And there I was on holiday with them when I got a call from the Queens Park Rangers manager, Neil Warnock.

QPR had just been promoted to the Premier League and Neil was sniffing around in my general direction, so this was an amazing chance to get back in the top flight – well, it would've been had he not called while we were all getting blind drunk around the pool.

I foolishly answered the phone, more than likely because I was half-cut.

'Hello Neil, how are you doing?' I said, putting on my best possible I've-not-had-a-drink voice, one which is so ridiculous that it doesn't sound like me at all and, if anything, makes the other person suspect that I've had a drink.

I mouthed 'It's Neil Warnock' to my mates and they all started laughing and shouting as I tried to move away from them so we could speak properly.

'Sorry Neil,' I said, 'I'm on holiday with some mates and we've all had a couple of drinks.'

'It's fine, you're on your holidays,' he replied.

But, by then, I was cracking up laughing too because my mates were winding me up something rotten. I also found it quite funny that Neil Warnock was calling me on my holiday, because sometimes I just revert to being a football fan who thinks it's hilarious to talk to all these famous people.

While we carried on chatting, the nutters were trying to tape me to a chair with the aim of then throwing me into the pool, so while I was on the phone about a potential transfer, I was simultaneously trying to fight them off.

He was talking at length about pairing me in the middle with Shaun Derry, another experienced player, but I was clearly unable to concentrate on the conversation thanks to my inebriated state and the close attention of my mates.

After about ten minutes, I could tell that Neil was starting to think this might not be such a good idea after all and began to make his excuses. The conversation had started with him talking to me about playing for QPR, but by the time we said goodbye, he was pretty much saying he didn't think it would work.

When I told my mates, they roared with laughter at the snub and some of them still talk about it now, winding me up that Shaun Derry was a much better player than me. Still, that's what mates are for, right?

Luckily for me, Ipswich got off to a poor start to the new season and the fans were calling for the club to re-sign me. You're always a much better player in football when you're not actually on the pitch.

The pressure was on Paul Jewell as the club had lost four out of their first five matches of the season, including a disastrous 7-1 tonking at Peterborough. A few days after that match, I joined the club on a permanent deal. Coming in on the back of a result like that, it would have been hard not to make an improvement.

I must've done something right because I came off the bench in my first match against Leeds with us a goal behind and we scored two late goals to take the three points.

I'd love to take credit for either of them, but the truth is

I wasn't really involved because the gaffer now had me playing in a much deeper role than when I had been on loan earlier in the year. He wanted me to sit in front of the back four more, rather than in my usual floating midfield role where I'd pop up all over the park.

We played a midfield diamond and during my loan spell, I had been at the head of it, just behind the strikers, but once I'd signed permanently, the gaffer played me at the back of the diamond. I think it was because he had so many attacking midfielders like Keith Andrews and Lee Bowyer, so he wanted to fit everyone in.

Obviously, I preferred to play in my normal position and I was a bit upset about it, but I had to be professional, get my head down and get on with it. I decided not to make a fuss at all as I was just so happy to be playing again. After all the problems I'd had at Hull, the last thing I needed was another argument with the manager – especially not one who's keen on shutting heads in doors.

So I got on with it and struck up some good friendships with my new team-mates, including our striker Michael Chopra, another brilliant character and complete wrong 'un, who reminded me of my old mates.

I got to know him pretty well as I used to stay at his place twice a week so I would be local to the training ground. That way, I didn't need to up sticks and move house again and could base myself back in Cobham with Diane and the kids.

I never knew whether to take Chops seriously because there was always a little bit of the wind-up merchant about him. At one point that season, things weren't going too well on the pitch so the gaffer called a team meeting after training to allow us all to air our grievances. The idea was that it would be a constructive way of letting the players get those little simmering tensions out into the open with the aim of improving team spirit, unity and, ultimately, results.

So Chops, who'd scored seven times that season, went off on one about the lack of goalscoring support he was receiving.

'You can't talk,' said the gaffer. 'You haven't scored for years.'

'To be fair boss,' said Chops, 'you're better off signing Lionel Messi to play with these bunch of monkeys. There's no-one that can put a through-ball in and the seven I did score, I set up myself.'

Now, I don't know what goes on in the average workplace because I was lucky enough to be a footballer, but I'm pretty sure you cannot say that to your colleagues whatever your line of work. You certainly can't say that to your team-mates in football.

Chops coming out with that in front of twenty other pros was animal behaviour. I was crying with laughter at the nerve of the bloke and even the manager couldn't hide the smirk on his face at Chopra's sheer audacity. But none of the other boys found it amusing and thought he was a bit of an arsehole.

Chopra actually had a far worse problem than worrying about what his team-mates thought of him though, because he was a serious gambling addict. So serious, that he owed a bunch of gangsters a hell of a lot of money – about £150,000 to be precise.

One morning, this shifty-looking character wearing desert boots came on to the training ground. I took one look at him and instantly thought he was trouble as he looked a right handy bastard.

The gaffer called security, who moved the gangster on, but he waited across the road from the pitches, on the way to the changing rooms.

I was walking up that road when training had finished and was stood just behind Chops, when this bloke reappeared and walked towards us. He grabbed Chopra by the scruff of his neck and said: 'Are you Michael Chopra?'

Quick as a flash, Chops replied: 'No, it ain't fucking me mate, it's him over there', and pointed to our young left-back Aaron Cresswell, who was behind us.

'It is you, you cheeky bastard!' said the gangster, tightening his grip on Chopra's collar. 'I know it's you cos I googled you. Make sure you get my fucking money back, okay?'

'Okay, okay, okay, I'll get it for you,' said Chops, as the bloke let him go and walked off.

A couple of weeks later, the gaffer got a phone call from one of the gangsters, trying to shake him down for Chopra's money. 'Make sure your boy gets the money because otherwise I'm coming to the club to see you.'

The rationale was that they were clearly never getting their money off Chops, but they certainly had a better chance of getting it from the club. The last thing Paul needed was gangsters on his case, so the club gave Chopra a huge loan in order for him to pay off his debts, on the condition that he went into therapy for his gambling addiction.

Off he went to the Sporting Chance Clinic to sort himself out. I felt sorry for him being stuck there, but he had a bad problem and it needed fixing. Which was why I was very surprised to see my phone ringing with his name on the screen after he'd been in rehab for only three days.

'Hello Jim, I'm better!' he said brightly.

'What? You've only been there three days, you mug!' I replied, almost laughing but I thought better of it.

'You know what they let me do today? They put me at the bottom of the swimming pool and let me find myself. And now I'm complete.'

Now I didn't know whether to laugh or cry.

'Fuck off, you need three years at the bottom of a pool to sort yourself out!' was the best I could offer in the circumstances.

After a fortnight of rehab, Chops was back with the club again but the clinic hadn't sorted out his problems at all as I discovered one night when I was staying at his place. For starters, when I was talking to him, he wasn't focusing on a word I said. I know I'm not that interesting, but it was obvious his mind was elsewhere, which was a tell-tale sign.

I woke up at 4am on that particular night as I needed a wee – it happens when you get older, trust me – and as I walked to the bathroom I saw Chops looking at the racing odds on his telly using the red button, or whatever replaced Teletext.

He sprung up out of his seat and rushed to turn the telly off, saying, 'It's for my mate!'

'So why turn it off then?' I asked him, once I'd done my wee – I had to get my priorities straight.

'Because I was scared,' was his rubbish response, which made me laugh.

'Look, you don't have to lie to me,' I said.

'Please, please don't tell anyone,' he pleaded with me. 'They'll sack me if they find out, you know what they're like.'

I told him I wouldn't and I didn't. I'm a man of my word but I'm not sure if I was helping him by doing that. Weighing it up, he didn't need to be given the elbow by the club. That would only have made things much, much worse for him. What Chops and I really needed was a good night out. Or, as it turned out, two good nights out.

He had his gambling problems, while I had suddenly found myself on the bench unable to get in the team. The sitting role that the gaffer wanted me to play didn't suit my natural game. When I just signed, I had a decent run in the team as we won five of the first eight games I played, but a shocking run of seven straight defeats saw me lose my place and, from then on, I was only ever in and out of the starting line-up.

The gaffer had changed a bit too. He'd had massive success in the early part of his career at Bradford and Wigan, but he had a bad time at Derby, and Ipswich wasn't plain sailing either, so we all saw a slightly darker, harsher side to him. If we'd lost and he was angry with you, he'd let you know about it. There was no pussyfooting around the issue.

And he wasn't best pleased one Saturday in February when we'd ended a run of four straight wins with a heavy defeat at Brighton, a game I watched from the bench. Chops had been planning a night out for the squad the following week and the gaffer knew about it.

So twelve of us went out in London on the Tuesday and had a good time. Ten players decided they'd had enough, and then there were two.

Me and Chops.

So we did what any pair of blokes would do in that situation and headed up to Newcastle the following day for another bender. Chops made sure we were well looked after in his home city and we had a blinding time. I forget where we went but it definitely seemed like fun while we were there.

Being the reliable, conscientious pros that we were, we made sure we were back at Chops's place near Ipswich in time for training the following morning. We'd done the hard bit, which was making it back from Newcastle, but then Chops forgot to order the taxi to take us to training, the dopey sod.

So we rolled in there late on the Thursday, having had an extra day of partying in Newcastle, all of which added up to a furious gaffer. Naturally, I didn't think it was such a big deal, but Paul took a different view and made us train with the youth team that day. Even worse, he called me into his office after training and told me I was suspended for two weeks.

'What? That's a bit harsh isn't it?' I protested.

'You need to be taught a lesson,' he told me and I couldn't argue because his mind was made up.

I was absolutely gutted about it – even though I hadn't been playing regularly, I still needed that daily fix of training and the dressing room nonsense with the lads. Two weeks without that was like a life sentence for me.

I was even more furious when I found out that Chops had only been fined for his part in the night . . . sorry, nights out. No suspension for him, he was free to train the following day and play at the weekend. The gaffer explained to me that if he'd suspended Chops as well, he'd have ended up in Ladbrokes in five minutes so he had to keep him close. He wasn't wrong – as I knew better than anyone – and Paul would no doubt have been delighted with his decision when Chops scored the first goal in a win against Bristol City two days later.

I understood where he was coming from, but it still didn't add up to me – you can't have two different punishments for the same crime.

But I took my medicine, kept my mouth shut and got on with it because, even though I'd been in and out of the team, I was really enjoying my time at Ipswich. It was a fantastic club, I had a great rapport with the fans who were brilliant and the chairman Marcus Evans was a top man too. I was aware my football career was nearing its end so I couldn't do anything other than relish it, in exactly the same way as I savoured every second of those early experiences at Peterborough.

The Newcastle bender was the beginning of the end for me at Ipswich, however. I was only involved in one more game that season and that was the very last match of the campaign. That didn't dampen my enthusiasm that much though and I resolved to come back in pre-season doubly determined to work really hard and get myself back in the first-team reckoning. I wanted to show the gaffer and everyone else exactly what I had.

The only problem was that, by then, what I actually had was one very dodgy knee and another one that wasn't particularly clever. I was definitely not the same player who was called into the England squad three years before. The injuries were taking their toll and there was no doubt that they affected my performances, both physically and psychologically. And I think Paul realised that too – my absence from the side in the latter part of the previous season spoke volumes. Having said that, while the Premier League may have been out of my reach, I was still very confident that I could do a decent job in the Championship. So I worked as hard as I possibly could in pre-season training, doing pretty much everything bar putting the cones and bibs out for everyone (I'm not that stupid).

I played in a few friendlies and seemed to be doing okay, then one night I found myself playing in a match with youth and reserve players and only one other senior pro, my old Wigan pal Nathan Ellington. I'm no private investigator, but even I could work out that was bad news, because we shared the same agent and I knew The Duke was leaving the club as the gaffer didn't fancy him anymore. So where did that leave me?

It left me on the bench a week later for a friendly at Southend. Which on the surface doesn't sound so bad – it was a warm-up game after all. But it was two weeks before the start of the season and I felt like it was now or never for me. If I couldn't get on and show Paul what I could do there and then, I just had a feeling the writing might be on the wall for me. I wanted the club to know that I was desperate to play and that I wasn't going anywhere. And that was the moment when I asked Chris Hutchings to put me on.

A couple of days later, I was sitting with Paul in his office when he broke the news to me that I'd feared my whole career.

'Look Jim, it's not going to happen for you here,' he said.

No. Please no. I didn't want to hear this.

'As things stand now, I can't see that you'll be getting a game here this season.'

No. No. No.

All I could think about was Lee Bowyer who'd also been

released by Paul a few weeks earlier and hadn't found another club. He never would.

I tried to collect my thoughts, but it was tough.

'How long have you known about this?'

'I decided about two weeks ago,' he said.

What? Two fucking weeks?

'Paul, you're killing me. You're ruining me. Most clubs have already got their squads sorted for the season now, why didn't you tell me earlier? We know each other so well.'

'Look, I'm running the football club and that's my decision.'

We had a few words man-to-man – some things are worth risking another trapped head in the door for – and he apologised for not telling me earlier and explained he'd been thinking about it for a long time because it was the hardest football decision he'd ever had to make. He even said he'd tried to find another club for me. I know he meant well, but I felt that was going behind my back again like Hull did.

Finding out you're not wanted for anything in life is very tough to take. All I could think was that I was going to be out of football as a result of this. On the scrapheap. Done and dusted at thirty-three. I was devastated.

I may not have been the same player he'd had at Wigan, but I honestly did not believe that my form and ability had deteriorated that much in the year since I'd signed for the club permanently. How could it? Ability doesn't change that quickly. And what's more, if he wanted to see the best of me, then why not play me in the right position? I think he was just after younger players and had decided to release the older pros, like me and Bowyer. I also thought I was definitely still good enough to play for Ipswich Town, but it didn't matter what I thought.

Paul had made up his mind that I was no longer part of his plans there.

And he was the manager.

Bollocks.

PILLAR 12

FROM ONE CAREER GROWS ANOTHER. AS LONG AS YOU CAN PLAY GOLF

'When you reach the end of your rope, tie a knot in it and hang on.'
Confucius

The International Course at the London Golf Club is a picturesque setting for sport, right in the heart of the Kent countryside. It's a fantastic place to play golf, especially when you're participating in the regional qualifying rounds for the Open Golf Championship, the daddy of all golf tournaments.

That's where I found myself one beautiful summer afternoon, very much looking the part in my finest gear I'd chosen specially for the occasion. Ian Poulter would have been proud.

I was playing a shot to the green from the fairway with a lob wedge as there was a bunker in the way and I wasn't taking any chances. I discussed it with my caddy, Lee, then went through my pre-shot preparation and got in the mental zone.

'Nice and easy,' I thought. 'Nice and easy, arc it up over the bunker and on to the green. Nice and easy.'

I swung the wedge, drove it straight into the ground, then made a slight contact with the ball, which trickled forward about four yards.

And the red mist descended.

Suddenly, I was the thirteen-year-old who'd just lost at pool and was smashing the cue and throwing the balls around.

I looked across at Lee, a six-and-a-half-feet tall, absolute animal who wouldn't take any shit from anyone, and he could see from my eyes that I had lost it. 'Get away from me now' is what those eyes were saying and, at that moment, it wasn't possible to be far enough away from me. There's nowhere you can go.

I flung that lob wedge as hard as I could and it skidded across the grass of that beautiful course and clipped Lee on the shin before coming to a rest in the middle of the fairway.

He looked at me and I knew what that look meant.

'If you ever do that again, I will never carry your bag for you,' he said.

I was lucky, because if it wasn't Open qualifying I'm sure he would have given me a black eye, no question.

There I was, a thirty-four-year-old retired footballer, still acting like a stroppy, sulking teenager. The only reason why I hadn't behaved like that on the football pitch throughout my career was because my parents had forced me to completely change my attitude.

Once I started playing non-league, I played games with a completely different psychological outlook thanks to advice from my mum and dad. That fear of losing actually hindered my performances. I was a far better player when I put the whole win, lose or draw thing out of my mind and just focused on enjoying the moment and entertaining through my football. Losing that uptight and tense feeling which was all based around the result, allowed me to play far better football as I was performing without inhibitions.

It's a weird thing to admit, but there was a small part of me that didn't care about the result – that had to be the way in order for me to play to the best of my ability. Of course I was desperate to win every game but, in order to play well, I had to force myself to believe that it wasn't the be-all and end-all if the result didn't go our way.

People would say to me, 'Jim, you don't seem to take games seriously as you always play with a smile on your face.' But that was what worked for me. You could count on one hand the number of times I got booked in my career and I was never sent off. But it's not like I never made a tackle. Different things work for different players. Look at Wayne Rooney – he needs that anger and petulance that can sometimes make him look like a sulking kid on the pitch. Without it, he wouldn't be the same player. Which is why it's pointless when people have a go at him for picking up yellow and red cards. That's his game.

I need to bring a bit of my calming psychological approach to football into my golf game because that was the sport I decided to focus on after I called time on my football career.

I'd always felt like golf was there in the background, ever since my dad had bought me my first half-set of clubs when I was eight. I used to caddy for my old man at that stage as he played regularly, but then we started to play nine holes together and a couple of years later, I got my first full set of clubs.

I was never a member of a club as a kid but I used to spend ages pitching balls with a seven iron in a field behind my house, next to the River Cray. Like the green in front of my house for my football, I learned so much about golf in that field. It was only when I signed for Peterborough that I started entering golf competitions as I became a member at Thorpe Wood. In one summer up there, my handicap dropped from six to two, which is when I started to take it a little more seriously.

With all the injuries, I had plenty of time to improve my game and even Fabio Capello was impressed that I was a scratch player. Plenty of people said to me over the years that I could be a pro golfer, but I never really took that idea seriously. Well, not until I suddenly found myself twiddling my thumbs at home every day.

So I entered a EuroPro Tour qualifying event – the tour is a couple of levels below the main European Tour – but I was told I'd have to pay to enter as an amateur. Sod that, I just turned pro instead. Occasionally, people have a pop at me for turning pro, saying I'm too big for my boots, but the only reason I did was so I'd be able to win prize money if I played well.

That qualifying event went like a dream for me. I was one over par with just two holes remaining of my third and final round, a score that would've been good enough to put me on the tour.

My drive from the seventeenth tee nestled in some rabbit droppings, and I wasn't allowed to take a drop so I stupidly tried to hit a four iron out of it and hooked it left straight into the rough from where I bodged another shot out and ended up with a double bogey. With only the par three eighteenth left, that was game over for me and I went mental.

Despite the presence of cameras on the course, I couldn't control myself and smashed my club into the ground again and again. Messing up on the fifty-third of fifty-four holes was too much to take, and I probably made another fifty-four holes in the ground in my frustration.

Luckily, none of the officials seemed to see my Basil Fawlty-esque thrashings and I was invited back to play the odd tour event that summer because I'd done so well in qualifying. As brilliant as it was, playing proper professional competitive golf turned me into a bundle of nerves and I struggled to play my best. But there were two good things about it.

First, it got me out of the house, plus it also put me back into that competitive sporting environment again which was really important. And although I've had mixed fortunes since I joined the Tour – meaning I've either done badly or really badly – I was learning all the time and decided to stick at it and keep believing in myself. After all, if I hadn't had that belief in my football when everyone around me was saying no, I would never have made it to the Premier League.

Sadly, that top-flight experience seemed a distant memory when I was released by Ipswich.

One minute I was about to start a season playing in the Championship, the next I wasn't even playing in my back garden. For the first time in my career I didn't have a club, which is a pretty crucial part of the whole being-a-footballer thing.

My old man was there for me as usual and, together with my new agent Simon Dent, we all rang round a load of clubs, letting them know that I was available, fit and raring to go for the new season. At that point, retiring was not a thought that had ever entered my mind as I still felt I could do a job at a high level.

There was a mixed response from the clubs we contacted. Reading manager Brian McDermott returned my call and we had a long chat – nothing ever came of it, but I really appreciated him taking the time to talk to me about my predicament. And the same can be said for Chris Powell at Charlton and Kenny Jackett at Millwall, who both made time for a chat, while I exchanged answerphone messages with Dougie Freedman at Crystal Palace.

As nice as all that was, plenty of others didn't return my calls and the overall result was that I was still a footballer without a club. A very weird feeling. Suddenly, I didn't have anywhere to go every day, no training ground, no matchdays. I tried to stay calm about the situation but that was hard as I was so keen to carry on playing.

My mood was up and down like a yo-yo and it was during a bit of a despondent phase when I picked up the phone to a random football agent I hadn't worked with before called Rob Segal.

'How do you fancy playing for MK Dons?' he said. 'They've got a really good up-and-coming manager called Karl Robinson, they play good football and . . .'

I was already halfway round the M25 before he'd even finished his sentence.

I was back. It didn't matter that MK Dons were in League 1, I just wanted to play.

Karl rang me and we had a good chat, he sounded like a top bloke. He also sent me out some discs of their recent matches to show me the way his club played, and they did look really good. They got the ball down and passed it, and the keeper always rolled it out. I was pleasantly surprised how well they passed it as it had been quite a while since I'd last played at that level with Peterborough and Wigan, but things had obviously changed.

I went up to Milton Keynes to meet Karl and he told me

he didn't have much money to offer me – he couldn't do better than £1,000 per game.

'Don't worry about it,' I said. 'I'll play for nothing. I just want to play football.'

Eighteen months earlier, I was still a £45,000 per week player at Hull, and now I was on £1,000 a week with MK Dons, playing in the third tier of English football again. Football really is mental sometimes.

The first thing I had to do was improve my fitness so I spent a couple of weeks training with my new team-mates, which meant I got to know them a bit before I had to go on the pitch with them.

I came on as a sub in a home win against Carlisle and had a twenty-minute run-out which was good. I even managed to make it into the opposition box, latching on to a loose ball and getting a shot in. The shot was blocked, but it felt good to be playing again and the fans were all brilliant to me.

Three days later, I started my first game, a Johnstone's Paint Trophy tie against Northampton, something of a local derby.

And that's when my career pretty much ended. Just like that. At Sixfields. With all due respect, it wasn't the most glamorous location for my swan song and there were only three thousand punters in the ground that night. What's more, none of them would've even known what had happened.

What did happen was that a little Northampton winger accidentally put his knee straight through the top of my right knee and I felt like I'd been shot. My right knee was the one which had been operated on twice and it wasn't a massive fan of collisions with anything, let alone with a younger, far better-looking knee, smashing against it at pace.

The pain passed and I carried on playing, but by half time my knee was stiffening up so I kept on my feet in the dressing room as I really wanted to make the best possible impression in my first start for my new club. But I only managed to last ten minutes of the second half before I had to come off as there was too much pain and stiffness to carry on.

I went to Northampton's medical room where I was given ice to put on my knee while keeping my leg raised. After a while, I plucked up the courage to lift the ice pack off my knee to survey the damage. That's when I realised the full extent of what had happened – the nightmare had returned.

I couldn't actually see my knee as it had swollen up so much. A virtual swimming pool of fluid had gathered there and it wasn't a pretty sight.

That was the moment when I knew it was over.

I wasn't prepared to put myself through that pain any longer. If I took another knock on that knee, I might easily do something so long-lasting that I wouldn't be able to walk properly again. I'd reached the point where it just wasn't worth it anymore.

The truth was that I couldn't do anything on the pitch that I was once able to. I was a very poor imitation of the midfielder who was called into the England squad and was once worth £5 million.

I was also well aware that I had been lucky to have the career I'd had. I had achieved things I never would have dreamed of and played until I was thirty-four so I couldn't really have any complaints. Especially when I look at someone like Dean Ashton, whose career was over at the age of twenty-six.

My surgeon, Steady, had told me that my knee wouldn't

ever feel the same again after the operations but that I would learn a different way to play, to make up for its deficiencies. He was right and it worked to an extent, but the psychological damage caused by the injuries was something that could never be healed.

The truth is I was a little bit scared of getting hurt again and once you acknowledge that feeling, it's impossible to feel like the same player, because you're always going to be playing slightly within yourself.

I couldn't train the way I wanted to and I had no pace. One morning during training, after the swelling in my knee had gone down, Alan Smith was leaning up against me during a match and I just collapsed on the ground like a bag of shit. It was so disheartening as I felt like a delicate, glass ornament. And in my experience, delicate, glass ornaments do not make good footballers.

More than anything though, it was just embarrassing. I had nothing left to prove to anyone. I did not need to be sitting on the medical bench three weeks after signing for a new club. The signs were all there, I saw them and I eventually acknowledged them and took action.

I managed one more sub appearance against Yeovil and was on the bench again for the following game against Notts County without getting on. But that Alan Smith moment had made up my mind for me and I woke up a couple of days later and just thought 'No, sod it'.

I called Karl and explained my decision to retire to him. He was surprised but he understood where I was coming from. The chairman Peter Winkelman was very good about it too and told me to take a few weeks to think about it.

But I knew it was over because my knees wouldn't allow me to play anymore. And every day since that I've woken up and been able to walk without any problems, I feel like I made the right decision. With all due respect to MK Dons, I was playing in League 1 and my football was never going to improve again as I couldn't see any Indian summers on the horizon for me.

Football had changed so much since I first started out. The game had become so serious, which sucked the life out of it for a happy-go-lucky player like me. There was a world of difference between the changing room spirit at West Ham in 1999 and Ipswich in 2012.

When I first started, the players used to stick together in the changing room and look out for each other all the time. If someone turned up late for training, instead of making sure that player was fined by the club, we'd all cover for that bloke and try to help him, even if it meant telling the odd porky to the gaffer.

By the time I finished my career, players were dishing out fines to each other left, right and centre for all sorts of nonsense reasons like not having exactly the right gear on or being five seconds late. Maybe I'm old-fashioned, but that's not the way it should be. If I was a club captain – okay, I never met a manager who thought that would be a good idea – and another player had stepped out of line, I'd go and see the gaffer with him and sort it out.

The lack of camaraderie and unity in the dressing room was another reason why I had no regrets about my decision even though almost every pro I knew told me that I would miss all that daily dressing room banter.

They were wrong. I didn't miss that side of things at all. Don't get me wrong, I loved that side of the game. Turning up at the training ground every morning and larking about with the boys. I probably spent more time laughing than playing football; I was privileged to be able to do that for a career.

But I have all my old mates I grew up with and I have exactly the same kind of relationship with them and can always get up to mischief with them. And that same daft spirit is there with all of my golf and fishing boys, too.

What I have missed the most, however, is the entertainment factor. Having the ability to perform in front of twenty-, thirty-, or forty-thousand people on match days was an incredible buzz, an extraordinary adrenaline rush.

And I really miss that. It kills me how much I miss it. But there's no replacing it. You cannot replicate feelings like those I had when I scored my first Premier League goal at West Brom. But you can cherish it at the time and remember it for all time – and, ask any of my team-mates on the bus with me after that match, I did exactly that.

Saturdays now fill me with a kind of horror, as I walk around like a junkie, desperately looking for that next fix with no idea where it's going to come from.

I've not watched much football since I quit because that kills me too. And, although I love him to bits and he's a top, top man, watching Jeff Stelling on *Soccer Saturday* does my head in as it just reminds me how much I miss playing. Stop it, Jeff – you're killing me, absolutely killing me.

I always have to get out of the house and do anything but watch that on a Saturday. I'll go to a mate's, go fishing, take the kids out, play golf – anything that will take my mind off

the fact that I'm not playing football in front of tens of thousands of people.

That's why I think that so many players struggle when their careers end because you have to be completely ready for that moment. That feeling of loss. Of emptiness. If you're not prepared for it, you'll find out about it very quickly and it will hurt.

It can be a very dangerous time and I can admit I struggled a bit here and there, but I'm lucky to have a lot of inner strength to get myself through low times. Others don't have that and that's why you'll see ex-pros go off the rails sometimes. They're looking for something to give them the same buzz, but they can't find it. And that's because it doesn't exist.

Another unique thing about football is that you build up very strong bonds with other players very quickly. Over a career, there will be dozens or even hundreds of people you'll become close to, but the minute you retire, where are they? Do you hear from them? Do you bollocks!

I found myself looking through old pictures and cuttings from my career. Incredible moments, winning trophies, receiving medals – highs that are way higher than I could have got in any other profession. Looking through the old stuff, I had a lump in my throat; I had a right moment before I pulled myself together and told myself to stop being such a soppy bollocks. Because I had no reason to feel disappointed by my retirement, not when I had inhaled every second of that amazing ride I went on.

From the first time I went to Anfield with West Ham, I drank it all in, every single moment. When I celebrated on the pitch, I always went over the top, just so I would never be able to look back and say I wished I'd gone even more mental.

I had an absolute ball, but life goes on and it was time for me to explore new avenues and opportunities. And keep myself busy, because it's the boredom that's really dangerous.

Golf certainly helps with that, but so does fishing. Angling can be a very lonely sport but when I go to my fishing club, I lose myself in it as there's so much to think about. If you're not into the sport, it's probably hard to understand what I mean by that, but there's a certain mystery to fishing. What's in the water and where in the water is it? You've got to work it out for yourself.

Fishing is one of the most natural things in the world. It's pure instinct because, once upon a time, we all had to catch fish to eat so we could live. So it's all about hunting and there's a proper craft to it which I love. That skill element shouldn't be dismissed – you're taking on a fish in its natural habitat, which is a huge challenge.

During my career, fishing helped me massively. If we were given a few days off in the middle of the season, loads of the boys would fly off to Dubai, but I would just drive over to my local fishery for a couple of days to switch off and get away from the world. While I was at Wigan, that meant a trip to Brookside where I became mates with a lot of the locals, including England international Stuart Conroy. We'd always meet up on a Sunday, go fishing, then go for a pint. It doesn't get better than that.

Down south, I fish for Dorking, probably the best club in the country if not the world. Imagine playing your football for Barcelona – that's what it's like to fish for Dorking. And because I'm still just a big fan at heart, it's like I'm fishing with all my idols when I go there. Former world champion Will Raison was someone I used to read about when I was a kid and now we fish together and socialise now and again. I know it may sound sad to you, but that really is living the dream for me.

A fishing competition is an amazing thing to be a part of as it's really down to who is the best hunter. It's properly primitive. There's normally around fifty people spread around a lake for five or six hours – you could be playing as an individual or as part of a team like I did with Dorking. Usually, the biggest weight of fish wins the competition – it doesn't matter whether you've landed loads of little tiddlers or one enormous catch. The best anglers are always the best hunters and it's fascinating to watch them. Will just seems to know everything that's happening under the water the whole time. It's actually quite scary.

My angling obsession has also taken me to some of the most beautiful places in the country, like the River Wye in Herefordshire, a truly picturesque location. The riverbanks are surrounded by fields of cattle and you have to really keep your eyes open at all times to take in the nature. I saw a forty-pound salmon leap out of the water right in front of my eyes, while buzzards flew overhead. It's almost like being in a fantasy sometimes as it's such a world away from, well, the world.

It's a different kind of buzz altogether, but, like the golf, it certainly helped me focus away from the fact that I'd retired from football.

I can't say the same for my post-football media career, though. If one thing is going to make you think about playing football, it's talking about playing football. But the fact that there were TV channels, radio stations and other corporate organisations out there prepared to pay me for my thoughts, softened the blow somewhat.

I was fortunate enough to already have an established media presence, so I felt fairly comfortable when *Sky Sports News* asked me to go into the studio and describe a Newcastle Europa League match to all the viewers. Until I got there, that is. Because they just handed me two sheets of paper with the teams written on them and told me, 'On you go Jim, you're live!'

I would've thought I might have needed a bit of training for something like that and given how Sky broadcast into so many people's homes, I just assumed things might have been a bit different. I'd never talked about a game live on the telly before so I was expecting it to be a little more structured; I could easily have frozen in the camera lights.

As the game kicked off I felt like I'd been chucked right in at the deep end, but I just said what I saw and relaxed into it after five minutes. In the end, I enjoyed it but I didn't really get any kind of buzz from it like I did from playing football.

I also did some presenting for BT Sport, which saw me go down to Poole to play with the England beach soccer team. That all came about through my mate Chris Nutbeam, who used to work on *Soccer AM*. He knows how my mind works and just asked me to be myself on camera, not to worry about swearing as they could edit it all out and just have fun. Those were the kind of instructions I would have got from Barry Fry before a match, so it was music to my ears.

Beach soccer was a breeze compared to my next assignment for them where I was taken for a spin by Elfyn Evans, the FIA World Junior Rally champion. That was definitely the best TV job I've had – I didn't know anything about rallying before and it was amazing to go behind the scenes of a sport like that.

Having said that, I think I'd rather have more knee surgery than sit in a car with that nutcase driving again. He flung me round corners at ridiculous speeds while the whole thing was filmed inside the car so I had to pretend I wasn't shitting myself. I didn't do a very good job of that and I felt lucky to get out of that car alive.

Almost as bad was my appearance on talkSPORT with Colin Murray. My relationship with the station began when I received a call out of the blue asking me if I wanted to do breakfast with Alan Brazil. 'No problem,' I told them, 'what time and where are we eating?'

Once they'd stitched their sides back together, they explained I had to be at the studios at 5.15am ahead of the show's 6am start. That involved getting up so early there was little point in going to bed. But I did it because it was always worth keeping my hand in with the media work and staying in the spotlight.

They sent a car to pick me up and I turned up at talkSPORT Towers in the middle of the night, all bright-eyed and bushy-tailed. There was no sign of Alan, so the producers stuck a load of papers in front of me and started to worry me by telling me to read this, look at that, do say this and don't say that. I started to think this was a bit of a mistake.

I was there for ages, getting myself into a panic and all that time nobody had any idea where Alan was. Suddenly, at five minutes to six, the big Scotsman rolled in and said to me: 'Right, take no notice of all these fuckers and just say whatever you want.'

This was more like it.

In the blink of an eye, we were sitting in the studio, the big, red 'ON AIR' sign had flicked on, I had a huge pair of headphones on my bonce and I didn't have a clue what I was supposed to do.

I needn't have worried though as Alan made it so easy for me as he waltzed through the show. He's a completely off-the-cuff character in a world which has become too formal, with everyone afraid of making mistakes; he taught me not to be too concerned with stuff like that, which probably explained why I ended up making a complete tit of myself by singing 'My Way' on Colin's show a couple of months later.

The timing of his programme was much more up my street, given that it started at 10am, when footballers usually arrive at training. I was on a couple of times with him, but there was one show where I was put on the spot and asked to sing live on air to raise £1,000 for charity. Didi Hamann wasn't available that day so they asked muggins. How could I say no?

So I belted it out the best I could and got a bit carried away because there was also a camera in there; I smashed Frank Sinatra's version to pieces and did likewise to the microphone which fell apart in my hands.

The one thing I tried to avoid at first among all the media work was out-and-out punditry, mainly because I didn't really get it. After all, how does anyone really know what's going to happen in a game? They don't.

When Wigan were promoted to the Premier League, no pundit, journalist or any other so-called expert believed we had what it took to stay up. I found that quite strange because I was pretty certain that the large majority of them had never seen us play in our promotion season. How could they have possibly known how we would do in the top flight?

I never spend that much time reading the papers, but the boys always kept me informed and it seemed there was a stone wall of pundits (I made that one up) telling us 2005/06 would be our first and last Premier League season. Last time I checked, Wigan stayed in the Premier League until 2013 so they were wrong about that one for starters.

Which brings me nicely to my theory about pundits – not to put too fine a point on it, they don't know fuck-all. That's right, they have no idea what's going to happen. No-one knows! All the pundits are guessing, which is why they were all wrong about Wigan. They're just surmising and doing their job. It seems sensible for them to assume that the promoted clubs would struggle in the Premier League, but football doesn't really work like that.

Who had a better chance of staying in the Premier League in 2005/06 – a team that was on the up with a bit of money to spend like Wigan, or a team like Birmingham who hadn't exactly set the league on fire the previous season? The answer is, of course, Wigan. And Birmingham went down. Isn't hindsight a wonderful thing?

I was asked to do a bit of punditry myself after I finished playing.

'So what do you think the score will be?' they asked me. How the fuck do I know?

That wasn't the exact answer I gave but it pretty much summed up what I was thinking.

The fact is that if anyone was a really good pundit, they'd be a top gambler, earning loads of money, but none of them are because they're no good at it.

I was also asked for my expertise at the 2013 FA Cup final

between underdogs Wigan and moneybags Man City on the Club Wembley stage, in front of all the corporate punters. I was representing my old club while Danny Mills was doing the same job for Man City, with Jake Humphrey presenting. Naturally, when Jake asked me what I thought of Wigan's chances, I told him that I thought they were going to win. I just had a feeling for them on the day and there was nothing more to it than that.

Fuck me. At least one thousand people went absolutely mad, heckling me and telling me that I didn't know what I was on about, adding that I was a mug for good measure.

The good thing about that gig was that you get to go back on stage at the end of the match to review the game, and I very much enjoyed my smug told-you-so moment, after watching Wigan dictate the game and outplay City to win the cup. Not one pundit predicted that because, ultimately, none of them had any clue what was going to happen. I just had a hunch Wigan would do it.

And that's when I realised that despite all my punditry theories, I was actually pretty good at it and I've been lapping up the opportunities ever since. I go with my gut, that's the only way I've ever known. Much like Chris Kamara, the only pundit I've always loved.

The man is a hero because he's completely spontaneous. You never really know what's going to happen next when he's on air. That, and we've both got great hair.

Which probably helped me to get noticed when I was a kid and also in my early career (not Kammy's hair, mine). If I was starting out again now, I honestly don't think I'd be given that chance again as the game has become so much harder to get into. It's now completely global and clubs have so much money that there's no need for them to take a chance on a local lad doing well.

And I did do well, exceeding all expectations, even my own.

But the funny thing is that in fifteen years of meeting fans in the street, I can count on one hand the number of people who have ever said something along the lines of 'What a player you were'.

What every other person says, without fail, are things like: 'What about you when you were looking at Duncan Ferguson, eh?'; or 'What about you when you cuddled the ref that time?'; or 'What about you when you did that interview and you couldn't stop laughing – what were you laughing at?'; or 'What about you when you were fooling around with Freddie Ljungberg? You're nuts, you!'

It's always about the stuff that I did around football, rather than the football itself. Those are the things that I'm known for in the game and I think because of all those incidents, people always saw me as much more approachable than the average footballer.

Some people say the fans identified with me more because of all that stuff, but I'm not sure about that. Does that mean they jumped over a load of people in the penalty area on a Sunday morning?

I think that people just recognised that I was a bit of a wrong 'un, not quite wired right, however you want to put it.

I love that and wouldn't have it any other way.

Je ne regrette rien.

Whatever that means.

PILLAR 13

ALWAYS LEAVE THEM WANTING MORE . . . HANG ON, I THOUGHT THERE WERE ONLY 12 PILLARS?

'The greater the difficulty, the more the glory in surmounting it'
Epicurus

'Jesus Christ! What is that?' I said, absolutely shitting myself in the near darkness of an underground tunnel that was almost fully submerged in water. There was a fabric sheet covering me, but something was walking around on top of it and, therefore, on top of me.

My heart was beating off the scale as I ripped open the Velcro on the fabric, and saw a load of water dragons leaping around and looking mean.

'Fucking hell!' I yelled as I leapt back behind the Velcro. This was not at all funny. Yet, on safe ground above me, I could hear Ant and Dec practically crying with laughter. Okay, it was quite funny, looking back at it now.

There I was in my swimming shorts, T-shirt and a pair of goggles trapped inside the Tunnel of Terror, being watched by millions of people on ITV's *I'm A Celebrity . . . Get Me Out Of Here*!

But I wasn't thinking about anyone on their sofas at home. I was just focusing on getting through this ten-minute ordeal that was turning me into a bit of a nervous wreck. And plenty worse was still to come.

With Ant and Dec's laughter ringing in my ears, I prepared to dive into the Perspex box that was full of water – and the dragons – to try to grab two stars that would earn my celeb mates (ooh, listen to me) and me some much-needed food. Not that I felt any pressure about that. I didn't give a monkey's really – I just wanted to do my best.

But as I started to enter the water, the little bastard dragons started leaping up at me.

'You're alright! You're alright! You're alright! Easy son!' I told them. I'm not sure if they understood me, but I got in the water, grabbed the stars and dived back out to the next bit of fabric that was separating me from the next box.

I opened that one up and was greeted by fifty giant eels. 'Look at the size of 'em,' I yelled to more guffaws from Ant and Dec. The eels were absolutely enormous; these boys were certainly not freshwaters. I got in the box and started kicking at them and they all came up round me. My heart was pumping so fast. And my swear count was going through the roof too.

Thanks to my Special-Forces-style combination of violence and extreme swearing, I managed to grab another star from among the monster eels, and a fourth from the next box that was full of crabs, who I correctly predicted wouldn't jump up at me.

Two stars to go. My heart must have been in dangerous territory, but I was right into the challenge now and I opened the last bit of fabric to see what awaited me in the last box.

Oh no.

Snakes.

My biggest fear.

I yelled. I swore. I closed the Velcro.

In between giggling fits, Ant managed to tell me that they were water pythons. There was no way I could go in that box with them. I had another look in. 'Bastards,' I screamed. 'Get out of it, will ya! Fuck off!'

I was more or less treating them like bouncers who'd kicked me out of a club. And we all know who wins in those situations. This one was no different.

I tried to calm my breathing down and considered making a leap for the last stars, but as I did so I felt one of the pythons on my shoulder. If viewers thought I'd been sweary before then they were mistaken as I gave it everything I had out of sheer terror.

I got out of there and Dec was laughing so hard I thought he was going to shit himself. The boys told me it was one of the funniest Bushtucker Trials they'd ever done and that I'd worn out the bleep machine. At the time I had no idea that I'd been swearing so much – the adrenaline rush was so big my head was still all over the place. Four out of six stars wasn't a bad effort so I was quite happy with that.

That was the first trial of the series – my adoring public had voted for me to do it, probably because of the way I'd reacted to putting my hand in some water when the show had started a couple of days earlier. At that point, I was on a Gold Coast beach with Melanie Sykes, having just been flown in by a chopper – a scenario which would've been beyond my wildest dreams just a few months before until, out of the blue, my agent rang me and told me I'd been approached to go on the show. It didn't take me long to say yes as I wasn't doing much at the time and this was the exposure I really needed to try to carve out a different career for myself.

ITV got back to me and told me that I hadn't been chosen among the starting line-up of ten people for the show, but I was on the list of reserves and I might join the show a bit later. I was happy with that and a film crew came over to my house to record interviews about what I was planning on doing in the jungle just in case I got called from the subs bench.

Being completely honest, I did have the odd moment of doubt about whether I should do it, but everyone goes through it. Only one footballer had ever been on the show – Neil 'Razor' Ruddock – so it was a great opportunity for me. Diane and the kids were right behind me, as were my mum and dad, although they were a bit nervous as they know I can be a bit mad and weren't sure how I'd react. They needn't have worried. Okay, maybe just a bit.

A few days before I was due to fly out to Australia, ITV called again and told me I had been promoted to the main cast for the show. I was ecstatic. From being a maybe to a definite was unbelievable for me. And off I went.

A lovely fella from ITV called Jonathan acted as my chaperone. He accompanied me on the flight and then spent six days in a hotel with me, the poor sod. We weren't allowed out as ITV didn't want anyone to know who was going in the jungle, meaning I drove poor Jonathan up the wall. I'd be up early in the morning, in bed late at night and barely let him sleep. I was too hyper, and by the end he couldn't deal with it. Another one I'd ruined.

I managed to escape from the hotel a couple of times, and

wondered off to a local restaurant but there wasn't a massive amount going on over there.

Then it was showtime. The first time I met my campmates was in a lovely villa. You had to cross a 'red carpet' style bridge to get there and I was so nervous that I nearly fell off the bloody thing into the water. Seeing all the cameras and crew on set didn't help either but a glass of bubbly soon settled the nerves. After the meet and greet, we had another night in the hotel and then the show started for real.

Which is how I ended up on a secluded beach with Mel. We were plunged straight into a task where we had to retrieve some letters from a load of crates that were filled with water and other creatures.

I was more than aware of what could have been there, but I probably shouldn't have jumped out of my skin when I put my hand into the crate and felt some water. It was always going to be hard to be taken seriously from that point and it was no surprise I was voted to do a few trials after that.

Luckily, Mel braved the water – and the eels, tiny crocs and crabs – and managed to grab every letter so 'we' succeeded in our mission.

We then had a long old trek to get to the camp. I'd always wondered what the camp really looked like and when we finally made it there, I couldn't believe how small it was. It was tiny. I looked up and there were trees 100 feet tall and as much space as you like, but down below, absolutely nothing. I couldn't work out how we were all going to sleep in there. And the noise was just deafening. I actually miss that jungle noise – and my campmates.

Sykesy was quality. She was more like a geezer, in the nicest possible way, and we got on very well. Well, she laughed at my jokes anyway, and we even went out for drinks after the show.

Then there was 'Foggy' – Carl Fogarty to be accurate – who I quickly became very close to as we have a lot in common. Yes, I know he's the most successful World Superbikes racer of all time, but we have other stuff in common, honest. We bonded very quickly and it was the same when the *X Factor* fella Jake Quickenden joined us in the camp. Those three were probably the people to whom I was closest, but I got on with everyone – and drove them all mad.

First thing in the morning, I'd be out of my hammock in a flash. And I wasn't having any lazy bastards still kipping on my watch.

It's not that I needed to be the life and soul of the party, but if I'm up, everyone's up – that's how it's always been with me, cameras or no cameras. Even when I'm going fishing at 7am, I get bored sitting in the van on my own so I'll call my mum and wake her up for a chat. I can't help it. That's why, back in the jungle, I was straight in everyone's faces – if I saw someone still asleep I was over there, waking them, shaking them, lying on them, even jumping on them if necessary.

I sang too. One morning, everyone was still in their hammocks so I tucked my t-shirt into my pants, then hitched the Y-front right up and started doing a little dance while singing *Pass The Dutchie*. I'm pretty sure that one went down well.

But it wasn't all fun and games in there. It's hard for people to understand just how tough it can be in the jungle when you're starving. We were existing on as little as three spoonfuls of rice for every meal. The only extra food you get given is a little sachet of salt and electrolytes to put in your drink every six days to stop you getting cramp. I struggle with my stomach at the best of times and at one stage in there, I didn't go to the loo for ten days – so they gave me some prune juice. There were no other extras, meaning it was so tough that I considered quitting a few times – especially when I started hallucinating.

One day, I was walking down to the swimming pool to cool my water bottle down. No word of a lie, as I walked down the steps towards the pool, I started seeing little pizzas on each step! I went into the hut to talk to the producers.

'I'm in a bad way. Either bring me some food or I'm gone. And get the doc . . .'

There was about five hours until dinner-time and I was advised to rest so I went to sleep and got through it. That was the closest I came to leaving, but however low I got in there, a mate like Foggy would always get me through it.

He was like a brother really as we saw things very similarly, and we had such a laugh together. We had a right howl, especially during the first ten days or so.

There's so much that goes on in the jungle that they don't show on the telly – probably with good reason. For example, we all knew Kendra and an ex-boyfriend had made a sex tape which had been leaked online. So I wasn't shy about winding her up.

'So did he use the old tripod or what?' I asked her with a completely straight face while Foggy started wetting himself. 'Or was it the old hand-held?' I continued, getting myself into a cameraman's position, really going for it with all the acting.

Kendra wasn't having any of it, but Foggy spent the rest of the day struggling to breathe as he was laughing so much.

He really cracked me up. I think he thought that the more he did in the show, the better it would be for him. He's like a whirlwind, a little Tasmanian devil. He'd be up bright and early in the morning and would go down to the bottom of the jungle, fetch some wood for the fire and come back. Then he'd go and do the whole thing again, and again. Three times he'd make that return trip. He'd then start the fire, come and sit down and say, 'Jim, I'm fucked here!'

'I should fucking think so, you ain't stopped,' I replied. 'No one's even brushed their teeth yet. No one's even got out of their hammocks to start the day.'

'My energy's up and down, Jim.'

'You've just run down there three times. You're living like you do in real life but you can't because you haven't got any energy in here,' I counselled wisely. Not that he listened. He just couldn't get it into his head so he'd be out of breath, like a big kid, and then he'd sit down for two hours and wouldn't move because he was shattered. Me and Jake would look at each other and say: 'He's off his head, this character.'

Jake also cracked me up. One day, he started punching himself in the face and yelling, 'I'm going mental in here!' He hit himself so hard he actually made his nose bleed which had me in stitches, as you'd expect.

Me and him dressed up as superheroes on another day. We just went off on one, running around the camp like a pair of nutters and made everyone laugh. Anything to pass the time.

Of course, when we weren't doing that, there was the

endless banter, mainly between myself, Foggy and Jake. And, funnily enough, that's what lead to me being turfed out first.

On a daily basis, there would always be a lot of piss-taking between us, most of which wasn't shown on the telly. Regular themes would be Jake and Foggy saying I was a shit footballer, me and Foggy having a pop at Jake for not being famous and we laughed at Foggy, well, just for being Foggy.

But the best banter always came after the trials, particularly if anyone had let themselves down. After that first tunnel of terror, I was back in the spotlight a couple of days later when I had to do an eating challenge with Kendra – and some of those horrific tastes and smells will live with me forever.

There were ten things to taste, and we had to throw a dart at a board full of L's and S's to see whether we'd have to have a large or small portion of each dish. Fortunately, this is where my darting prowess came in very handy. Or so I thought.

To be honest, I still don't like talking about this trial as I can still taste certain things in the back of my throat that I never want to taste again. But seeing as you asked . . .

It started with Kendra having to eat a deer's penis, which she did relatively easily although she did stop in the middle to inform everyone watching that: 'The penis is in my throat.' I erupted, and Ant and Dec did a very good impression of a couple of giggling schoolboys too.

My first plate was a pair of cow's lips – as I'd hit the small section of the dartboard, I just had to chew down a tiny bit which I did, no problem. It tasted quite beefy actually . . . as it would, being meat from a cow.

It got worse on my next go which was a witchetty grub.

The problem was that the wriggly little fella was very much alive and kicking. 'Outrageous,' I gasped, closed my eyes and bit into it, managing to chew it down and swallow.

After I coached Kendra through eating a fish's eye, I stepped up to the oche and completely missed the small section, meaning I had to eat four pig eyes which I managed to do without too much fuss.

Kendra then had to eat a pig's nose during which she moaned: 'It tastes like I'm swallowing farm!' I loved that. What does farm taste like then?

Then things became really unpleasant when I had to eat a sheep's testicle. It stank. It absolutely hummed as I put it in my mouth and started chewing.

'Is there a taste to it?' asked Ant.

'That's just fucking filth,' came my reply as I pulled all manner of disgusted faces but finally swallowed it down.

With my final dish came the promise that all my campmates would have a drink if I was successful. Which was all well and good, but then they brought me out a camel's hump. I only had to eat a small part of it, but I was feeling pretty sick at this stage.

'Fucking hell, I could do a lot of things but that . . .' I said, as I trailed off contemplating my fate.

I started chewing it and it was vomit-inducing. Even now it makes my stomach turn just thinking about it. It was a bit like a pork scratching with 50% fat and 50% meat, and parts of it stuck all over my gob. Horrible. As I finished it, I grabbed my water bottle, took a swig and spat out the water. 'Sorry boys,' I said to the approaching Ant and Dec, 'I'm in trouble here.'

I kept having to rinse my mouth out as I couldn't get rid of the taste. Kendra rushed over to me to celebrate completing the trial while I had a load of water in my mouth. She hugged me and I just gobbed a mouthful of water straight over her shoulder. Smoothly does it.

I was on top form at my next trial, when I was invited to do a bonus round of the 'Critter Cube' after Jake had absolutely rinsed it and won all ten stars. The bonus was for another round of drinks – the only problem was that I had to solve an easy puzzle while putting my hands in a plastic box full of pythons. Knowing how scared I was of the snakes, they gave me two chances – I bottled the first one, but finally got my shit together and conquered my fear second time around. I celebrated like I'd just scored an injury-time winner, jumping on Jake shaking my fist in the air, and gave Dec a huge hug too. It was a feeling of pure relief.

I wasn't so good at being locked up in a dark box with only rats for company though. I don't mind rats when I'm fishing as they just shoot off and they're part of the furniture out there in the wild, but they threw in some particularly inquisitive little fuckers when I was in the 'Terror Tomb'. Or maybe that's just what Aussie rats are like?

As I was being locked in the box, I bravely shouted: 'Come on then you fuckers, let's have it!' But that was probably more stupid than brave.

The second I was in the dark with rats crawling over me, enough was enough. Even though Foggy was encouraging me from the outside, I wasn't having it at all so I started yelling, what I thought was 'I'm a celebrity, get me out of here!' but, looking back on it, I think I said something more along the lines of 'Celebrity jungle, get me out of this fucking shithole!', such was my state of panic.

It was about this kind of time that Foggy, Jake and I started to really wind each other up about the trials and there would be a lot of banter if any of us failed, which I did a fair bit.

When I lost to Vicky Michelle (her from *'Allo 'Allo*) the two of them really let me have it with stuff like: 'You won fuck all, you only played for Wigan.' I laughed it off and said, 'Your time will come . . .'

The next day Foggy had to do a trial against Edwina. They had to keep their fingers on a button while having gunk and creatures poured on top of them. Foggy is the worst loser I've ever met – as an individual sportsman I think he had to have even more about him than anyone playing in a team – and I don't say that lightly as I've been around sportsmen for a long time. Any defeat niggled away at Foggy for an age.

So when he was off pushing buttons with Edwina, I was willing her to win, even though it would work against me as he was on my team and the losing team would be put up for a public vote to get kicked out of the jungle. I couldn't help it as I thought the opportunity to take the piss would just be too good.

Sure enough, Foggy ballsed it up and I had a field day. 'You're seven-times world champion, you're not worth a pump! You just got beaten by Edwina, a politician. You're a disgrace. You shouldn't even be in camp!' I destroyed him while he sat around gutted. But it was all in good spirits; he knew that and I knew that.

Which was why when Jake made a joke about me having the same body as sixty-eight-year-old TV newsreader Michael

Buerk, my reaction was just as strong. But also in good spirits. The problem is that ITV hadn't shown the public any of those bits before, and they just showed me rinsing Jake which, on its own, obviously didn't look good.

Vicky had mistaken Michael for me and Jake seized upon it, saying me and Michael must have similar physiques.

'Alright fucking He Man,' I shot back to him, 'just because you're all fucking muscles, you fucking prick.'

'You can't take it, can you?' he replied.

'What have I got to take? That I look like him [Michael]? I don't give a fuck.'

'But you bite so fast,' he said.

'Are you sure?'

'You do, don't you?' said Jake.

'Just because I'm the governor of banter . . . you just get hurt, you lanky piece of shit.'

'You bite so quick.'

'I ain't biting.'

And so it went on. Lots of to-ing and fro-ing between us. At one point I said the lines which were in all the papers: 'The more I get to know you. I'm thinking, 'What the fuck is this prick doing in here? What's he offering?' Why the fuck are you in here? What sort of skill have you got?'

Once again, on its own, that's not great. But we carried on laying into each other, and it finished with Jake calling me a 'Mr Burns-looking cunt' in reference to the old boy in *The Simpsons*. That made us both crease up. Hardly the outcome of a bullying episode, is it?

The problem was that by only showing that incident, it seemed as if it was an isolated one-off, but the two of us were going on like that the whole time. I know I can be vicious in those situations but never with people who can't take it, and I knew that both Foggy and Jake could take it, and Jake was way tougher than the show made out.

After the show, my position was always to wait and see what Jake had made of it all, and when he came out they asked him about the supposed bullying to which he replied: 'Nothing like it, Jimmy was one of my good mates in there.'

But the damage had been done. A couple of nights after that incident, me, Foggy, Mel and rapper Tinchy Stryder all faced the chop. My campmates were saying I was going to win the show, but I was having none of it. The way I saw it we all had a twenty-five per cent chance of going because none of us had any idea what the public was being shown. Unfortunately, I was proved right as it was me who was first out.

But I have no complaints. I was privileged to be in that position, on that show, in that environment. That's why the jungle is so good. If there's a big shock with who goes out, then that's it. Boom! That's why we like watching it – it's off-the-cuff stuff.

And I always said that as long as people in the camp know what I was really like then I was happy, no matter what the press wrote. When I looked at the footage of the camp after I was voted out, they were saying things like: 'We've lost a good man.' Their reactions meant so much more to me than what was said and written by people who weren't there with us.

I was gutted to leave but it really didn't take me long to get over it – about half an hour, to be precise. That was the point when I was tucking into a Full English breakfast. I knew I was done the moment that first bacon rasher slid down my throat – you can't get that in the jungle. They'd have had to drag me back in there kicking and screaming.

I'd done what I set out to do which was make an impact. It would have been lovely to win but that wasn't what I went in there for. I'm not ashamed to admit that I did it to gain more exposure and to open more avenues for work. I certainly didn't do it for the money – my appearance fee of £25,000 was very nice but I know it was one of the lowest paid to the contestants.

Since I've been back from Australia, I've been stopped in the street by mums and daughters, instead of fathers and sons. I'm now being recognised as Jimmy from the jungle rather than Jimmy the nutcase footballer. And my TV gigs have been changing too. Okay, I got to do *Match of the Day* which was a dream, but I've also been on general interest shows like *The Xtra Factor*, *Reality Bites* and *Lorraine*. Check me out!

Being chucked out first certainly didn't dampen my enthusiasm for acting like a pillock either. We had six days in the luxury of the Versace hotel after that which was like a holiday after the hardship of the jungle.

One day, my manager Jim and I were a bit bored, and Foggy's wife Michaela had told us that she was going to be live on *Good Morning Britain*. Jim and I looked at each other – here we go.

I waited until she was on air, hitched my Speedos right up so that my arse cheeks were on show, and walked up to the camera, interrupting her interview.

'Morning everyone!' I said. 'How are you? Go on Foggy! What a lovely day,' and then turned around, presenting the Bullard backside to the nation, and walked off. They cut back to the studio in London where presenter Ben Shephard was cracking up laughing, and his co-anchor Susanna Reid had her hand over her mouth in shock. Too easy.

I'd also served up a couple of crackers in the jungle too – you may have heard about them, although there was one incident that was certainly not shown on the telly.

Edwina Currie joined the group at the same time as Jake, and the politician – famous for shagging a former Prime Minister – was definitely not the shy, retiring type. But then neither am I. One day I was a bit bored and, completely unplanned, just rocked up to her and asked, 'How was it with Major? Worth the rattle?' Unsurprisingly, she didn't offer much of a response.

She wasn't that fussed either when she came back from that button-pushing task with part of her hair covered in some disgusting, fluffy slime.

'She looks like she's got a dead parrot on her head,' I said and Sykesy nearly wet herself laughing.

One afternoon, Edwina was having a massage – don't worry, I didn't do a 'Bouba Diop' on her. I'm not that daft. I think.

Before Edwina knew what was going on I'd swapped places with the masseuse and started rubbing her back. She'd twigged it was me but I took my bathrobe off and jumped on her anyway – she loved it. Worryingly, I think I did too.

Edwina had the thickest barnet I'd ever seen. Her hair was like one of those foam things my mum sticks flowers in. It was like a sponge, and I always said to her – in a nice way

– that if she got in the pool there'd be no water left. Funnily enough, the time she did get in the pool in our jungle camp saw me absolutely lose it. You've probably seen the clip . . .

I was massively hyped up as I'd just won a trial and we were all in the pool, larking about. Suddenly, I just grabbed Edwina and lifted her in the air, screaming, 'Politics? Fuck politics!'

It's all a bit embarrassing as I got slightly carried away.

But then that's me. That's what I do. And I'd like to think that when people talk about me on the show, they talk about the daft stuff like me and Edwina in the pool, rather than a silly bit of banter between me and Jake.

Always leave them wanting more.

No problem. I'm off.

☺